CAN I KEEP
MY JERSEY?

CAN I KEEP MY JERSEY?

**11 Teams, 5 Countries,
and 4 Years in My Life
as a Basketball Vagabond**

Paul Shirley

Introduction by Chuck Klosterman

VILLARD Ⓥ NEW YORK

To my father, Ken, for telling me to use the backboard;

to my brothers, Dan, Matt, and Tom, for being my best friends;

and to my mother, Jane for everything else

Published in the United States by Villard Books,
an imprint of The Random House Publishing Group,
a division of Random House, Inc., New York.

VILLARD and "V" CIRCLED Design are registered
trademarks of Random House, Inc.

ISBN 978-0-345-49136-7

LIBRARY OF CONGRESS CATALOGING-IN-PUBLICATION DATA

Shirley, Paul.
    Can I keep my jersey? : 11 teams, 5 countries, and 4 years in my
life as a basketball vagabond / Paul Shirley.
        p.   cm.
ISBN 978-0-345-49136-7 (hardcover : alk. paper)
    1. Shirley, Paul.   2. Basketball players—United States—Biography.
I. Title.

GV884.S45A3 2007
796.323092—dc22
[B]

2006101184

Printed in the United States of America
on acid-free paper

www.villard.com

9 8 7 6 5 4

Book design by Mary A. Wirth

Introduction

by Chuck Klosterman

There are 6 billion humans on the face of this planet. About 2.5 billion of these humans are farmers; another 800 million are starving; an unrelated 18 million more purchased Boston's debut album. Existence is inherently alienating. However, the overwhelming majority of these unwashed (and semi-washed) minions still share one unifying characteristic, and that characteristic is this: they are all relatively terrible at basketball.

For chunks and stretches of the early twenty-first century, Paul Shirley has played in the National Basketball Association. The NBA has 30 franchises, and each club carries 12 players; this equates to a fraternity of just 360 people. These are the strongest, quickest, richest basketball players in the world. Even if your census includes (a) superstars who retired in their prime, (b) the best players in college, (c) any undiscovered hoop geniuses still hidden in Eastern Europe, and (d) every Earl Manigaultesque washout roaming the frontcourts of playgrounds and prison yards, Shirley was (and perhaps still is) among the top 500 basketball players alive. How many people do you know who are in the world's top 500 at *anything*? It's easier to get into the U.S House of Representatives than it is to get into the NBA. But this is what Paul Shirley accomplished. And that's really weird, because Paul Shirley would never define himself as a basketball player, even though that's what he scrawls on the bottom of his tax return; he loves basketball, but he despises basketball players. And that peculiar detachment is what makes this book unlike anything you will ever read about professional sports.

This is not a situation like *Paper Lion*, where George Plimpton was given the chance to pretend he was a Detroit Lion. It's also not like Jim Bouton's *Ball Four*, because Shirley never contributed to any NBA club as much as Bouton contributed to the Yankees, nor was Shirley particularly close to any of his teammates (when I briefly met the author in 2006, he had the name of exactly one professional basketball player in his cell phone, and I think the dude was Russian). Shirley is neither a dilettante nor an insider; he's more akin to the most deeply imbedded reporter in the history of sport. Every on-court experience he had was authentic and consequential. Every off-court conversation he overheard was casual and unrehearsed. He has guarded Ron Artest on the perimeter, and he has listened to Amare Stoudemire discuss politics. He did not merely have exposure to basketball culture; he had complete emersion. Yet it is clear that Paul Shirley never *became* a pro basketball player. He never lost his perspective on the unreality of the NBA. He never stopped being the skeptical, reasonable person that farm kids from Kansas tend to be. He never drank the Kool-Aid; in fact, he openly mocked the Kool-Aid on the Internet. And this probably hurt his career. But it also made him an exceptional and hilarious journalist.

As stated earlier, Paul Shirley was (and might still be) among the 500 best hoop specimens alive. And that, of course, is an ironic reality. Because we live in a world where everything is relative, Shirley is usually classified as a strikingly mediocre basketball player. This is the deepest insecurity of his life; the pages of *Can I Keep My Jersey?* are saturated with self-deprecating references surrounding Shirley's on-court shortcomings and his eternally tendril future. He may have made the NBA, but he is not a confident athlete. He is, however, a remarkably confident intellectual. He writes about racial politics with a clarity that will make some readers uncomfortable. His hatred for religion (and the way it has infiltrated athletics) is on par with Vladimir Lenin. He doesn't like fans (or fandom) because he doesn't like stupid people. And he is *obsessed* with details, probably because the details are pretty much everything.

There is, I suppose, a glaring paradox to this three-year diary, and it won't be lost on any serious reader: it often seems as if Paul Shirley did everything in his power to attain a life he never really wanted. The NBA he imagined as a thirteen-year-old had no relationship to the NBA he experienced at twenty-seven. He traveled around the world in the hope of throwing a leather sphere through a metal cylinder, and that never stopped seeming ridiculous. He did everything in his power to become a better player, even though he couldn't relate to the type of person he aspired to become. It's a contradiction that even Shirley struggles with; I'm still not sure he could adequately explain why he was so driven to become someone he couldn't understand. But here's the good news, and here's what matters more—it didn't happen. Paul Shirley never became that type of person, which is why this book exists.

Like most of the world's 6 billion humans, you will never be paid money to play basketball, and you will never have access to the rarified humans who do. But the following pages explain what such an experience might feel like, assuming you managed to remain the same person you are right now.

CAN I KEEP
MY JERSEY?

always dread the paperwork at the doctor's office. I know I'll have to walk the secretary through the spelling of my last name. To save time I usually explain that it's just like the girl's name. Then, nodding slowly, I agree that third grade was about the time my classmates realized why that was funny. Which made for three long years of boyhood abuse, since it wasn't until sixth grade that I developed a grasp of the witty retort.

But that isn't the part I dread. I hate the section that asks for employer information. I feel guilty about my response in the box marked "Occupation."

I always write, "Professional basketball player."

Because that's what I am. As absurd as it may seem, people pay me to play basketball. Thus, I am a professional basketball player.

(I use such gravitas. My tone would have been more appropriate if I had written something much more intriguing, like "I am an undercover assassin" or "I am a ninja.")

When I tell someone that I play professional basketball, I know that I will have to provide an explanation. I suppose it is better than many of the alternatives; saying that one is a data specialist rarely stimulates much of a conversation. But my story has always proved to be a difficult one to tell. When a person learns that my job is to put a three-dimensional circle through a two-dimensional one, the next question—invariably—is, "So who do you play for?" My response usually involves some stammering, the shifting of my feet, and some thorough consideration on my part. Much of the time, I don't have an answer. Although it is fun to make something up, as in "I play for the Tampa Bay . . . Dirty . . . Devil . . . Hawks," just to see what happens.

My life—the life of a professional basketball player—is not as sim-

plistic as it appears. I suppose it's easy to understand the life of an
NBA superstar. He goes to practice, collects the biweekly check de-
rived from his multiyear, multimillion-dollar contract, and, generally,
knows where he will be from year to year. Likewise, it isn't difficult
to comprehend the life of the college hero who wasn't quite good
enough. He tried it for a year, failed, and quit to become a vice president of the hometown Denison State Bank.

My story is not so simple. I am the in-between. I've played for
eleven teams in my four years as a pro. I've been at the top, playing in
NBA games with three different teams . . . and the bottom, released or
otherwise rejected eight times. But I keep going back. Much like a
drug addict, a battered wife, or a guy who thought playing basketball
for money, while sometimes maddening, remained a far better alter-
native to life in a cubicle.

In the end, I'm a lot like everyone else. I've had to prove myself
over and over, which makes me no different from a real estate agent,
a surgeon, or a garbage collector. (Well, a garbage collector who belongs to the worst union in the world and happens to live in the most
waste-disposal-performance-conscious city on the planet.)

The only difference between my life and everyone else's? Instead
of taking my first job in Peoria, I took one in Athens. Instead of morbidly obese co-workers named Patti and Bernice, my "colleagues" are
large men who go by Kobe, Amare, and Viktor. Simply put, my professional life has been a lot like that of most people—filled with ups and
downs. My ups and downs have just been a little more interesting.

My initiation into the world of professional basketball came about
in the locker room of the defending world champion Los Angeles Lakers. I was a fresh-faced rookie from Iowa State where—while no
star—I had been well known and loved by the crowds who packed
Hilton Coliseum to its capacity of 14,092. Standing in the Lakers
locker room, I was nobody. Strangely, my introduction to a life of
being paid to play a game was much more comfortable than I expected, thanks to a man named Shaquille O'Neal.

I grew up as a shy kid in a small town. Actually, that's not really
true. I grew up in the country, not a small town, but we all have to

claim somewhere as our home. For me, that town is Meriden, Kansas. It is my hometown only by default. My parents raised my brothers and me at the intersection of two unnamed gravel roads. As a child, I was fascinated to learn that the placement of our mailbox governed our address. Our mailbox was on the east side of our property, so I wrote "Grantville" in the upper left corner of my letters to Santa. Had our mailbox been on the north side, I would have written "Meriden."

Address confusion notwithstanding, I went to school in Meriden. So when I started my first game as a sophomore at Iowa State, I heard, "and at center, six-ten, from Meriden, Kansas, Paul Shirley."

I learned the basics of the game of basketball on a gravel driveway. (I realize that this is all sickeningly quaint. But I can't go back and make my parents move to the city.) My childhood heroes were of two types. They were either (a) members of the University of Kansas basketball team or (b) Larry Bird. My brothers and I watched the former group play televised games on cold Saturday afternoons, keeping track of players' statistics in intricately named columns like "Points" and "Fouls." At halftime, we would report to the basketball goal suspended from the deck and imitate our favorite players. Our ill-advised excursions into the elements invariably resulted in, at minimum, one jammed finger or one basketball to the face. Neither occurrence was especially pleasurable when the air temperature was hovering around freezing.

By high school, I was a fair basketball player. (Note: That was an example of self-deprecation. It will remain a theme. I was really good. Obviously. I wouldn't be telling the story of my professional basketball career if I'd been a bad high school basketball player.) I wasn't able to lead my high school team to a state championship, but we won far more games than the citizenry of Meriden was used to. I remain disappointed by my failure to achieve the ultimate small-town basketball triumph. Without a state championship, my story derails from the hokey, vomit-inducing course it was taking. I'm sure that when the movie is made, a gaudy, yellowed banner reading "State Champs" will hang in the Jefferson West gymnasium.

And then I went off to college. I was not a hotly pursued recruit, so my options were limited. (Averaging a load of points against tiny

schools in northeast Kansas is not a shortcut to a scholarship at
UCLA.) Fortunately for me, a man named Tim Floyd saw in me a bargain from which he could hardly walk away. It turns out that I am not
a complete idiot; I was a National Merit Scholarship finalist. I don't
even really remember what that means; I think I did well on a test. At
any rate, Coach Floyd used my qualifications as a non-imbecile to secure for me a full academic scholarship at Iowa State. The arrangement worked out well: he wasn't forced to use an athletic scholarship
on a skinny kid with potential, and I didn't have to pay for college. It
was a good deal for both of us.

I survived two head coaches, eleven assistant coaches, forty-nine
teammates, and approximately three real dates, and graduated from
Iowa State with a degree in mechanical engineering. By the end of my
career in Ames, I was fed up with basketball. I told my mother—on a
forgettable January morning—that my senior year of college would be
my last season of basketball.

My athletic career at an end, I retired to the woods, where I lived
peacefully among the forest creatures, dining on scavenged acorns
and pine sap for the rest of my long life.

And so, it would seem that I've reached the end of my tale, in just
under four pages. The remainder of the book will be spent in the craft-
ing of knock-knock jokes and haikuy. . . .

Fortunately for the sanity of the reader (and me), that bizarre departure from reality never transpired. I recovered from my one-day
bout with early-twenties angst and allowed myself to be convinced to
play a game for money. It was a tough sell.

When I would shoot baskets in my parents' driveway as a child, I
always dreamed of playing in the NBA. It was an absurd dream—and
the impossibility of it was hammered into my classmates and me on
nearly any available occasion. I think our high school football coach—
who doubled as the calculus teacher—even had a poster hanging on
his wall that spelled out a statistical breakdown of how unlikely a job
in professional sports was. And he was right. Then again, he did not
post a chart specifically for those in his class who would grow to a
height of six feet ten inches.

If I had followed through with my plan to give up basketball after college, my math teacher would have been proved correct. Because I am a stubborn bastard, I couldn't allow that. And if I had quit after my senior year of college, my little-boy hopes would have been dashed forever.

Jesus Christ. If that wasn't the worst goddamned line ever.

My team at Iowa State was fairly well known on the national stage. I shared the floor with players named Marcus Fizer and Jamaal Tinsley, who would both go on to be starters in the NBA. We won back-to-back conference titles my junior and senior years. At the end of both years, we were ranked in the national top ten. Sometimes, I was a big contributor to our cause. On other occasions, I was simply along for the ride. I spent much of college playing with injuries to various locations on my body and limped, both literally and figuratively, my way to the end of my career. (And a tragic end it was. It came at the hands of tiny Hampton University. Or perhaps it's called Hampton College. In fact, it could actually be Hampton Technical School. No one had ever heard of the place before it became only the fourth team seeded fifteenth to win a first-round game in the NCAA tournament.)

When my college days were over, I was invited to play in the Portsmouth Invitational Tournament. My invitation was probably not by virtue of my individual ability. I was invited because I had played on a really good team. In fact, because two of my teammates were also invited to the showcase for college seniors, Iowa State had the largest contingent at the event. In all, sixty-four players are invited every year to the tournament. We were divided into eight teams, and each team played in three games over the course of the weekend.

I didn't have much fun playing basketball in college. I enjoyed the winning and the accomplishment of certain goals, but the actual act of playing the game rarely brought about much joy. I took my collegiate career—and myself—entirely too seriously. When I left for Portsmouth, I decided to change my ways and forced myself to let go. In the least-shocking news ever, my plan worked. No longer encumbered by a mind-numbing attention to the implications of every play, I allowed myself to enjoy the game in a way I hadn't since high school.

The Portsmouth tournament was a glorified meat market. Agents and scouts—both from overseas and the NBA—swarmed the games like Puerto Ricans at a cockfight. The players involved were generally midlevel; anyone good enough to know that he would be drafted skipped the event and waited for the NBA's more high-profile scouting opportunities. Obviously, I was not in that category. I needed some help to get my fledgling career off the ground. During the week, I met with two agents who approached me, and I signed with one of them.

The one I chose, Keith Glass, didn't sugarcoat his analysis. He told me that he had been pleasantly surprised by my basketball abilities but that life as a white professional basketball player would be a constant struggle. He listed off some of his clients and noted that he generally represented good players who are decent human beings. Since I can often fool people into thinking that I am both, he didn't have to say much else to convince me that our styles might mesh. Keith told me that he thought I had a chance to play in the NBA but that he couldn't guarantee it would ever happen. (Something about hell freezing over . . .) He compared me to one of his clients, a player from Marquette named Chris Crawford, who had just signed a long-term contract with the Atlanta Hawks. In the same breath, he said that such an event wasn't necessarily likely. (Which is just what I needed—another realist in my life.) But if I fell short of the NBA, it seemed likely that I would find a home in Europe. Keith claimed to have contacts all over that continent.

After Portsmouth, players who stimulated interest from NBA teams were invited to individual workouts in NBA cities. Some attended as many as fifteen such workouts in the run-up to the NBA draft. Number of scheduled workouts for me: zero. As draft day approached, it became apparent that my name would not appear on the television broadcast of the event. The Cleveland Cavaliers had expressed some interest, but their second-round pick came and went with no fanfare.

The NBA runs summer leagues as an opportunity for teams to work with draft picks and young players and to try out free agents. A member of the last category, I was invited by the Cavaliers franchise to play with its summer league team in Salt Lake City. I was a nervous wreck when my mother dropped me at the airport in Kansas City. My overriding fear was complete embarrassment—which, now that I think about it, is probably everyone's main fear when they start something new. So my experience was really no different from that of the guy who goes off to a new job as an investment banker. Fortunately, summer league isn't exactly the full-on NBA. Or Deutsche Bank. I held my own. In fact, because I was a complete unknown, anything I did beyond successfully putting on my own uniform and/or not defecating in that same uniform was viewed as an improvement on expectations.

When what I thought to be a moderately successful summer league ended in late July, I returned to Kansas to consider my options. My home was the less-than-glamorous confines of my parents' basement; I had moved home from college while I awaited the next step in my life. I worked out in Topeka and thought about my future. Keith told me that there were European teams interested. On the opposite end of the career-path spectrum, I had been accepted into the MBA program at the University of Kansas—my default option in case a life in professional basketball did not come calling.

Just about the time I discovered that the old Nintendo stashed in the utility room was still functional, my life heated up. The Los Angeles Lakers invited me to an individual workout. I flew to LA. When I woke up on the morning of the workout, I was so nervous I could force nothing down my gullet but a piece of Marriott-served honeydew and one-quarter of a cinnamon roll. It proved to be enough food, though, as I became a workout god when I got to the Lakers' practice facility. If it had been a job interview, the HR guy would have offered over his youngest daughter for abusive sex—I was that impressive. I made shot after shot and picked up exactly what they taught about the ephemeral triangle offense. I left the Healthsouth practice facility on Sepulveda feeling quite good about myself.

When I got back to Kansas, I learned that my fantastic showing had caused the Lakers to . . . do absolutely nothing. No training camp invite had been proffered; in fact, the team, for all its on-site affection, seemed lukewarm about my basketball abilities. I was dismayed, mostly because my pre-workout anxiety had caused me to miss out on a free breakfast.

Fortunately, my other half-assed suitor—the Cleveland Cavaliers—continued to lurk. The team invited me to training camp and, as September wound down, I resigned myself to a trip to Cleveland. I knew that there was very little chance I would make the team, as the Cavaliers had a nearly full roster, leaving little room for interlopers such as myself. Two nights before I was to depart, I got a call from Keith. He told me that the Cavaliers had de-invited me to training camp. He didn't know why, he only knew that I was now without a basketball destination. I had turned down at least one basketball job in Europe and was getting antsy to begin my "career." Losing out on my one training camp invite was not the rip-roaring start to the NBA career I had envisioned for myself. I decided to drown my sorrows in a trip, with my family, to my youngest brother's flag football game. Debaucherous.

When we got home, a message from Keith was waiting. My fortunes had reversed: the Lakers had called with an eleventh-hour training camp invitation. (Side note: shouldn't the cliché involve the twelfth hour? The eleventh hour runs from ten to eleven, which makes it a lot less urgent and suspenseful and more just irrelevant.) The Lakers had called without any prodding and had inquired about my availability for their training camp. Because of the Cavaliers' rejection, Keith was able to tell them that I was, in fact, free to come, and had been so for all of an hour and a half.

I packed a bag and, once again, got really nervous. I was met at the Los Angeles airport by a limousine. The driver was a nice guy; he told me that he had read my name in the day's transactions and showed me a copy of the *Los Angeles Times* sports section. Under "Transactions," I found the following: "Los Angeles Lakers sign F Paul Shirley." (*F* stands for *forward.*) Of course, my situation looked better to my driver than it did to me. My contract with the Lakers was valid only if I was on the team's opening-day roster. Since the team was leaving for Hawaii—the location of training camp—the next day, my driver rushed me to the hospital for a physical. After an in-depth examination, I found myself in the team's locker room, faced with a Lakers jersey with *SHIRLEY* sewn on the back. Even though it was only a seam ripper away from returning to its normal, uninteresting state, there was something special about the realization that I was the possessor of an official Los Angeles Lakers jersey with my name on it. (Of course, this was all sort of the opposite of the plan. In my childhood vision, the first and only NBA jersey I would ever don would be that of the Boston Celtics. But I wasn't going to complain.)

When the mild erection I was nursing subsided, I took note of my surroundings . . . and a bunch of very large humans who sort of looked like they wanted to kill me. The old version of me would have stood quietly in the corner of the locker room and waited for instructions. But the new edition—the one who had decided that he was going to try to enjoy basketball again—took over. I mustered my courage and walked up to the biggest of the bunch, the most famous active basketball player in the world, Shaquille O'Neal. I stuck out my hand and said, "Hi. My name is Paul Shirley."

My whole future seemed to hang in the balance.

I waited.

And then he said, with a smile, in that famous gravelly voice, "I know who you are."

And I nearly fell to the floor.

But I didn't. I said, "Nice to meet you." And walked back to my locker. The enormousness of the exchange struck me immediately. Shaquille O'Neal, arguably one of the top five most recognizable humans on the planet, had just put me at ease. He didn't have to. He could have said, "Hi, I'm Shaq," and it would have sufficed. But he made me feel like I belonged. Maybe he followed college basketball so intently that he actually knew who I was, but I doubt it. It is possible that he had read my name in the transactions page. It could be that he just said it. Whichever it was, I was grateful.

I lasted three weeks of training camp/preseason with the Lakers. (The term "training camp" is used to denote the time from the beginning of practice until the first regular season game.) Because the Lakers are, well, the Lakers, the team's first two weeks of training camp were held in Hawaii. I was nearly as completely out of my comfort zone as was possible. I was staying alone in a hotel suite large enough to house my entire family. I rode on the daily bus to workouts with players who will someday be in the Hall of Fame . . . and their bodyguards.

Kobe Bryant actually had bodyguards at training camp. (Note the plural.) His personnel would exit the hotel before him, with one man maintaining a lookout position from a balcony above. When he was safely stashed on the shuttle to practice, they would retire to a trailing car. If I had remained completely true to my new philosophy, I would have asked him, "Are you serious? You have *multiple* bodyguards? You really are one pretentious son of a bitch." My reticence would come back to haunt me in practice one day, when Bryant blocked a poorly executed shot of mine and, in the process, knocked me to the floor. (Probably due to an uncoordinated recovery on my part, not because of a foul on his.) I found my temporary nemesis standing over me, legs straddling my midsection. He began venting his rage at the gall it had taken for me to challenge the area around the basket with my ill-conceived, pathetic attempt at a basketball shot. The sentence(s) he used included the following words: *bitch, ever, don't, weak, shit, bring,* and *in here.* The order in which he used them remains unclear. I was completely taken aback. I was so confused that I froze. I had no idea why he felt so threatened that he was yelling at me, the white guy who would probably be the first player released. Given it to do over again, I'd have punched him, or at least kicked him in the testicles.

In general, I was out of my element with the Lakers. Soon after we returned to the mainland, I was released. It didn't come as much of a surprise. I had done nothing of note during training camp

After my release, I found the Lakers' equipment manager in his office. Still dazed by the team's rejection, I asked him if I could take my jersey home with me. I assumed that my request was a mere formality; my surprise was probably obvious when he said, "No, we're not a club that does that." Shocked, I couldn't even come up with the obvious response: "What the hell are you planning to do with a Los

Angeles Lakers jersey with *SHIRLEY* stitched on the back? I don't think it will bring much in the way of revenue." Since I had no experience in the matter, I walked numbly out of his office and found my way back to the storage room that had served as the auxiliary locker room for two of my fellow rookies and me. I grabbed my backpack, surveyed the room's cache of shoes, and took the first two pairs that caught my fancy. As retribution goes, it wasn't much, but it seemed appropriate at the time.

When I got back to Kansas, it took Keith very little time to parlay my brief stint in the Lakers' camp into a European job. (Any contact with the NBA is like crack to European coaches. I think it helps with public relations to be able to add "former NBA player" to the back end of a player's resume, even if it is only true by the loosest definition of what an NBA player is.) I left the United States on Halloween to join my new team in Athens, Greece.

I had very little access to the Internet in my first weeks in Greece. Actually, access was available—I was just too cheap to buy it. In my defense, I had just graduated from college; ten dollars an hour for use of my hotel's computer seemed like a steep price. (I was going to be cute and convert that to Greek drachmas, but I can't remember the exchange rate. Opportunity lost.) But I needed to tell someone about the absurdities I was encountering on a daily basis. So I began writing about my experiences, sending my journals home whenever I felt flush enough to fork over some money to the girl at the front desk.

Eventually, I moved to an apartment complete with a working Internet connection. I had found that I enjoyed the catharsis of writing about my adventures in Greece, and oddly enough, my friends and family enjoyed reading them. So I continued writing.

After seven months in Greece, I left a beautiful three-bedroom apartment in one of the most chaotic cities in the world and returned to my parents' basement in Kansas armed with the cynicism provided by a year of professional basketball. I had made a little money, so I could justify to myself the summer workouts with which I tortured myself.

I was happy with my first year as a professional basketball player.

But playing in Greece had not been my goal as a child. As the second fall of my professional career approached, I was determined to find a place in the NBA.

What follows is the story of the next three years of my professional basketball career. It isn't a reproduction of my journals verbatim. (That would have been a lazy move.) But it follows that format.

At the time, I thought my year in Greece would be my strangest ever. In truth, it was the dullest I've had since I graduated from college. The miniature cycle of rejection and rejoicing I endured in year number one would be repeated over and over as my basketball career continued. However, the stakes rose as I got better and more well known. ("More" should be taken to mean "slightly more" or even "infinitesimally more.")

In the course of the three years chronicled here, I played for eight different professional teams. I went back to Europe—twice—and found myself in the minor leagues exactly two more times than I would have liked. (In a joke that is only funny to four-year-olds, I of course played for two minor leagues.) More important, I made it to the NBA. (Ruined that surprise.) And I figured out that I could play at that level. I even made a basket or two. But unfortunately, not too many more than that.

Along the way, I learned what basketball could do for me, what it could do *to* me, and just how little control I had over which of those actually happened.

And I learned that writing about it all seemed to help me understand it.

I dislike confusion when I read. I think some writers strive for it. Since this is my book, I will try to avoid befuddling the reader. Thus, even though it makes me feel like the barker for a nineteenth-century production of *King Lear,* I will set the stage, as it were.

We find our hero . . .

Wait, that was terrible.

My second year as a pro started in training camp with the Atlanta Hawks. I had a better chance with the Hawks than I'd had the year before with the Lakers. But I was by no means a shoo-in for a roster spot.

Now let's pick it up with me in Atlanta, as I wrote about it back then.

But more clearly, and with editing.

YEAR 1

September 15

My home here in Atlanta is a hotel connected to the CNN Center—the epicenter of the world of cable television. As such, one would think that I have a plethora of televisionary options to fill my non-basketballing time. Not so. I think I have two channels that are not somehow related to CNN. And I doubt that either of them is going to show the Kansas City Chiefs game that I am fixated on watching, if only because it would breathe some normalcy into my current existence.

I'm here trying to make the Atlanta Hawks. My days are filled with basketball workouts, obsession about the repercussions of those workouts, and avoidance of the out-of-doors—strangely, it's really hot in the South. My chances of success in this endeavor weren't great to start with. (Chances of making the team, that is. I'm pretty good at staying inside.) However, I'd feel better about my odds of making the team if I had the use of all of my digits.

I should explain.

My brother Dan volunteered (was coerced) to take me to the Kansas City airport. As I robustly tossed my duffel bag into the trunk of his teal Grand Am, an as-yet-unidentified metal protrusion in that trunk nearly tore off the top of my right index finger. I said, "Darn it," and went back inside to patch myself up before he drove me to the airport. Obviously, worse events could have befallen me—a car accident, a tornado, or a raging case of syphilis each would have caused me far more strife. Nonetheless, I could have done without an additional hurdle in an already uphill climb.

My seemingly insignificant injury resulted in a condition wherein I now occasionally have no idea where a basketball will go when it leaves my hand. Which would have been fine had I not been bound for an NBA training camp. (Additionally, I am struggling to type the letters *Y, U, H, J, N,* and *M.* So perhaps I should amend the previous statement—stenographer's boot' camp would have been a challenge as well.)

Most players in the NBA do not fight for their jobs each year. Generally, they have guaranteed contracts—often for multiple years. For one of those players, training camp is merely the season's beginning. That player endures the twice-daily practices safe in the knowledge that he will be on the team for the entire year. Because the team has already committed to paying him a salary for the season, it would make no sense to release him. I have never been the player in the example.

Most teams maintain one or two open roster spots and allow players like me, who will jump at the chance to make an NBA team, to fight among like-minded souls for the remaining slots. (Note: it is not an actual fight . . . although that would make camp more interesting. I envision gladiator-style arena battles for the final roster spot, audience participation, a vote at the end . . . it could work.) The team guarantees the combatants nothing more than a per diem and a fair shot. It is debatable how fair that shot really is, but at least the per diem isn't bad—$95.

The difficulty in wrangling even an unpaid NBA training camp invitation amazes me. Last year—my rookie season—I had to fly to Los Angeles for a two-day tryout with the Lakers before they would commit exactly zero dollars for my training camp services. This year, I needed to impress the Atlanta Hawks coaches in yet another tryout setting. To this end, I went early in the fall to a two-day workout with the Hawks in order to fight for a position as low man on the proverbial totem pole. While I was there I played well enough that the team invited me to training camp, starting October 1.

Camp with the Hawks will be populated by several players in a like situation—guaranteed nothing and hoping to remain on the team through the madness that is two-a-days, preseason games and practices that seem—and might be—make-or-break. If I manage to survive the laid-back atmosphere and find a roster spot on the Atlanta Hawks when the first game of the actual season finally arrives, I will have accomplished the most outlandish goal I've ever had—to play in the NBA. Not that I'm taking this too seriously or anything.

I spent the summer loosely affiliated with the Cleveland Cavaliers. Again. The NBA holds a brief summer league each year. Although summer league teams play under the banner of NBA teams, only a few of the players on each squad wind up playing for the team in the winter. The summer league is a chance for a team's personnel to get an early look at players they drafted, young players who may be in line for a longer contract, and jackasses like me who are hoping that someone watching might take a liking to what they see. I played quite well in the NBA's summer league in Salt Lake City, but Cleveland wasn't interested in paying me to play for them during the season. (Such is my assumption, anyway; I think I would have noticed the six-year contract if it had arrived in the mail.) I surprised the Cavaliers' coaching staff by keeping pace with one of the team's new toys—their first-round draft pick, Carlos Boozer, of Duke fame. As I displayed my basketball wares alongside fellow free agents, rookies, and near-rookies, it was apparent that I belonged on the court. But the team drafted Boozer and so has a vested interest in his future success. Consequently, he returned to Cleveland safe in the knowledge that he had a shiny two-year contract that would pay him roughly $1 million. I returned to Meriden, Kansas, safe in the knowledge that I had a lopsided bed in my parents' basement and access to my old high school gym from ten to eleven every morning. I played far better this summer than last but—as seems to be the trend in my life—had nothing more to show for it.

When I went to training camp with the Lakers last year, I thought there was a 5 percent chance that I would make the team—odds similar to the survival rate after a diagnosis of pancreatic cancer. This year with the Hawks, that probability has improved to 20 percent. (Lymphoma.) Neither number is sufficient to warrant heavy action in Las Vegas, but it is encouraging that the trend is not the opposite one.

(Source: my own warped view. I have no evidence to back up my statistical claims.)

After passing my late August audition with Atlanta, I returned to Kansas and continued the workout routine that I had embraced for most of the summer so that I would be prepared for training camp. The Hawks offered to let me join the team's pre-preseason training sessions anytime after Labor Day. I would have rather stayed in the warm uterus of the heartland, but the Hawks' offer was not one to be spurned by an unguaranteed free agent who has never played in the NBA. To that end, I packed and prepared for an indeterminate amount of time in Atlanta.

I spent my first two days here in Atlanta participating in a mini-camp with the Hawks. The NBA recently decided to allow such events sporadically throughout the summer and fall so that each team can get together for extra work and/or confirm that none of its respective players has been recently incarcerated. Since my mini-camp experiences with the Hawks, my time has been consumed by individual workouts and pickup games while we prepare for the beginning of training camp in two weeks.

Mini-camp consisted of laid-back practices where, according to NBA rules, the drills could not go beyond three-on-three. So the two days ostensibly were not too difficult. However, it always re-surprises me that such a high level of concentration is required if one wants to have any success at the NBA level. The slightest wandering of the mind—especially when one is trying to learn a basketball system or philosophy from scratch—makes catching up a challenge. Over the years, I have come to understand that there are two intelligence-level options among basketball players: (1) A player can be relatively intelligent, and so can concentrate for long periods of time, or (2) he can be a Neanderthal. In the latter case, a coherent thought rarely sails through the participant's brain. The relative emptiness inside that player's cranium makes it easy to focus on simple activities. For example, when one has no other worries, the instruction "Put ball in basket" becomes a fairly easy command to follow. The rest of us are balancing the need to call about health insurance, concerns about our dinner plans, and confusion about our purpose on this earth. Meanwhile, the moron already scored and is pointing to the sky on his way back down the court.

Surprisingly, many NBA players fall into the former category—the smart-guy group. I make note of the unrecognized good fortune of the idiot only because I am envious. Such ease of focus has been demonstrated to me by many former teammates; it proves maddening for me to admit that it is so effective. The proverbial blank canvas, perhaps. For better or worse, I fall more easily into the category of the relatively intelligent soul. Thus my need for extreme concentration at all times, if only to dumb myself down. What a waste of brain cells.

September 22

Late this week I signed a contract with the Hawks, which sounds a lot better than it really is. As previously mentioned, my contract is valid only if I am on the team's roster at the end of training camp. I will admit that it is somewhat intoxicating to sign my name to a contract that states that I will receive $512,435—the minimum yearly salary for a player with my experience. Because I went to training camp with the Lakers last season, I am no longer considered a first-year player—even though I was not on an NBA team during the regular season. The NBA regulates minimum salaries according to years of service. (Which makes it sound like the army. Life in the NBA is decidedly dissimilar to life in the armed forces.) I now qualify as having had one year of that service, so my salary escalates according to a preset scale. Unfortunately, that financial boon isn't quite the benefit it would seem to be at first blush. While my potential personal financial gain does increase, the team is required to pay me more than a player who has never been to a training camp, so the system could work against me. I wanted to offer the Hawks some sort of Kevin McHale/Joe Smith arrangement whereby I would return some of the money if those in charge would allow me a spot on the team. But I chickened out. I still do threaten to someday go to the GM's office and give him my best PowerPoint presentation, entitled "Why Paul Shirley Should Be an Atlanta Hawk." Some of my key bullet points would include:

- I will never be pulled from the charred remains of a Ferrari at 5 A.M.*
- I will never complain about playing time or my role on the team.**
- The importance of actually learning the plays is not lost on me.***
- I have no illegitimate children for whom I need complimentary tickets.****

I think it's a foolproof plan.

I have been impressed with the work ethic of most of the Hawks. Perhaps the most impressive is displayed by Shareef Abdur-Rahim. As far as I can tell, he is almost always the first player at the gym and he appears to actually work hard. In real-world logic, this would seem appropriate—he is set to make $20 million this year. I have found, though, that basketball logic is usually the exact opposite of its real-world counterpart. Usually it goes that the more money a player makes, the less effort he puts forth. Shareef is a thoughtful guy; we have had a couple of decent conversations—probably more because his locker is right next to mine than anything else. It turns out that he was a collegiate teammate of Kenyon Jones, the other American on my team in Greece last year. In fact, now that I think about it, I believe Kenyon once told me that he owes Shareef some money but, in his words, "I don't think he's missing it." Anyway, Shareef and I were relating college experiences recently. I have always maintained that mine was not exactly a normal collegiate existence, but I can hardly imagine what he thinks of his. He was at Cal for only his freshman year. In essence, since he probably did not stay around much longer than April because he was headed to NBA pre-draft camps and the

* I will not, however, rule out a tragic Corsica accident.
** Until I sign a multiyear deal. Then, watch out.
*** To be honest, it is. If the ball comes my way, I'm shooting it.
**** See second footnote. The groupies won't know what hit them.

like, his college experience lasted eight months. Because of his short stay in college, the man is all of one year older than me and is now entering his seventh NBA season.

(Side note: When talking to Shareef, most people call him "Reef." I have a hard time latching onto nicknames, so I stick with "Shareef." I contend that if I wasn't around for the coining of the nickname, I am not allowed to use it. I think it is sound policy.)

Our pre-training-camp workouts continue to go about as well as could be expected. As is usually the case, my standout abilities in these situations are showing up early, touching the lines when we run conditioning drills, and staying longer than everybody else. Pickup games? Not my strong suit.

As I played with the Hawks in an informal setting, I examined the phenomenon of the pickup game in my mind. It is a strange beast, this pickup game, but it seems to follow set rules all through the basketball world. A pickup game can be loosely defined as an informal scrimmage where the number of players is greater than ten, leaving players on the sidelines to "pick up" players from the losing team for the next game. There are no referees, and scorekeeping is done by the participants. For illustrative purposes, we will allow that, in some cases, there may only be ten players available, in which case the same players stay on the floor (and the games get uglier and uglier as the players get tired). Some general rules apply:

1. Teams shall be picked by either the two tallest or the two eldest players participating. A shortage of players should not be looked upon as a hindrance to the beginning of action. If need be, bystander(s) with any level of basketball skill can be drafted, without regard to effect on the level of play. Eligible bystanders include coaches, ball boys, and all bipedal organisms from the class Mammalia.

2. After teams are established, the members of neither team should in any way differentiate themselves from members of

the other team. The concept of "shirts and skins" shall remain just that—a concept. Which isn't confusing at all.

3. There shall be, at minimum, two arguments concerning the score. At some point in the game, players will be forced to count up individual baskets in order to come up with an aggregate score for the team. (Understandable; it is easy to lose track when all baskets count as one point and the winner is the first to score the astronomical number of seven.)

4. No player on the court shall ever know whether the offensive or the defensive player is responsible for calling of fouls. In most cases, the opponent will have taken the ball to the other end of the court before it is established that a foul was called. Here, the player who calls the foul must stand up for his cause. The slightest hesitation or lack of conviction will result in forfeiture of future foul-calling rights, in addition to public ridicule. And manhood-questioning.

5. Upon conclusion of any one game, if players on the sidelines wish to join the game, they must make a case for inclusion with force and speed. If not, there exists the possibility that the players on the court will "run it back" and start a new game with the same participants as the previous game. When entering the field of play, the new player or players shall select, from the losing team in the previous game, enough participants to fill a new team. At this point, no one shall tell the players who were not selected of their gross ineptitude. Instead, they will be ignored until they make their way to the sidelines, heads held low.

6. If a number of games to be played has been established prior to the start of play, that number shall be ignored upon arrival at said number. No player shall admit that he is "tired" or that he "needs to do something else" or that "the games have deterio-

rated into nothing more than full-court layup drills" for fear of being viewed as weak in body and spirit.

7. Nothing resembling a coherent offensive plan will be employed on the court. Instead, players will limit themselves to a strict regimen of bad shots and ugly play at all times.

8. The author of these rules shall, at all times, participate in pickup games with the overriding goal being the avoidance of the shaming of his family's name. He realizes that this is not a ticket to success and promises to try to find a better outlook. Next week.

I played in a pickup game with Dominique Wilkins recently. He is some sort of "special assistant" for the Hawks, so is often lurking around the practice court. More accurately, the Hawks keep him on the payroll in the hope that prospective ticket buyers will associate his former glory as a player with the potential glory of the current regime. At one of our recent workouts, we did not have ten for a pickup game (see Rule 1 above), so Dominique jumped into the fray. He didn't stretch at all—he simply walked onto the court and started playing. During the game, I was not party to a single highlight-worthy dunk. But I didn't leave disappointed. No matter the outcome, I got to play in a legitimate basketball game with Dominique Wilkins. As a kid, I used to watch on television as he would shock even his own team-mates with his on-court acrobatics. Ten years later, we were sharing a court.

Sometimes even I realize that my life can be amazing.

September 29

Workouts continued this week. Formal training camp finally starts in a couple of days with a practice here in Atlanta, followed by an inexplicable trip to South Carolina for three days of practice. (Feels like escape-from-the-wives time for a particular coaching staff.) Upon reentry into the greater Atlanta region, a few practices will be had before the first preseason game. This geographically diverse activity will bring me closer to knowing my fate with the Hawks. I don't know the exact date that those in charge will decide who will occupy the team's roster spots, but the more practices I can get under my belt, the closer that mysterious day will be. And that is good. I mean, this state of mind—no earthly idea of where I will be for the year—is fun and all, but I'm willing to let someone else try it.

As camp begins, my mental and physical condition are both good. (Apparently, I am the Terminator now. *Mental and physical condition: good.* What a jackass.) My attitude is the time-worn, clichéd, "nothing to lose" one. Unfortunately, I think it applies in this case. My chances of actually making the team waffle between poor and very poor, but I will put everything I have into the opportunity; I don't know if I will do this un-guaranteed training camp thing again, so I will "leave it all out there" as best I can.

(Apologies for the hokeyness of that paragraph. It would appear that I have lost my mind. I probably could have written, "Blah, blah . . . I'm going to try hard to make the team.")

October 6

There is a somewhat obscure movie called *Gattaca* that stars Ethan Hawke and Uma Thurman. *Gattaca* is about a future in which every person's destiny is preordained based on the genetic potential he displays at birth. It is one of my favorite movies. The plot follows the life of a man named Jerome who, it has been determined, will rise only to the level of laborer but who wants more than anything to defy his birth and become an astronaut. In order to do this, Jerome buys another man's genetic identity. In the end, he fools everyone around him into thinking that he belongs in his station in life through all manner of tricks involving faked blood and urine samples. Jerome does not have some of the capabilities of his colleagues, forcing him to put an extraordinary amount of effort into anything he does.

I was reminded of the movie a few times this week during my first few practices of training camp. On more than one occasion, I asked a teammate what he thought of practice. He would invariably reply, "Oh, piece of cake. How about you?" Meanwhile, I was actively considering that my effort to make the Atlanta Hawks is the most idiotic thing I have ever attempted. Instead, I replied with, "Um, it was okay." The movie has a happy ending, wherein Jerome realizes his dream and becomes an astronaut. I will continue to hope that such is the case here. (The realization-of-the-dream part, that is. I don't want to be an astronaut. Very cramped existence.)

Actually, when compared to some of the torture I endured in college, Hawks' practices are not nearly as terrible as I make them out to be. In fact, so far, the use of curse words in a violent manner has been limited, no one has questioned my testosterone levels or familial origin, and I have not once been made to run a sprint over again because some moron did not touch a line on the court. I suppose that practices are made difficult if only because I—as I have mentioned before—must maintain a rather high level of concentration in order to have any chance. Also, the players are moderately large and strong and tend to balk when I suggest that they get out of my way.

October 13

During one of our first preseason games, I found myself on the court with Shawn Kemp. He was wearing an Orlando Magic uniform, which was odd—Shawn Kemp will always wear a Sonics uniform in my mind. But the strangest aspect of Kemp's appearance was not his uniform. It was what was under it. Shawn Kemp is *huge.* And not huge like tall and strong—huge like Oliver Miller. Huge like Chris Farley, post–*Saturday Night Live* and pre-overdose. Kemp is listed at 280 pounds in the media guide, but he looks a lot bigger than that. I think they weighed him on the moon.

And so another rung in the belief system ladder is destroyed. Shawn Kemp was the "Manchild"—the high-flying power forward who was the anchor to my entire NBA Jam dynasty. (Best basketball video game ever made.) Now he has been reduced to lumbering up and down the court like a drunken brontosaurus, holding on to the glory days so that he can support the gaggle of children he has fathered. (And, to be sure, this is no large Mennonite family. In fact, I'm sure there is nothing even remotely familial about the situation.)

We won the game against Kemp and Co. by twenty-five points or so—not that anyone cares. Preseason games serve only as a chance for the coaches to try out new plays on unsuspecting foes. Players who know they will be on the team for the whole year use them to slowly work back into game condition. Players like me just hope to get into the game.

I was sent into the game late in the second quarter, which was encouraging because, after the first ten players, I was the next one in. I was a bit spastic in my first-half action. In a move that will surprise no one who saw me play in college, it took me all of four seconds of game action to commit my first foul on Tracy McGrady as he flew toward the basket. In good news, I settled down for some garbage minutes at the end of the game. It's the little victories that keep me going.

We've played three preseason games. The home game against the Magic was followed by a trip to Florida for a return engagement, which we lost by ten. Once again, I did not play until the end of the game. (It seems that I'm really making an impact.) After returning from Orlando, we flew to Indianapolis for a game with the Pacers, which we lost by two. I played the last six minutes of that game and did a good job of doing what I was supposed to do. (Story of my basketball career—I pretty much do what the coaches tell me to do; anything beyond that might be an iffy proposition.) While in Indiana, I ran into a former college teammate, Jamaal Tinsley, who plays for the Pacers. We had a meaningful, in-depth, thirty-second conversation and then both went on our way. We are not close. In fact, I consider very few of my college teammates to be good friends of mine. My college experience wasn't quite what I expected it would be, which is sad. I have met players who were very close to their college compatriots. I am always quite envious.

I have to take the blame for some of the emotional distance between myself and my fellow alumni. When I was in school, surviving in both basketball and class was much more important to me than anything else and so completely dominated my life. I rarely went out—I didn't have time. Resting for the next practice or studying to keep up with the über-dorks who were the bane of my engineering existence took up most of my discretionary hours. Of course, I didn't have much motivation to hang out with my teammates. Many of them were only short-term additions—one guy survived all of six weeks before giving up and going home. And a large percentage had few interests outside of basketball, with the distinct exception of the chase of the Iowa-bred sorority girls who had never seen a black person before.

Jamaal is the starting point guard for the Pacers. I am happy for him, I suppose. While we will never attend PTA meetings together, I would not have had some of the success I now enjoy if not for his contributions, so maybe I shouldn't be so hard on him. (And by my "success," I mean "questionable success." Or perhaps "burgeoning success.") Now that I have reasoned this all out, maybe our next talk will last an extra minute.

Aside from my own personality flaws, there is a veritable catalog of reasons I don't get along particularly well with my fellow basketball players. Religion and stupidity are near the top of that list. Shockingly, those with a severe case of the latter often develop a strong belief in the former. The result is never a good one.

The religious fervor of athletes continues to amaze me. It is a phenomenon I have observed for years. Unfortunately, it seems to be worsening. I am surrounded by Bibles, crosses, and tattoos with religious overtones. My problem with all of this dedication to religion is the blatant hypocrisy inherent to it. I have known many a basketball player who will rarely miss saying grace before a meal but who will also give no second thought to cheating on his wife on a road trip. (I've vaguely heard of these commandments that religious people embrace. I feel like there's something about adultery in there.) In the same vein, the player with the "Only God Can Judge Me" tattoo is often the first to find the sports page so that he can read what the beat reporter thought of his last game.

The omnipresent Bible scares me as well. I recently noticed that a teammate of mine carries a copy of the Good Book in his car. I cannot imagine the scenario wherein biblical guidance would be helpful while driving: "Well, I don't know if Route 79 connects to this road or not. But it sure is a good thing I brought my Bible—I think there was something about that in the second chapter of Corinthians."

In other news from the imbecilic front, the following was an actual occurrence in a locker room during a recent halftime: A teammate of mine asked the trainer for something to spray in his nose because of some congestion therein. (*Congestion* is my word, not his. Aren't I an elitist ass?) The trainer told the player in question that the best he could do was an oral decongestant. The player furrowed his brow, and said, "Oral? What does *oral* mean?" It was no sex joke, either. He truly did not know what the term *oral* meant.

And another example to drive the point home: After we landed in Indiana, a different teammate, a kid fresh out of the University of Houston, followed me down the stairs from the private 737 the Hawks own—conspicuous because of the gigantic Atlanta Hawks logo painted on the side. When we got to the tarmac, he realized that he had left something on the plane. He thought for a minute and then asked me, "Are we taking the same plane back to Atlanta?"

It's shocking that I don't spend more time with my teammates. They have so much to offer in a conversation.

October 20

I probably ought to define what it means to "get dunked on." (Side note: I usually avoid the use of colloquialisms and slang because reading them makes me want to suck on the barrel of a shotgun. Here, though, the term is the least offensive of the available options.) To get dunked on is to attempt to block the dunk of an opposing player . . . and fail. To watch a player dunk the ball from near the basket is not to get dunked on. To remove oneself from the play by ducking out of the way is not to get dunked on. (It is to be a pussy, but "being a pussy" is not the subject of the current debate.)

Most of the time, getting dunked on occurs according to a prescribed order. A defensive player (for the purposes of this exercise, I will call him Paul) notices that a teammate has just been beaten to the basket. Paul's innate basketball sense tells him to help his teammate protect that basket, so he rotates toward the goal. At this point, the Fates have measured his length of string; the end result is decided, depending on two things—how late he has arrived and how good his opposition is. (Read: how much higher than Paul he can jump.) But Paul doesn't know that the result has already been determined—his basketball pride tells him that there is still a chance. He arrives at the moment that may or may not haunt him for the rest of practice. He makes the unconscious decision to challenge the opposing player. He jumps, hoping that his Dikembe Mutombo moment is at hand. The dunker realizes that Paul has arrived at the scene of the crime in a cable-repairman-like manner (late) and sends the ball through the rim, leaving Paul flailing like a marionette whose ropes have been cut. With some luck Paul survives the experience without further insult, such as a foul call or an injury caused by the ball's impact with the top of his head. Regardless of his physical and basketball well-being, the emotional scars will remain with him for the remainder of the day. His teammates—noble comrades that they are—will be sure to help him through the difficult time by reminding him frequently of his ineptitude.

Immediately post-event, Paul trots in as stoic a manner as possible back down the court, pretending that what just happened did not. In the locker room after practice, he may even try to deny that the event ever occurred: "No, man, I wasn't even in that play." Or "Oh, he didn't dunk on me; I got out of the way." Bad form, Paul. The experienced player takes the high road, admits that it happened, and leaves the locker room with much haste, hoping that the next day will bring with it some amnesia on the part of his teammates.

I discuss the fundamentals of the dunk-on because I was a party to the wrong end of the experience in a recent practice. It was ugly. It hadn't happened in a while; I had nearly forgotten what it is like. (Remember, I played in Greece almost all of last year. The players there are decidedly more ground-bound.) The feeling returned in a hurry.

The offending party was the oft-mentioned Shareef Abdur-Rahim. He put a wicked back-door cut on the player guarding him and, just as described above, I came over to help my fallen comrade.

Unfortunately, my arrival was a late one. After it happened, my pride and my chin both really hurt. I resolved to show no weakness, but then someone noted aloud that I was bleeding all over the court. The trainers opted for some newfangled skin superglue instead of stitches, so Shareef's elbow has given me a memento by which I can remember the event when I am shaving for the rest of my life.

Of course, that I am around to be humiliated on the basketball court is not the worst turn of events. So far, three players have been released by the Hawks—leaving four of us free-agent types on the chopping block. Unfortunately, it is likely that the team will get rid of all of us, but I am glad that I still inhabit my hotel room above Centennial Park. (Six weeks now—a new same-room record for me.) Beats being the first one cut.

I speak from experience. One year ago in the Lakers' training camp, when Dennis Scott and I were ushered into the basketball offices, I was the first to be wrestled into the guillotine. Head coach Phil Jackson and general manager Mitch Kupchak made up something about how much they had enjoyed having me in camp, and then I asked them what I could do to improve my chances of playing in the NBA. They told me to consider taking up water polo, and I went on my way. But at least Dennis Scott was there. At one time, he held the record for three-pointers in an NBA game. Of course, by the time I knew him, he weighed about 275 pounds and could barely tie his own shoes, but I prefer to dwell on the positive so as to feel better about myself.

After our first spate of preseason games, we members of the Atlanta Hawks played in two more meaningless encounters—in Alabama, of all places. I suppose the Hawks organization is trying to expand its fan base. However, their target audience appears to have been poorly chosen. I'm not sure anyone in Alabama actually has enough money to buy an NBA ticket. I also think Alabama is one of those states that is always forty-ninth or fiftieth in high school graduation rates and per capita income. When I really put my brain to the matter, I'm not entirely sure why the United States continues to allow Alabama statehood. On our way to Birmingham, we drove by Talladega Superspeedway (NASCAR), which is home to one of the biggest white-trash conventions in the world every year, so it's got that going for it, which is nice.

I write "we drove" because we actually took a bus from Atlanta to Birmingham—on game day. We left at 10 A.M. and I rode for two and a quarter hours with my headphones on, trying the entire time to drown out whatever movie was being shown. (There will come a time when I reach the higher level of understanding that allows me to comprehend why movies shown on buses are played at such a high volume. Unfortunately, that time is not now.) Upon arrival at our hotel in Birmingham, a couple of teammates and I wandered around a nearby strip mall. One of the participants is my main competition, a fellow named Antonio Harvey. He is thirty-two and is the prototypical journeyman, having played for six NBA teams already. We are the only two remaining unguaranteed inside players. (For future reference: *inside players* is synonymous with *bigs* and *posts*.) We both know that if the team is going to keep a player from the pool of non-guaranteed guys, it would most likely be one of the two of us. NBA teams are generally anxious to keep around as many bigs as possible; the bell curve of height would predict such behavior (i.e., there aren't enough tall guys to go around). While Antonio and I are rivals for what is potentially a very lucrative job, we are also teammates. Additionally, we have a fair amount in common; I'm like him eight years ago. He waffles between giving me guidance and being standoffish. He knows that I could easily usurp his position of authority if the transaction winds blow the wrong way. (Wrong way for him, that is.) Such relationships are always bizarre. I would never admit it to him, but I stay on mental guard. I don't want to admit weakness or confusion. I'm sure he does the same. It's a very healthy dynamic for two adults. Our relationship is probably similar to that between two cubicle groundhogs gunning for their boss' affection in order to get the big promotion to vice assistant to the traveling secretary. Except we're taller.

The team bus left our hotel at five for a seven-thirty game. Since I knew I wouldn't be filling up the "minutes" column on the stat sheet, I put myself through an intense-ish pregame workout. After working up a good lather, I proceeded to sit on the bench for the next two and a half hours, the times I stood up to cheer notwithstanding. It was eerily similar to the bus ride but less constructive—at least on the bus I was able to listen to some music. With about five minutes remaining in the game, I was sent in. My job: release the energy I had been dying to use the whole game by compacting it into a five-minute period, but without blowing out any of the muscles that had been busy atrophying for the better part of three hours. Ouch. I successfully avoided snapping any tendons, we lost, and no one cared. Again, it's preseason.

Our next outing was to Huntsville, Alabama, for another matchup with the Indiana Pacers. Before the game, coach Lon Kruger found me and said, "Paul, we have to start getting into our regular-season rotation, so there may not be a lot of playing time to go around." Translation: "Find a good seat because you'll be watching this one." Which is exactly what happened. In discouraging news, Antonio Harvey got to play, if only for three minutes. I will now enjoy several days of obsession regarding the possible implications of his 180 seconds of nonglory contrasted with my own lack of playing time, which will be good neither for the quality of my sleep nor for my sanity.

I probably ought to clarify the mess that is the contract situation here in Atlanta. During the regular season, an NBA team is allowed to have up to fifteen players under contract. Of these, twelve suit up for games. Three players are placed on the inactive list. The Hawks currently have thirteen players signed to guaranteed contracts, including DerMarr Johnson, who broke his neck in a late-night car wreck and is out for the year. It would seem, then, that two spots are open. Not really. An NBA team is not required to keep fifteen players on its roster. The only real requirement—at least to my knowledge—is a roster of twelve. Given that information, one might wonder why I would willingly subject myself to a training camp under the conditions outlined. The answer: like every other cliché-spouting basketball player, it has been my dream to play in the NBA since I was a skinny, freckle-faced ten-year-old shooting baskets on the goal mounted on the deck of my childhood home. To me, it is worth the gamble. So I battle on. Other people think they're going to drop twenty-five pounds in two pre-wedding months; I think I'm going to play in the NBA. We all must have something with which to delude ourselves.

October 25

I had a feeling that it might not be a good day when, after practice, one of the assistant coaches found me and asked me if I was still in contact with my former team in Greece. My dire premonition was con-firmed when Lon Kruger sidled over as I was shooting post-practice free throws. He flashed his ever-present smile and said something to the effect that it was "cut day" and that he needed to see me in his of-fice. My brain wanted me to say, "Tell you what, Coach, how about we skip the niceties? Let's shake hands, I'll tell you to kiss my ass, and we can both go our respective ways." My mouth said, "Uh, okay." I deal with rejection in a very healthy way.

And so I got the axe.

I was literally the last player cut. As previously theorized, the choice came down to Antonio Harvey and me. They picked him. Ouch.

I knew before practice that one of us was going to make the team and that one of us was going to clean out his locker. I talked to my agent, Keith Glass, the night before my demise; he told me that final cuts would happen in the morning. He related that the team had just learned that one of its post players was injured severely enough to re-quire surgery. Consequently, they would keep either Harvey or me until the injured player could return. It was shaping up to be a story-book ending.

Keith's next words were disheartening. He had learned that the general manager of the Hawks, Pete Babcock, wanted to keep me, while head coach Lon Kruger wanted to send me home in favor of Harvey. I felt a little betrayed. Actually, a lot betrayed. Lon Kruger is from Silver Lake, Kansas, which is about twenty miles from my child-hood home. I grew up playing against his nephew. In fact, that nephew helped Silver Lake eliminate my high school team in the sub-state semifinals during my junior year of high school. Additionally, Keith advises Kruger. I didn't expect these connections to help if I wasn't close to making the team. However, given the obvious ambivalence displayed by everyone involved, it seemed to me that it would not be difficult for Kruger to look the way of a fellow small-town Kansas kid. Apparently I was wrong. If our families lived in Tennessee, I think a hillbilly hollow battle would now commence.

Armed with Keith's confusing information, I went to bed anticipating an interesting day. As I fell asleep, I really had no idea what would transpire. I woke up feeling relatively good about my chances— an odd emotion for me. The choice was between two players with very similar abilities, who had played nearly the same number of minutes in the preseason games. I thought that either my hometown connection with Kruger or my low cost to the team would make the decision easy and carry me to the fruition of my basketball dreams. (And then I considered grabbing the pen at my bedside and stabbing myself in the eye for ever thinking of the phrase "fruition of my basketball dreams.") Additionally, I had Babcock—the team's general manager— in my corner. I had also placed calls to both my college coaches, Tim Floyd and Larry Eustachy, the night before. I hoped that either would be able to call in a recommendation.

I went to practice expecting some news before we took the court, but no information was forthcoming. Nobody mentioned any cuts, so I readied myself to scream at Keith after practice for sending me into a panic and making me call in favors on short notice. And then it all came crashing down around me when Lon Kruger found me after practice. During the obligatory hyperpositive meeting with the GM and head coach, the usual phrases were tossed about from their side. Some examples: "great to have you in camp," "really love the way you play," "great future in front of you," and my favorite, "let us know if we can do anything to help you." To which I wanted to respond, "Oddly, there is something you could help me with. I've always kind of wanted to play in the NBA. Anything you can do on that end?" I managed to find my way out of the office and then participated in one of the most uncomfortable fifteen-minute periods of my life. I had come directly from the court to the coaches' offices that adjoin the locker room. I hadn't had time to shower or dress. So I prepared myself for departure from the locker room—and the Atlanta Hawks—while the real team showered and got ready to go home, finished with another average day in their lives. It wasn't awkward at all. My former teammates tried not to say anything that might send me into an uncontrollable rage, but I could practically hear the little voice from afar saying, "Dead man walking!" as I exited the shower. I would have found the whole mess quite funny, had I not been so sad.

And was it really necessary to tell me all this jolly news *after* practice? It's not like I needed the extra exercise.

November 17

I am relatively new to an existence as a professional basketball player. Now that I am unemployed, answering the obligatory second question— "What team do you play for?"—just became much more difficult. I wonder if I am eligible for unemployment benefits.

The next step is in sight, however.

Keith got married recently. Because of the subsequent honeymoon, he was able to answer one of my recent calls and the requisite question about his well-being with, "Well, we're on a gondola in Venice." My response was, "Yeah, well, I'm in my parents' basement in Kansas. Again. Stick that in your pipe and smoke it."

I feel some ownership for his marriage because I was around for the beginning of it. When I was playing in Greece last year, he came to Athens to browbeat my team's management into paying what they owed me. To that point, I had received less than half of the $100,000 I was supposed to receive for the year. I had begun to consider the firebombing of the team's gym to stimulate some transactions when, thankfully, Keith decided that a trip to Athens was in order. He had several clients there in a similar predicament. (Not to mention that none of the teams with which he was dealing had paid him either.) I was happy that he cared enough to visit and was hopeful that a resolution could be reached without any harm befalling the team's owner or his family.

While in Greece, Keith met a woman with whom he had been set up—a Turkish sports broadcaster by the name of Aylin. (Last name of . . . something with a bunch of *t*'s, *k*'s, and *c*'s with extra appendages.) He a fifty-year-old Jewish agent/attorney from New Jersey, she a forty-year-old Muslim sportscaster from Istanbul—a match made in heaven. With all the similarities, I was amazed they didn't meet sooner.

Keith brought Aylin to the United States and married her. As we have all noticed, Armageddon was not brought on by this, the ultimate cultural and theological clash, and both parties seem to be quite happy. After the wedding, the happy couple was forced by the chaos in their respective lives to delay their honeymoon—it was the beginning of basketball season and the groom is, well, a basketball agent. Keith probably thought it was safe to take off for the honeymoon in early November. Most of the players in his stable can keep a job. Their honeymoon is also a chance for Keith to visit some of his players in Europe, while also checking the market for prospective suckers who could be deceived into employing one Paul Shirley. For better or worse, he has not encountered many teams in Europe clamoring to shell out large amounts of cash. That knowledge, coupled with the fact that I was rather close to making an NBA team leads us to think that it may be prudent to stay on this continent for the year.

I would probably be more apt to return to Europe if not for the swindle to which I was subjected in Greece. As I mentioned, I signed a contract that was to pay me $100,000 for the period beginning November 1 and ending at the close of the season. That salary—as is usually the case with European contracts—net of any taxes. The team agreed to pay income tax in Greece, leaving me responsible for any difference between the American tax rate and the Greek one. I received my first payment in whole and on time. It would prove to be the only such instance, as the team began half payments in December. I complained mildly at first but assumed that my illustrious agent would take care of the situation.

My team's non-adherence to my contracted pay schedule was not the only problem. Additionally, the conditions of our gym left something to be desired. At some point, vandals broke out the windows next to the court and the temperature inside equalized with that of the out-of-doors. Winters in Greece are not frigid. Nonetheless, outdoor basketball is not recommended. The open-air arrangement did provide some relief from the massive cloud of smoke that usually hung over the court. It would be my opinion that Greeks dislike two things: lung health and authority. No Smoking signs were displayed prominently at our gym but were universally ignored. Apparently, it was too much to ask for a two-hour hiatus so that the participants in a basketball game might be spared the inhalation of massive amounts of cigarette smoke while playing.

Their love for Philip Morris aside, the Greek people were great, I liked most of my teammates, and I liked Athens. I justified the lack of remuneration by recalling that I was being allowed the free use of a car and was paying no rent for a very nice apartment. And I was being paid *something;* after a lifetime of no real income, anything seemed like a fortune.

I left Greece with $52,000 of the $105,000 owed me. (The extra $5,000 was a contracted bonus for my team's advancement to the playoffs.) I was told that we would sue the team and that I would receive the money eventually, although it could take several years.

The lawsuit went to trial that summer. I won. The team appealed—on what grounds, I do not know. I won the appeal. Still, I felt no confidence that I would receive the missing money. In my time in Athens, I learned that the Greeks—at least the ones in charge of my team—are a duplicitous lot. Team officials would lie to me with no hesitation. For example, sometime after the team finally found an apartment for me, a knock at my front door roused me from the pathetic e-mail I was composing to some girl back home. My Greek landlord was in the hall, holding an eviction notice. He told me I had to leave the apartment that weekend because the team hadn't paid rent in three months. When I informed the team's manager, he assured me that the man would be paid soon. He wasn't—making my every trek through the lobby of my building a tenuous one.

Several teams were in similarly dire financial straits. As I wrote above, Keith had players on some of those other teams. The financially troubled teams petitioned the Greek minister of sport regarding their problems. The Council of Sport, or whatever it is called, decided to help its basketball teams and passed a new policy on player salaries. In the process, the teams were forgiven their respective debts and made to promise not to allow themselves to get into arrears again.

I will never see the missing $53,000.

Thus I am somewhat leery of a return to Europe.

Because Keith and I had decided soon after my departure from the Hawks that it was likely that I would stay in the United States to play this season, I explored the options here to the best of my ability. In our country, someone who does not make the NBA basically has two choices. Neither is especially attractive. There is the CBA (Continental Basketball Association), which has located its franchises in vibrant cities like Gary, Indiana, and Boise, Idaho. The CBA is chock-full of talented players who are missing something that keeps them out of the NBA. Whether what a player is lacking is an opportunity, a jump shot, or the ability to put down a crack pipe is determined by NBA scouts that travel to games.

The other option is the NBDL (National Basketball Developmental League), the year-old minor league that is the baby of the NBA. The NBDL hopes to develop as a more legitimate minor-league system for the NBA by playing its games in destination cities like Mobile, Alabama, and Fayetteville, North Carolina.

Keith and I think the CBA is less terrible than the NBDL, and after careful consideration, it seems that I will soon join the Grand Rapids Hoops for the rest of the season. That is, assuming that the team will change its nickname. The Grand Rapids *Hoops*? Jesus Christ.

November 22

Tonight I realized, while crossing a blustery street in frigid South Dakota in search of food, that I may have reached rock bottom in the world of professional basketball. This epiphany presented itself while

I pondered how the person who programmed the electronic marquee for the Sioux Falls Convention Center (it's on the way to the deli I was visiting) could have come to the conclusion that the British rock band's name is spelled Def Leappard.

I am now a member of the Yakima Sun Kings of the CBA. We (I am able to say "we" now that I have been a Sun King for all of three days) are at the beginning of a Dakotas road trip that includes two games in twenty-six hours, with about four hundred miles of highway in between.

The careful reader would note that I thought I would soon be joining the Grand Rapids franchise of the CBA. That plan fell apart when Keith got a bad feel from the Hoops about how I would be used on the court . . . and treated off it. So he went to Plan—well, I would think it's about Plan K, and set me up with coach Bill Bayno and the mighty Sun Kings. (Plan A: making the team with the Hawks. On through Plan J, which was to play basketball anywhere other than Yakima, Washington. I think Plan L might be to take up goat herding.) I acquiesced; I did not have any loyalty to any of the franchises in question and was fairly tired of living in my parents' basement. I even found a silver lining in the plan. Maurice Carter, one of the players who, like me, had been cut from the Hawks at the end of training camp, played for the team in Yakima. We had become friends, so I knew I would have at least one ally on the team.

I was supposed to leave on Thursday morning—which I learned on Wednesday afternoon at four-thirty. I was a little apprehensive; the entire scenario sounded relatively miserable.

After a sleepless night, I was primed and ready for my first CBA experience. I flew to Seattle, where I joined the team, which was traveling home from a game in Illinois. I had learned the night before my departure that my friend Maurice had recently decided to return home because of an injury, thus ripping out any lining, silver or otherwise, from the situation. The team made the three-hour bus ride to Yakima, where I was shown to my quarters. A major kink in the original Grand Rapids plan had been that team's inability to arrange a roommate-less situation for me. The Sun Kings did find a place I could call my own—a hotel room. Actually, I mislead. It's a *motel* room, as in the door to my room opens to the world. The entire team is staying at the palatial Cedars Inn and Suites for the balance of the season. I don't think my room is one of the suites . . . although it does have a microwave and a refrigerator. Let me reiterate, for emphasis, though—my door opens to the parking lot.

After taking in my new digs, I was whisked off to the city's premier eating establishment for a meet–the–Sun Kings engagement. And so I sat in the Burger Ranch in Yakima, Washington, and signed autographs until the hunger of the massive crowd of nine was sated (or maybe it was until my basket of chicken strips came out of the fryer), and wondered if my life could possibly get any better.

On Friday, game day, we had a midmorning shoot-around to prepare for the night's contest. I signed a lucrative CBA contract thirty seconds prior to the quasi-practice and my career with the Yakima Sun Kings was under way. (Nine hundred dollars a week, before taxes. Not exactly the NBA.) In my first action, against the Great Lakes Storm (coached by former Iowa State legend Jeff Grayer), I was extremely sluggish and my timing was off, but I managed to score nineteen points in a supporting role. Unfortunately, I was not around for the end of the game. My eyebrow had a rather forceful encounter with the forehead of an opposing player with about six minutes left in the game. I made a bloody mess of the court and then retired to the locker room, where a surprisingly proficient doctor stitched me up. It was a nasty gash; it gaped impressively, but it was directly in my left eyebrow, so the scar shouldn't hamper the modeling career on which I plan to embark upon the conclusion of my Hall of Fame–caliber basketball career.

I realize that there are worse things than being paid to play basketball. But three days into this, in a Best Western in Sioux Falls, South Dakota, I am struggling to see the forest for the trees. Or the light at the end of the tunnel. Or whatever euphemism that most eloquently expresses that I am not quite sure why exactly I am doing this to myself. The proverbial NBA dream seems a long way from here.

December 1

We recently had a Sunday off. I was looking forward to a pleasant day of contemplating the tensile strength of one of my belts if used as a noose when one of our assistant coaches informed me that he was driving to Seattle to work with a player who might join our team. The workout was to take place at the Sonics practice facility; said coach worked for that team for eighteen years and had access to their courts. He asked if I would go along. Apparently the Sonics brass had expressed some mild interest in my basketball stylings. I was not thrilled to spend an off day driving to and from Seattle, but as I have no real life and kind of want to play in the NBA, I thought I could sacrifice one lazy Sunday afternoon. We set out early in the morning and made the fog-filled journey to Mariner-ville. Upon arrival in the city, we picked up the player who would theoretically join us in Yakima, a Greek player named Giannis Giannoulis, pronounced tar-JEEK casstee-LEE-dis. (Not really. I was just checking to see if anyone was paying attention.) Giannoulis played for Panathinaikos in Athens last year but was suspended from competition for two years by the Greek sport authorities because he tested positive for a controlled substance. He maintains that he was given a cold medication by his team doctor and then took it as directed, resulting in his positive test. I tend to believe him. Most everything even remotely medicinal will taint the blood in some way, in the view of international guidelines. Acetaminophen (Tylenol) is a banned substance in European basketball circles. Seriously.

Giannoulis went to training camp with the Toronto Raptors this year but was cut before the start of the season. His only remaining option in the world is to play in the CBA. (Basketball option, that is; I suppose nothing is stopping him from becoming a mortician.) Evidently, American leagues do not have to abide by the rules the rest of the world holds dear. Through a friend of a friend, Giannoulis ended up in contact with coach Bill Bayno and took the trip over the ocean hoping to continue his basketball career.

After we picked up the Greek in Seattle, we drove to the arena where our assistant coach worked us out for an hour . . . without viewage from any Sonics personnel. Ostensibly, I was there to help test Giannoulis for the benefit of the Sun Kings, but my only real motivation was the hope of some contact with the Sonics higher-ups. I was miffed when our workout ended. But just as we were leaving, the general manager, Rick Sund, appeared. When he was introduced to me and we had dispensed with the usual pleasantries, he said, "You know, Paul, we knew you were coming up here today with Steve [our assistant coach]. Had one more of our guys been hurt, we were going to sign you for a day." The Sonics were down to eight players, and one of those was questionable for the night's game. The NBA requires eight players in uniform for any one game. So my fate—at least for one day—was determined by how one millionaire felt about his groin injury. Dammit. After talking to Sund, Giannoulis and I re-fired the inner furnaces and went through a brief secondary workout. (Giannoulis was about to pass out—he "not in so good shape.") Sund watched, but I didn't catch him running off to find a pen and a contract, so I returned to Yakima less one day of rest but having gained a little exposure.

After my brush with the NBA, it was time to think about a more important issue, namely, Thanksgiving. Or, more accurately, the avoidance of suicidal thoughts as I spent Thanksgiving away from home yet again.

For my money, the only thing more depressing than an Indian reservation casino filled with people who can't afford to be there is a Thanksgiving dinner held at one. This was Thanksgiving number seven in a row away from my family. Fortunately, I was able to spend a part of the day with a hundred or so of my closest Mexican, Indian, and white-trash friends. I would have considered the food there pretty good . . . if I were a Sudanese refugee. In fact, it was the worst Thanksgiving dinner I have ever consumed.

I am faced with the situation yearly, yet I never learn. I see turkey, mashed potatoes, and stuffing on some buffet table and I think of Grandma's turkey, mashed potatoes, and stuffing. While my mind is envisioning a delectable meal, the cold reality of what is about to be perpetrated upon my stomach is slightly less than that. In this year's case, I made it about halfway through the turkey loaf, instant mashed potatoes, and cold stuffing before giving up and trying the dessert table. It is hard to screw up pumpkin filling in the process of scooping it from the can to the pie shell.

December 15

Of late, my life has been a blur of bad hotels, empty arenas, and long bus rides. I'm not sure who decided that every CBA team should be located in a city near the Arctic Circle. I do know that I'd like to have that person shot. Logistics also seem to be a difficult task for the CBA front office. In my short time with the Sun Kings, I have already played in two back-to-back sets of games—but with a six-hour bus ride in between each. The first, during which we played in Sioux Falls one night and Bismarck the next, seemed somewhat acceptable, since we did play two different teams. However, I can't justify dual games against the Idaho Stampede—one in Yakima, one in Boise. After the first game, both teams loaded onto buses to drive across eastern Washington and Idaho. We slept through the day and then donned the opposite uniform as the night before—home became road, and vice versa—for a game in their home arena. I can't exactly imagine Allen Iverson agreeing to such an arrangement.

Lessons learned in the past week:

1. Bismarck must be in Saskatchewan. Such is the only explanation for how far it is from Sioux Falls.
2. Ordering from a Wendy's drive-through—on foot—on a late December night in South Dakota is a poor plan.
2b. Fast food should not be a part of anyone's training diet.
3. I hate sleeping with another person in my room.
4. I would like an NBA team to sign me—I am ready and willing. I've already had enough of the CBA.

The bones in my foot did an awkward little dance during one of the games that made me hate the CBA. I started a game against the Dakota Wizards like a ball of fire, scoring my team's first four points. After that, I pretty much took the night off. I could tell before the game that I was out of sync, but I couldn't tell Coach Bayno that I didn't have my best stuff—I'm not a middle reliever. I muddled my way through the first half and into the third quarter. Then, after a rare steal by me, I took off on the subsequent breakaway, but in a shockingly slow manner. It seemed like I was running in mud. When I got to the other end of the court, I attempted to make a move to the basket. In the process, I somehow managed to come down on the side of my foot. I jogged back down the court before I realized that something was wrong. After a brief discussion on the bench, I retired to the training room, where it was determined that I needed some X-rays, pronto. After the game, I went with much trepidation to the local clinic, where the physician's assistant who happened to be at the game examined my films. By his reckoning, I had an avulsion in a bone in my left foot. (An avulsion fracture is a condition wherein the ligament pulls a piece of the bone away from the main body of the bone.) To him, though, it looked like an old injury. The acute pain I was feeling was, he was 80 percent sure, an aggravation of the old problem. I was relieved. Kind of. I would have been more relieved if he had been a real doctor. A person doesn't usually *choose* to stop short of medical school in order to become a PA. The fear of a certain standardized test often has something to do with his decision.

Before the X-ray, I had some time on the bench to contemplate my possible fate. At the time, the outlook was pretty grim. The trainer and I were afraid that I had really done something nasty to myself. As I sat there and tried to imagine what I would do for the rest of the year if I had to rehabilitate an injury, I was struck with the realization that, for all my hatred of the CBA, I would be devastated to have my season cut short right now. I would be less disappointed if the team grew tired of me and released me. At least I would have given this my best effort and would be leaving because of something I could control—my own ability to play. A two-month rehab period at this point in the year would do very little to help my basketball career. In fact, it would probably destroy the season for me. I haven't exactly made enough of a name to withstand such a setback. This really is a fragile existence.

After my initial examination by the team's faith healer, I rested for a day and then saw a real doctor. He ordered an MRI to determine the exact nature of the problem in my ankle/foot. Because I have spent a relatively large portion of my life waiting on the results of X-rays, MRIs, and bone scans, I've had time over the years to reflect on my mood prior to learning about my frailties. It's a strange set of feelings. In my experience, I never want to be badly hurt, but I usually want something to show up on whatever piece of film is being utilized. I suppose it is a silly, macho, sports-related mentality, but I never want to have begged out of a game or practice for no reason. No one wants to be the crazy old lady who hears things that others do not. While I analyzed my own neuroses, I waited at the doctor's office, hoping that I wasn't going to need a screw put in my foot, but also hoping that the doctor wouldn't return to his waiting room to find an overly tall crazy person waiting for him.

As suspected, the injury to my foot was merely the aggravation of an old problem. The MRI showed a piece of bone that is capable of dislodging from time to time. When I came down on my foot strangely, it moved to a location that struck a nerve. (Literally, not figuratively. For a change.) But the piece of bone is able to naturally find its way back into the puzzle-like space it normally inhabits, and all is well. Getting out of bed at age sixty is going to be great.

December 25

Someone wearing a yarmulke just walked by. I wish I had one of those on my head right now. If I did, I wouldn't mind that I am sitting in an airport on Christmas Day, waiting for the delayed connection that will take me to Seattle to meet back up with my team. My Christmas visit at home was great—I was so happy, it felt like I was on heroin for two days. I suppose the lows of the return trip are worth the highs of the time at home, but sometimes I wonder.

One would think that I would be better at leaving home after Christmas by now. I've only had to do it for the last seven years in a row—minus the two I was not at home for Christmas at all. Unfortunately, I am not good at it. This year, I thought I was in good shape as we left for the airport, but the fact that I was leaving hit me hard when I watched my mother and brother wave good-bye from behind the glass at the gate in Kansas City. Apparently, twenty-five-year-old males are not yet emotionally developed enough to leave home without sinking into a mild depression. Perhaps life in basketball has stunted my maturation. Then again, maybe I just don't like going back to situations that are terrible. Seriously, it's Christmas Day. I'm supposed to be lying by the fire right now, digesting my Christmas dinner. I'm not supposed to be waiting for a connecting flight to Seattle.

I knew when I signed up for this basketball gig that one of the hazards of the occupation is missed holidays. But I suppose one can never prepare fully for the feeling of leaving any situation in which one is comfortable, whether it is Christmas Day at home or a warm bed in the morning. (Well, I guess some people can prepare—they're called "well-adjusted.") I do know this: when my basketball career comes to an end, I will certainly make myself enjoy a little geographical steadiness and will keep myself away from airplanes, out of hotels, and home on Christmas.

December 29

By bus, the Dakotas look a lot like Poland. Flat. And barren. The Canadian army would not have a hard time conquering this part of the world—if Canada does, in fact, have an army. I've had plenty of time to observe the Dakotan, er, scenery during a recent trek from Bismarck to Sioux Falls and back again. We played in North Dakota on Friday, in South Dakota on Saturday, and then again in Bismarck the following Tuesday. Again, one would think that some CBA scheduling genius could have put the two Bismarck games together so we would have to make only one long ride across the plains. Obviously, geniuses are in short supply.

With a few tweaks, the CBA could be really good. Well, tolerable, at least. But it must lose all of its talent—both athletic and administrative—to the NBA. It makes sense. The best players are called up; I would guess that the same rules apply to administrators, secretaries, and trainers. Even the best floor sweepers probably don't last long. By the nature of a society that rewards those who succeed, a minor league's pinnacle is mediocrity.

Regardless, to the naked eye a good CBA game is not much different from an NBA game. The players are really tall and the action is just as fast-paced. Fans do miss the recognition of stars, but I contend that teams are just as marketable—especially in cities completely bereft of any entertainment options. I now know from experience that there is nothing better to do in Yakima than to go to a minor-league basketball game.

Sadly, the CBA suffers from a shaky reputation. It has long been a holding ground for minor-league lifers—players who will probably never play in the NBA and have enormous flaws in their games. But these same players know how to win at the minor-league level, so it is difficult for a particular team to turn them away. Those who don't fit the stereotype of the long-term failure are likely to be transient participants; players move in and out every few weeks and fans struggle to relate to an ever-changing roster.

I contend that many of the league's problems could be solved by a good, cheap marketing plan. If revenue increased, players' salaries would follow, attracting better players who would, in turn, attract more fans. Unfortunately, I haven't seen many ads promoting the Sun Kings around Yakima. I feel like a weekly trip to the schools to hand out tickets might not be a bad idea. Maybe even the occasional blood drive for publicity. Or semen drive.

I came to these groundbreaking conclusions during my latest bus ride across the tundra. I would have rather been sleeping, but bus-bound rest is a near impossibility. Buses are most definitely not built with six-foot-ten-inch people in mind. Someone my size can't sit facing forward without his knees grazing his Adam's apple. But the seats are too lumpy to lie comfortably across. The walls of the bus are invariably equipped with protrusions of the sort that make it impossible to rest one's back against them, and the pairs of seats across from one another are never lined up correctly. When one tries to sleep by stretching out across the bus, his legs have to shift one direction or the other, making cramps and spasms a way of life for the duration of the attempt at slumber. The aisle, meanwhile, is just wide enough to provide a chasm into which one's ass will forever slip. All in all, the ergonomics of the bus make trying to sleep in one like trying to sleep on a staircase.

Temperature control is often a problem as well. It is always too hot on a long bus ride. Always. I think this is due to an overcompensation for the frigid weather outside; I haven't spent a lot of time on buses in the South—trips across Alabama notwithstanding—but I suspect that I might be onto something. Another constant is the spilled drink that makes its presence felt from the front of the bus to the back. The drink in question is always soda. Anything less sticky is simply unacceptable.

One nearly ubiquitous facet of the bus ride has actually been challenged on our trips of late: the bad movie. Generally, the people who pick bus movies think that since tastes are varied among the prospective viewers, the movie should be aimed at the lowest common denominator—no taste at all. As I said, however, we at the Yakima Sun Kings have rebelled of late. Our assistant coach, inexplicably, has decent theatrical taste—we've actually watched the odd good movie now and then. The phenomenon has opened up entertainment options I didn't know existed on buses.

When I leapt into this minor league experience, I expected to hate my teammates. (I am such the optimist.) With a few exceptions, my fears have not been realized. I've been shocked at how well I get along with most of my compatriots. I assumed that I would be riding around on buses with sullen ex-cons. Of course, I can out-sullen nearly anyone, so perhaps that was the wrong adjective to use to describe people I wouldn't like. At any rate, I really do like most of my teammates. How very bizarre.

Now, I cannot advance the theory that these colleagues pay much attention to the world around them. I barged into our locker room prior to a recent game to find some of my teammates embroiled in a heated debate. They could not come to a consensus regarding the number of states in our country. (That would be the United States, in case of reader confusion.) Two thought there were fifty, while the others contended that fifty-two was a more likely answer. But neither party could win the support of the other. When I arrived on the scene, the group appealed to my vast knowledge of third-grade social studies for a final answer. After an initial reaction of incredulity and, actually, indignation, I set them straight and then decided to press the issue a bit. (I am such an ass, thinking I know so much about facts that could be taught to a baboon.) So I asked whether anyone knew how many stripes are on the flag. (This, after I clued in those present to the tidbit that is the correlation between states in the Union and stars on the American flag—a shocking revelation to some. I wish I were joking.) The first response to the stripes question was thirty-three. But that hypothesis wasn't voiced very convincingly. There were no other guesses. As we move through the season, I think I'll keep the conversations away from history and the social sciences.

We added a player named Alex Jensen to our team recently. He is my roommate on the road now; we get along famously. It is striking how similar we are, even though he belongs to the cult that is the Mormon Church. He is like the teammates I thought I would find in college. (But didn't.) He is just as baffled by the whole minor-league experience as I am, which is to say very baffled. Oddly, we don't complain about our lots in life at all. That last sentence was a lie.

Alex and I spend a lot of time together. As such, I was surprised when I returned to our hotel room in Bismarck and found my nose to be immediately assailed by the pungent aroma of marijuana smoke. After a brief bout with confusion, I realized that Alex had not fired up a joint—he's more of a Quaaludes guy. (Slander prevention: I'm joking, of course.) Two of our illustrious teammates were next door producing enough smoke to filter under the adjoining door, thoroughly devastating the air quality of our room. Skill of theirs that needs work: discreetness.

While I do have to battle the occasional contact high, my life could be worse. For most of the season, the Sioux Falls SkyForce—one of the other seven teams in the CBA—has employed a player named Korleone Young. He was recently released by the team. I took note because Korleone was a nemesis of mine in high school. He went to a much bigger high school than I did, so our meetings came only in summer AAU tournaments. Korleone and his high-profile teammates regularly thrashed my team of small-school white kids in gyms across the Midwest. Young was touted as a surefire pro; I was touted as a surefire college intramural player. (Perhaps *nemesis* was the wrong term earlier. "Destructive force to my basketball self-esteem" may have been more appropriate.) He went on to be a second-round NBA draft pick directly from high school. But for Korleone, the high school days and the fame they brought were the highlight of his career. Since then his stock has fallen dramatically. Meanwhile, I have gone from his whipping boy to—currently, anyway—having a much better chance at a successful professional career than he. Strange how these things work out. Despite my efforts to the contrary, I remain a vengeful bastard. As such, I take no small amount of pride in our role reversal.

I will never forget the disdain I saw in the faces of Young and his teammates back in our younger days. They were not exactly respectful to my AAU team. (Polite understatement. They rarely acknowledged our existence.) And while I joke about our skill level, we weren't bad at all. But we were all white and none of us had scholarships waiting for us when we were sixteen. To be honest, Young and his teammates were the bullies of our AAU world. Back then, I exacted my revenge by being clever and figuring out ways to score that didn't involve direct athletic confrontation. Now, I find satisfaction in knowing that my way worked. I kept getting better while he floundered, happy with what he had accomplished. It does pain me to admit that I take some pleasure from our changed fortunes—it's not the most enlightened view. Then again, maybe he should have been nicer.

January 5

When we are in Yakima, a minibus takes us from the motel to practice and games. The shuttle is driven by a bearded older fellow named Paul who seems to have quite a lot of time on his hands. He is an unbelievably nice guy but is something of a hillbilly. Like many of his ilk, he has an easily stereotyped berm house surrounded by fourteen weed-covered cars in various states of disrepair. When Alex and I found out about Paul's automobile menagerie, we asked if he might be able to find us some transportation; the man obviously has connections within the very-used-car market of Yakima, Washington. We were hoping to find a car that personified the CBA experience. Paul came through nicely. He pulled a beauty from his own domain—a 1980 Chevrolet Malibu. In maroon. Cost to us: $50. The Malibu came to Alex and me fully loaded with a blue left front fender option along with a standard child-protection lock on the driver's-side door (i.e., it cannot be opened from the inside). It has a fully cracked windshield. I think the dealer threw in the matted dog hair on the seats for no additional charge. It suits our needs perfectly. We now have a car that seems custom-designed for the CBA.

On a recent sojourn, we noticed that our trusty maroon steed was in need of nourishment, so we pulled into a local Amoco. After some head scratching and several furrowed brows, we discovered that the gas intake was on neither the left nor the right, but in the rear under the license plate. (What a great era for car design. No engineer could have been expected to foresee that a rear-end collision might turn the vehicle into a fireball.) After locating the car's receptacle, Alex and I began fueling the car as we watched passersby ogle our chariot. Then another engineering flaw came to light. In the rear-tank setup, the spring-loaded license plate is held away from the entry valve only by the nozzle that is doing the fueling. That night, the force of the spring was greater than the hold the nozzle had on the gas entry valve and, voilà, the nozzle popped out, spewing gasoline all over the ground . . . and my pants. Alex and I looked at each other, gave thanks that we were not tap-dancing on nails at the time of the incident, shrugged, and resumed the gassing process, taking care to hold the pesky license plate at bay.

January 12

I'm at a loss for words.

I usually fail when I try to express the emotions surrounding positive events in my life. For whatever reason, I am more effective when the chips are down. With that in mind, I will now attempt to describe the achievement of the one goal I have ever had.

I am now in the NBA. The Atlanta Hawks signed me to a ten-day contract.

I wish I could write that I will probably make too much out of this. In fact, I probably won't make enough of it.

As a child, I wanted nothing more than to one day play in the NBA. I don't know why, but being among the best basketball players in the world captured my imagination. Of course, I wanted a few other things along the way. From age six to sixteen, I expressed a desire to be a construction worker, an aeronautical engineer, and a cardiologist. Those desires never stuck. The goal to play in the NBA did.

It was a stupid goal. Kids who grow up in rural Kansas don't ever play in the NBA. But I thought I might as well give it a try. So when my eighth-grade basketball coach sent me home with a list of drills and then asked me how long I had practiced each night, I could say, with pride, that I had been dribbling and shooting from the concrete slab underneath our deck for an hour, or an hour and a half, or two hours. My brothers and I played out the NCAA brackets in games of one-on-two. (They're younger, and so made up the two.) I created little games to test my shooting—a shot from the short corner, a side three-pointer, a jump shot from the elbow, a three from the top of the key, and a free throw.

Of course, lost in all of this self-congratulatory bullshit is the help I had along the way. My parents never let on that my goals were idiotic ones, and my coaches never allowed me to settle for anything less than greatness. (Or at least, really-goodness.) And, along the way, I grew.

I probably wouldn't be writing this if I were six-two. It's possible—just not as likely. I theorize that each additional inch of height increases one's chance to play in the NBA by an order of magnitude. Incremental changes in height are to the NBA what the Richter scale is to brick-and-mortar houses in Kazakhstan.

I should write it again: I am in the NBA. Not a tryout, or a summer league, or training camp. I am a full-fledged member of the Atlanta Hawks during the regular season. Of course, the Hawks are a sinking ship—a team adrift and without the head coach who favored cutting me at the beginning of the season. Leo Kruger was fired at Christmastime after it became apparent that the playoff guarantee the team delivered to its season-ticket holders was not going to come to fruition. I can't say that I was disappointed by Kruger's departure. (I need to work on this ever-present need for vengeance.) And the Hawks could be the worst team in league history for all I care. I'm just glad they are going to let me have a uniform.

Forgive me if I seem awed, breathless, and swept away. I am. I can't help it. I'm as happy as I have ever been. I have wanted nothing in my life more than this.

My call-up came as a complete surprise. I did know that the period when NBA teams are allowed to sign players to ten-day contracts was approaching, but I had lost track of the actual date. The NBA seemed a world away from the long bus rides of the CBA. I was in endurance mode; my goal had shrunk to lesser ones like "Get out of bed" and "Don't kill self."

We (the Yakima Sun Kings) played at home on a Tuesday against the Dakota Wizards. We won the game and then boarded a bus for Boise, where we would play the next night. We lay down for the "night" at 6 A.M. and slept until 12:30 or so. While Alex and I were contemplating our breakfast/lunch options in the hotel restaurant, our assistant coach sidled in wearing a beaming smile. He told me that Coach Bayno wanted to see me. I had no idea what was going on; I thought maybe he was trying to make me think I had been released. (I was functioning on very little sleep.) When he ushered me into the hotel bar where Bayno was waiting, phone in hand, I could tell that something positive had happened. Bayno handed me the phone and said, "Congratulations, buddy." Obviously, the Hawks were on the other end—this story would not go too well with the theme here if not. I listened in disbelief as the assistant to the GM told me that the team was going to sign me to a ten-day contract.

It is quite possible that I spoke to Alex and/or one of the coaches after I got the call, but I can neither confirm nor deny such an event. My brain switched into a different mode. I sprinted down the hall of the hotel to my room and gathered my luggage. (In truth, I may have broken into a skip. There is also the distinct possibility that I pulled off a heel click à la Dick Van Dyke in *Mary Poppins* at some point.) I bid farewell to my teammates and was at the Boise airport within an hour for my 3:00 flight. Because of the most easily endured flight delay ever, I did not arrive in Atlanta until 2:30 A.M. I got to bed at 3:30 but didn't really sleep; I knew I had to get up at 6:30 for a physical and was as excited as I had been . . . ever. The relaxation required for actual sleep was elusive at best. I passed my physical in the morning and was whisked off to the gym to sign my contract. I did not have to sell my soul, nor was it all an elaborate hoax, and I became a contracted NBA player. Amazing.

We (the Atlanta Hawks) have played two games since I have been in town. Both were at home, both were wins. The Paul Shirley era is off to a rousing start. I haven't played—I don't know if I will play. The Hawks signed me because a player who was supposed to return from an injury sooner was not ready and was put on the injured list. Additionally, a few of the Hawks' other players are a little beaten up. So the team needed a player for practices and for game-time emergencies. That player is this guy. And that job is just fine with him.

For once, I cannot come up with anything cynical or sarcastic to write about the events of the last week. My call-up to the NBA is truly one of the most amazing events of my life, and I won't trivialize it. So that's it. For the next six days, I will be a player for the Atlanta Hawks.

After that, I don't know—the team could sign me to another ten-day contract or it could send me on my way. I will do my best to make sure that the former happens, but for my own sake, I will try to enjoy this dream while I am living it.

January 19

It was set up perfectly. I had just entered the game and I had the ball. I had played one minute and twenty-three seconds the night before in Milwaukee but hadn't found a chance to shoot the ball. Now was the time. I was in Boston, where Larry Bird and Kevin McHale had shown me via television waves the way to play basketball in the 1980s. It was not the Boston Garden—that arena had been torn down to make way for a new one with less personality and more luxury boxes—but it was close enough. With my back to the basket, I calmly took two dribbles to the middle, setting up a jump hook. I gracefully turned into what would have been my shot, but since I was in Boston, I gave my best McHale fake and turned to step through toward the basket. I left the floor with visions of glory and . . . threw up a complete brick. The ball didn't even clip the rim. I guess I can't have everything.

Yet.

(Wink.)

I was only in the game because we were getting bashed handily by the Celtics. I entered the game with four and a half minutes to play and managed to cast up four shots. None of them went in, but no one can accuse me of timidity in my first real NBA opportunity. (Incidentally, I was fouled on the aforementioned fairy-tale first shot, but I didn't really expect a call. Referees are not generally sympathetic to a rookie twelfth man who gets his only minutes in garbage time.) I am actually kind of proud of myself. I often wear a Rage Against the Machine T-shirt that carries the following quote by Emilio Zapata: "It is better to die on your feet than to live on your knees." And while I am not a Mexican revolutionary, and while the above quote is both overkill and overused, I do figure if I get the ball, I may as well shoot it.

I find myself suppressing smiles these days. While sitting on the bench during a game or standing on the sideline during practice, a realization that I am finally in the NBA hits. The result: the overwhelming urge to break into a huge grin—not an impulse I often have. Thankfully, I am usually able to successfully stave off reactions of jubilation and maintain the illusion that I belong here. (Or at least the illusion that I am maintaining the illusion.) Actually, such moments are not new to me. During my freshman year of college, I would often find myself reacting in the same way I do now—with complete amazement. (This was, of course, before I became spoiled by it all, back when the idea of playing for a Big 12 basketball program was the be-all and end-all.) I'm glad that I remain capable of such childish glee. And I'm heartened that I never became overwhelmed and was able to achieve goals I never though possible as a skinny college freshman.

The achievement of one's goals is like the progression of dating. None of us is ever really satisfied. Let's say I spy a girl waiting in line at a music store. She's beautiful—tall, with brown hair and blue eyes. Since I'm ready to leave, I get in line behind her. I make a remark about the band on the T-shirt she's wearing. She turns slightly, laughs, and brushes the hair out of her eyes. Inside, I'm jubilant; she hasn't given me the "I have a boyfriend" stare-down, so I have a chance. I introduce myself. We make small talk. She dawdles after paying, and I walk with her to the parking lot. She gives me her number and then drives away. For a moment, I am ecstatic. If a fellow music store customer had told me that I would end up with the beauty's phone number, I would have (1) asked him for advice, and (2) made a self-deprecating remark about my ability to approach strangers.

I call her, we go out. During dinner, I can think of nothing except to wonder how I might be able to kiss this girl at the end of the night. I can't concentrate on the conversation; I just want to know if she likes me. I walk her to her apartment. I consider my move as we chat nervously. (I have a Y chromosome and so have no real ability to read her emotions. She might be nervous or she might hate me. I can't tell.) She stands on the first step and I move in. If, back at the restaurant, our waiter had told me that I would now be kissing this gorgeous creature, I would have (1) asked him for advice and (2) slapped him for speaking in such a way about a lady.

We make plans to meet at a bar with some friends one night. After a few drinks, she's sitting on my lap. She whispers in my ear that it is time for me to walk her home. I do and then follow dutifully up the same stairs where I kissed her a week earlier. I wander around her apartment, looking idly at pictures, and wonder how I'm going to segue from whatever conversation we are about to have into a trip into her bedroom. She returns from the kitchen. I grab her hand and tell her that I am going to give her a tour of her own apartment. We collapse on the bed and before we know what has happened, everyone is naked. If back at the bar . . . well, I think I've made myself clear.

For now, just being in the NBA is plenty. But every achievement is quickly lost in the quest for the next. Which is good. Without short memories, we would accomplish nothing. We would be content with whatever we had just done. Without a short memory, my basketball career would never have made it this far . . . and I never would have had sex with the girl in the story.

After my first few days in Atlanta, I realized that I was facing a clothing shortage. When I got the call from the Hawks, I was on a CBA road trip. I didn't exactly have time to peruse my closet for the choicest clothing selections before my trip to Atlanta. This made the requisite dressing up for games and plane rides somewhat difficult. Because I had packed for a ten-day CBA trip, I did have enough extraneous items—socks, underwear, and the like. But I was lacking in the real clothes department—I had only a pair of khakis and two decent shirts. And those were last-minute additions; I had planned to wear my new Yakima Sun Kings sweats for about 85 percent of the trip. (The semi-nice clothes were packed only because my minor-league road trip was supposed to include a trip to the CBA all-star game. Which is like being named a cover model for a plus-size fashion magazine. *Vogue* it is not.)

By my second game with the Hawks, I had exhausted my clothing options and so felt that it was time to embark on a shopping trip in order to save myself the public ridicule that was sure to follow if I pulled the wear-the-same-dress (*Seinfeld* reference) routine. I did some research and learned that there was an Eddie Bauer store in a mall near my hotel in Atlanta. Because half of my wardrobe comes from Mr. Bauer's racks—due to their remarkably vast selection of clothes that fit six-foot-ten guys—I was pleased, and set off on a quest for some items that would open up my options. I braved the Atlanta subway (aka the moving homeless hotel) and found the correct mall. Upon arrival, a pleasant-enough man asked me—while I was staring with puzzlement at a color-coded mall map—if I needed help. "Why, yes," I said, "the phone book says that there is an Eddie Bauer at this mall . . . but I don't see it on the map." He knowingly replied, "Oh, that closed a while back." Strike one. I moved on to the next option: Macy's. Uppity stores like Macy's no longer have a presence in Topeka, so I was not particularly familiar with the chain. But I thought I could fake my way through the encounter. I sauntered into the men's department, only to have a man there tell me that not only did they not have anything that would fit me, but that I would fail everywhere else in the mall. Strike two. I was becoming somewhat flustered: we had a game in a few hours and I did not have time to be wandering around malls aimlessly.

From the depths of my memory, I remembered a time when, by some fluke, I had found some clothes at the Gap. I dodged some teenage loiterers and found my next potential savior. The racks were filled with clothes neither large nor long. In fact, I think a pathetic Napoleon may have taken the reins at the Gap and decided to seek retribution on all larger examples of humanity—not only were the clothes too small, they weren't even close. Strike three. (This baseball analogy would be useful only if someone changed the rules and it took five or six strikes to strike out.) I was getting desperate. My next plan involved homage to one of my college coaches, Larry Eustachy, and the mock turtleneck he wore for games. Or at least a long-sleeved T-shirt. I didn't think that two sporting goods stores would fail me. But they did, miserably. (Am I already at strikes four and five?) At the end of my mental rope, in a foggy, recycled-air-induced haze, I thought, "What the hell, I can wear a plain T-shirt with khakis." I found a five-for-$20 stand at another store and finally secured a few well-crafted selections. So what if the next road trip was to Milwaukee? It isn't cold there in January.

The beauty of the whole situation is that because I am in the NBA, if I wear a ring-necked T-shirt, everyone will assume that I paid $35 for it at Kenneth Cole. They have no idea it cost me $3.99 at a mall chain store that doesn't exactly specialize in dress clothes. And so I wore my new shirts with pride and survived the next few days without any further wardrobe problems. And that was great, for shirts. My pants options were limited to khaki or khaki, which was fine, because I'm white and middle-class and think that khaki pants will go with anything. But I ran into a snag when I woke up the morning after the game in Boston to find a mysterious oily stain on the left thigh of my one pair of decent pants. I solved the problem temporarily by carrying my laptop bag in front of me on the left side anytime I had to move—from the bus to the plane, and so on. When we arrived in San Antonio that afternoon, I summoned a hotel worker and sent my pants off to be dry-cleaned. My trousers came back the next morning. I was quite pleased with my efficiency—my pants had been on the disabled list, but they were going to get healthy just in time for the game. But, alas, the healing process had gone awry. Someone in the laundry room had allowed me to keep the stain and had added a random hole for no extra charge. I was nonplussed. I called the service people and told them my story. They were quite agreeable and—after an hour or so—called back to ask for a quote. At first I thought they wanted to hear some Shakespeare, but the lady quickly righted me and said they needed to know how much the pants had cost. She didn't care what I said next. I could have said $100, $150—she wouldn't have minded. The hotel's cleaning was done by an outside firm, so my quote wasn't going to come out of her employer's coffers. So, of course, I said, "Oh, $40." I hung up the phone and immediately gave myself an internal verbal lashing. But I got over it and found a nice big and tall men's store nearby and found the exact same pair of khakis. For $55.

While suiting up for our game in Milwaukee, I heard some shouting and carrying on next door. It sounded like a maintenance man was being whipped for insubordination. In fact, a Bucks player was leading members of both teams in a religious service. As previously noted, I struggle with the embrace of religion in sports, but I have learned that it is part of the circus. (In Yakima, our coach—prior to leading us in prayer—said exactly the following on several occasions: "Let's go get these motherf——s! Now let us pray.") Whether or not religion is appropriate to the basketball court is not my current debate. It would be a good one to have; right now, though, I'm more worried about whether I will see some sinning. I made it to the NBA. I want to see some NBA behavior. I need to watch a player use the halftime break to snort cocaine out of a bathroom stall. I want to see—or at least hear about—a pregame rendezvous with multiple groupies. Allow me to catch wind of some kind of scandalous behavior. Teammates I had in college were not afraid to come to practice drunk or to kick the odd policeman in the teeth from time to time; it doesn't seem too much to ask for the exaggerated version now. Instead, I get pregame prayer groups. I'd like to see the real NBA now. While all this religion and saintly behavior probably looks great on television, it is not nearly as interesting as one might think.

I am learning that most NBA players understand the stakes. Each player knows that one mistake could jeopardize his next contract. Beyond that, he understands how important the public-relations machine is. A lack of godliness on the part of a particular player could result in one fewer endorsement contract. Opportunity cost, as it were.

There is some debauchery—it just goes on behind doors that are closed to me. Groupies exist. They are not, however, awaiting the team in the hotel when we arrive at the next hotel. Believe me, I've been paying attention. Instead, it seems that most groupie action happens thanks to careful planning. For example, when we arrived in Milwaukee, someone with a decidedly feminine voice was waiting for the player staying immediately to my right in the hotel. And I don't think she was his girlfriend. Nor do I think that the moaning I heard was caused by a deep-tissue massage.

The NBA experience is rather amazing (I think I may have

mentioned that), but there are some depressing aspects. It really is great . . . as long as I don't have to be around other NBA players too much. Most of them are decent enough fellows, but there is something missing. And I think that "something" is the ability to relate to the average person. It is apparent that many of them were really good guys at one point but have become so jaded by an insular lifestyle that they now cannot remember what it was like to be just another guy. I relate the following as evidence of the problem: I sat in the locker room, preparing to watch another game while wearing a uniform. As I anxiously anticipated another pregame warm-up, I spoke to Shareef Abdur-Rahim, who is one of the Hawks I like and admire the most, while he idly opened some mail. He found a huge manila envelope, tore it open, cursorily examined the contents, and then tossed everything in the trash. I asked him what he was doing. He said that he had just thrown away the letters that fans sent him. I was taken aback and was offended enough to say, "You realize that people took time to write you those letters, and you just disregarded all of them." He thought about it, looked at me, and said, "Yeah, that just doesn't make any sense, does it? It's sad, but I do it anyway." I could tell that he regretted it, but I certainly did not see him digging through the trash to retrieve his fan mail.

It is true that I do not know what it is like to be a star in the NBA. I can't understand the pressures or demands. But in my opinion, if a person cannot even take the time to open a note from a fan and give it a glance (and this doesn't even address answering that mail), then he may need to rethink his priorities.

On a more positive note, I have been extremely impressed by the bag-handling procedures in the NBA. Before each road game, a bellman from the hotel in which we are staying comes to my door and says, "Bag pickup." Then he actually takes my bag and puts it on the bus. After the game, someone else takes my bag and puts it on the plane. The reverse is true as well. I never have to handle my own luggage, except to move it to and from the bus at the beginning and end of our trips. Will wonders never cease?

In truly fantastic news, the Hawks have decided that they haven't had their fill of me after ten days and have decided to sign me to another ten-day contract. Yippee! (Remember, I do not use exclamation points lightly.)

January 21

The sequence of events regarding the signing of my second ten-day contract went something like this . . .

Thursday, San Antonio, 4 P.M.: Atlanta Hawks general manager Pete Babcock to me: "Paul, we are going to sign you to another ten-day contract when this one is up. Yours expires on Saturday; since we won't practice on Sunday, we'll sign you on Monday."

Sunday, Atlanta, 2 P.M.: Atlanta Hawks assistant coach Steve Henson states the following upon finding me in the weight room on our off day: "Chris [assistant to the general manager] will be in tomorrow before the game to get your contract signed."

Monday, Atlanta, 9 A.M.: Assistant to the general manager Chris Grant appears in the locker room. He produces my next ten-day contract and then says, "Hang out for ten minutes and then we'll get this signed; I have to go talk to Coach Stotts real quick."

Monday, Atlanta, 9:10 A.M.: Head coach Terry Stotts calls me into his office. "Well, Paul, we're not going to sign you just yet. We're not cutting you; we're just not signing you." Stotts and Grant explain that the Hawks' starting shooting guard, Ira Newble, has some knee inflammation. The team does not fully understand the state of his injury. They apologize and tell me that I will have to wait a day until they learn whether Newble's injury warrants rest. If it does, they will have to find a guard to sign to a ten-day contract. If his knee is okay, I will be $30,000 and ten more days in the NBA richer. I watch the afternoon's game against Chicago in street clothes from behind the bench. I am nervous, confused, and apprehensive.

Monday, Atlanta, 4:30 P.M.: Chris Grant calls my hotel room and tells me that no determination has been made. The team doctor wants to check Newble's knee on Tuesday morning.

Tuesday, Atlanta, 9:30 A.M.: I bravely march into Coach Stotts' office and ask him about the situation. He says, "We don't know yet, Paul, so go ahead and dress for practice and we will let you know."

Tuesday, Atlanta, 10:15 A.M.: Chris Grant finds me on the practice court and tells me that Newble's injury is going to require the team to "shut him down" for seven to ten days. They will have to find a guard to replace him. I will not be signing a second ten-day contract. Grant continues to

speak, but my brain ceases to function, so I cannot accurately report on
the remainder of his soliloquy.

Tuesday, Atlanta, 10:45 A.M.:   I remove my practice gear and make a
humiliating walk through the locker
room. I give my now-former teammates my best wishes and, miraculously, manage to leave without saying
anything I would later regret. Or assaulting anyone.

And so I am, once again, unemployed.

January 29

Now that I don't have a job to which I need to attend, I have time for
more mundane activities, like watching my thirteen-year-old brother
play basketball. When I journeyed to Perry-Lecompton Middle School
to do just that, the ghost of Luke Fergus appeared before me. Luke Fergus was the kid every middle school class has—the man among boys.
When we were both in seventh grade, he had hair in all sorts of strange
places, the likes of which I would not see for at least three years. He had
muscles bulging where I had smooth little-boy skin. He could run and
jump and generally looked like an athlete; I was still somewhat baffled
by the dueling basketball concepts of offense and defense.

As the game began, the inspiration for my flashback to my own
middle school days took position opposite my brother Tom, his
overdeveloped triceps pushing out of his size medium wash-and-wear
jersey. And, alas, like so many years ago, the Perry Kaws jumped out
to a commanding lead—eight to four. But in the end my fears were
unfounded. Tom's opponent was, in fact, that more common form of
over-testosteroned thirteen-year-old—the one who looks good in a
uniform but can't actually play. Tom's side pulled its act together after
the shaky start and ended the game on a 54–15 run that culminated in

a thirty-five-point victory. And so my brother did not have to suffer the same humiliation that I did in seventh grade. Back then, we had no experience on which to draw, and little (or big, as it were) Luke Fergus showed us a thing or two about the game of basketball and, in the process, decimated our team.

There is more to the story.

We finished that seventh grade campaign with a discouraging 3–7 record. Our eighth-grade season would not bring much success either, but we did exact our revenge against one Luke Fergus in the very gym where I would later watch my brother Tom play. That afternoon, we carried our unvictorious eighth-grade record proudly into the Kaws' arena, hoping to avenge the loss of the year before. I was fearful of another thrashing at the hands of young master Fergus and his comrades, but my trepidation was unwarranted. My rival had already done all of his growing. And most of my teammates (author not included) had done some maturing of their own in the previous year. As mentioned, testosterone remained a foreign substance within my own body. At five foot nine and perhaps ninety-five pounds, I was barely considered a full-fledged human. But my coaches had noticed that I had developed some hint of ball-handling ability and had (mercifully, for all those viewing one of our games) moved me to point guard. I learned a lot about the game of basketball that year—mostly that being responsible for advancing the ball down the court every time is not an enviable task. I learned one more thing that night in Perry— that muscles and hairy armpits do not guarantee success on the basketball court.

My team was a well-oiled machine. For one evening. We shrugged off the pressure of (what seemed like) a brutally hostile environment and played with a fierceness not previously seen (by our parents). Late in the game, we made some key plays and walked off the court with our first, and only, win of the year. I finished the game with twenty-three points, a career high that would stand until my junior year of high school, and a tremendous feeling of satisfaction. I knew that I had overcome my pre-pubescent lack of athletic ability and had beaten the five-foot-ten behemoth that was Luke Fergus. All he really had going for him was muscles, zits, and the need for daily deodorant use. In the end, those may have helped him with the eighth-grade girls, but they did not make him a lock for success on the court.

There is probably something profound to be found in the above tale—a relation to my current situation, perhaps. Maybe something about how I will overcome rejection by the Hawks, just like I helped my Jefferson West Middle School Tigers overcome the Perry Kaws so long ago. But that seems like a stretch. Right now, I am more concerned with figuring out my next basketball destination.

When I arrived home from Atlanta, I had time enough to walk through the door before being greeted with a note that said, "Call Keith. Urgent." I made the call. My agent told me that a Spanish team was interested in securing my basketball services for the remainder of the year. He did not know the details exactly but wondered if I would be interested. Since I am always open to the prospect of a trans-Atlantic trip on short notice, I assented and told him to gather some information.

I awoke the next morning ready to contemplate my future, still trying to convince myself that, since I had never actually possessed it, I had not actually lost $30,000 because of the turn of events that had prevented the signing of a second ten-day contract with the Hawks. Keith rang in with news that the Spanish team in question was head-quartered in a town just outside of Barcelona. The team's situation was an odd one. Their American player, Maceo Baston, had left Spain under the pretense that his father was sick. I was shocked at what I was hearing—Maceo Baston is not spelled Macy O'Baston. All this time I'd thought he was an Irishman. My whole worldview was shaken.

The team, Joventut (that's SJUE-ven-too, for those playing at home), had not heard from Baston in about three weeks and needed a replacement. Keith's Spanish contact told him that they wanted to sign me to a month's contract, with the understanding that I would be signed through the end of the year as soon as the team got out from under Baston's contract. If for some reason this did not happen, the team would pay me an additional sum of money at the end of one month and send me home. I considered this treasure trove of information and spoke with Keith again that night. Because the team was asking me to go on faith regarding the balance of the year, he thought he might be able to negotiate an out clause, which would allow me to return to the United States if an NBA team called in the next month. He told me to think about it for the night and then tell him in the morning. He woke me up on Sunday morning prepared to talk to the Spaniards. He wanted to know if I was willing to go, contingent upon him getting this out clause. The Spanish would want me to leave on Monday morning, so decision time was impending. As soon as I hung up with Keith, Coach Bill Bayno called from Yakima. We had spoken earlier in the week about me returning to my CBA team. At the time, I had asked about the situation there. He told me that he really "had a good rotation" and "felt good about the chemistry" that he had. Essentially, he told me that the team was doing fine without me. I can understand that; I do have a history of really mucking up the chemistry of teams, with my me-first, everyone-else-can-go-to-hell attitude.

When I spoke with Bayno Sunday morning, he reiterated what he had said earlier in the week. He told me that he might be able to "squeeze me in" but that he really "liked the rotation right now." Okay, loud and clear. I am not wanted in Yakima. Got it. I left the conversation with Bayno feeling pretty good about a trip to sunny Barcelona. But, after some thought and discussion, I decided that I could leave the country only if I retained the ability to return if called by an NBA team. I told Keith that if he could negotiate an NBA buyout clause until March 1, I would go. (In theory, if an NBA team such as the Hawks called, I could buy out my contract by returning some of my salary to the team and leave at any time, but only until March 1— differing from Keith's proposal, which would have given us only one chance to leave: on March 1 specifically.) And so I waited.

Let us review. I had said that if the team agreed to my terms, I would be willing to leave for Spain the next day. (Remember that half my worldly possessions were in a motel room in Yakima.) If Keith called back and said that the team had given the plan the go-ahead, I would be bound by my word to leave. I was a little nervous when I picked up the phone. Unfortunately (or maybe fortunately—we'll see), the team's front office did not like our proposal. No beach time in Barcelona for me, apparently.

February 13

The UPS man had no idea of the effect his delivery would have on my life. I was outside playing with the family dog when his magical brown truck made an appearance. (I say magical because a visit from the UPS truck is always cause for excitement out in gravel-road land.) He carried an overnight letter from Atlanta—my paycheck from the Hawks. I promptly began trying to guess what would be to the right of "Pay to the order of . . ." Since the contents of that envelope ultimately influenced my next destination, I will be forthright. I'd signed a ten-day contract worth $30,150. As I tore open my prize, I guessed— pessimistically—that I would end up with $20,000 after taxes. Realistically, I thought I would get $22,000 or $23,000. (Note that I thought that this check might be the only real money I would make for the year—my few weeks in the CBA did not augment my bank account significantly.) When I looked at the check itself, the first number that leapt off the page was $3,500. I thought, "Oh, they are going to pay me in installments. That's not as exciting, but whatever." Not so much. That was the first deduction—some kind of NBA escrow penalty, which has something to do with the NBA's luxury tax. I do not understand the ins and outs of it; I know only that I will never see that money again. My gaze next fell to the net pay line at the bottom of the stub. I nearly had an aneurysm: $13,800. What the #*%@? I felt like someone had kicked me square in the genitals. I actually had to lie down and put on some music so that I could digest the news.

I had spoken the day before with both my agent and with Bill Bayno. (I should seriously consider employing a secretary.) Bayno had called in the morning and asked me when I was coming back to Yakima. This confused me; I mumbled something regarding the disdain he had shown for my return. He told me that the team had wanted me back all along and that he had just needed some time to sort things out. Like a battered wife, I decided then that I would tentatively plan to return to the Northwest the next Monday, contingent on Keith's approval. But as soon as I got off the phone with B.B., Keith called from somewhere in the world. (I think the man is actually in his office about thirty minutes a day.) He had just spoken with the CBA office to find out if the Sun Kings had any hold on me. In the CBA's somewhat questionable view, Yakima did in fact have my "rights" until that very day; the team had been informed of its rights that morning. (Which explained Bayno's call to me and subsequent explanation/ groveling session, as well as why he had earlier been pushing me to go to Spain—he did not really want me back, but he didn't really want anyone else in the CBA to have me either.) So I was bound to Yakima and, unbeknownst to me, had been so since my ten-day contract with the Hawks expired. (Evidently this is why people always say to read the fine print on a contract.) Keith mentioned offhandedly that the team in Spain was now willing to guarantee the remainder of the year and was probably willing to pay the buyout to which the CBA was entitled. (Because I was still property of the Yakima Sun Kings, a foreign team would have to pay $25,000 to get my "rights.") I thought nothing of it at the time, because my mind had committed to finishing my exile in Yakima as best I could. But then the UPS truck came.

I realize that $13,800 is a lot of money for ten days' work. However, it is not all that much if it has to last a person an entire year. I also realize that I was somehow mistakenly put in the Rupert Murdoch tax bracket and that I will be refunded some of the $10,500 I contributed to the state and federal governments. But I don't enjoy giving out fourteen-month interest-free loans. Part of the motivation behind a return to Yakima was the possibility of another ten-day NBA contract. I thought at the time that two of them would make for a good year's work. And if I could secure another ten-day, it was possible that a team might sign me through the end of the season. It could happen—someone might be desperate for replacements after his entire team contracted the Ebola virus.

That Friday night I was torn. But I thought I should find out what my options were, so Saturday morning I called Keith to have him find out if the Spanish team was still interested and would be willing to pay the CBA buyout. He told me that I had to decide if I would be willing to go if that were the case—that we would have to commit to that course of action if the team assented. (I really don't know why he continued to act with such gravitas toward the situation. I was starting to feel like I was in the Old West, with all the word-giving. Keith's seriousness made me think that backing out on the Spanish team was going to result in them sending Boba Fett after me.) I thought about it some more, and some more, and some more. (I do have an engineering degree, remember, and we engineering types are not prone to snap judgments.) On Sunday afternoon, I told Keith that if the team would buy out my CBA contract and would still guarantee my contract through the end of the season, I would go to Barcelona. I justified my decision with the thought that the trip to Spain would allow me more freedom in the summer, at which point I can do what I want with regard to my basketball career. If I feel that the NBA is still worth chasing, I can do that without feeling like I should be a responsible human and take money offered to me from European teams. And so, I waited for a phone call. Again. It came, Keith told me they had agreed, and I got ready to go to Barcelona to join the team I had spurned a week earlier.

February 10

There was one problem with my theoretical trip to Spain: most of my possessions were still in Yakima, Washington. Because of some further bureaucratic hassles regarding the transfer of my rights from the CBA, I had three days after the end of negotiations to prepare for a change of address. (My new Spanish team was able to buy my contract at half price because Coach Bayno—true to what he had told me at the outset of my stint in Yakima—waived the team's share of the buyout. Cheers to him.) I thought the extra time might allow me to have some important items shipped overnight from Washington—my midgets and amputees porn collection, my lube, and all the rest. I spoke with the team trainer, Kyla McDaniel, whom I had found to be one of the few coherent employees of the Sun Kings, and told her about my problem. She put me in touch with the team's front office. It appeared to me that the process had been set into fluid motion. I wanted only a few items sent, namely, some of the limited clothing options I own. My plan called for someone to go to my motel room and call me, whereupon I could direct that person regarding the items to pack.

When I finally got the call, I heard the friendly voice of Paul the Bus Driver—the utility infielder who had loaned/sold us the Chevy Malibu. Paul the B.D. is a great guy, but he is a little, well, old and isn't exactly detail-oriented. I asked him if he was in my motel room with my things. He said, "Well, I've got your stuff, but someone just threw it all in three trash bags and gave it to me, so I'll have to dig through them to find what you want." Resigned to my fate, I told him what I wanted and hoped for the best. Amazingly, he came through. The items I needed arrived Wednesday morning, boxed up just as ordered. Score another one for the old folks.

I spoke with the general manager of DKV Joventut on Wednesday. She told me that my flight was the next morning at 10:15 A.M., informed me that I would be flying business class across the ocean—producing an inner cheer from me—and wished me a good trip. She e-mailed an itinerary, which I quickly printed before rushing to the bookstore and loading up on the requisite guides to Barcelona and Spain. I retired for the night in an uncharacteristically positive state, emboldened by my previous European experience.

It snowed that night, so after readying myself for the trip in the morning, I checked Delta Airlines' Web site at about 7:10 A.M. to make sure my flight would not be delayed or canceled. My subsequent inner dialogue follows:

"That's strange, this doesn't show a 10:15 flight to Cincinnati. And here's my flight number, flight 1018. But it says, 'Boarding.' I'd better check that itinerary she sent. . . . Oh, [insert string of curse words here], I'm about to miss my [insert similar string of words here] flight."

My flight was at 7:15. I am no genius, but I do know this: it takes longer than four minutes to drive from Detlor Acres in Grantville, Kansas, to the Kansas City airport. Like an hour and a half longer. In my efficiency the day before, I had not even looked at the itinerary e-mailed my way. I had filed the time given to me over the phone by my Spanish contact as incontrovertible fact and had put the itinerary in my backpack, for use at the airport.

The good news: I now have a pretty good idea what a heart attack must feel like. I very nearly passed out on my feet when I discovered that I was about to miss my flight. When I realized the depth of my stupidity, I immediately called the general manager from Joventut. She, of course, did not answer. Thinking quickly, I left her a well-reasoned, eloquent message: "Hi. It's Paul Shirley . . . IamsostupidandI missedmyflightpleasecallmeandtellmewhattodookaythanksbye." I next called Delta and made my case. Shockingly, Ms. Phone-Line Reservation Lady saved me. She managed to find a 9:55 Northwest flight through Detroit that would get me to New York in time to make my original connection. I rejoiced, and immediately regretted my call to the Joventut GM. She'd never needed to know of my idiocy. Or at least she didn't need the early warning.

My father and I arrived at the airport with just enough time to spare. I waited in line at the Northwest counter (my new airline), glad that the day's stress was behind me. When I got to the front of the line, the unhelpful fellow behind the counter got my boarding pass ready and then said, "How are you going to pay for this?" (Cut to: confused face on me.) I told him that the Delta phone lady had told me that my ticket would transfer just fine. "Well then, I need that ticket." (Cut to: slightly panicked face.) "You were supposed to go to Delta and get the paper ticket before coming here." (Cut to: really panicked face.) Theoretically, I had thirty minutes to get to a different concourse, grab the ticket, come back, check my bags, and board the flight to Detroit. I was told it would be faster to walk, so I set off. (It should be noted that whoever designed the Kansas City airport mistakenly thought it would be cute to leave the concourses disconnected.)

Midway into my trek through the ice, snow, and biting wind, as the shoes I was wearing—shoes I had not really worn before—tore into my Achilles, I was ready to give up on the entire trip. (My usual footwear had not made it into the box sent from Yakima.) But I had to find some warmth anyway, so I pressed on to the B concourse. When I got to the Delta counter, this nice gay guy laughed and laughed at the idea that I would get back in time for my Northwest flight. He found a seat on a Delta flight to Atlanta at 10:25 but could not access it. I thought about asking, "Why then, sir, do you have that computer? How is it helping?" But I doubted that such an outburst would help my cause, and held my tongue. He told me that he would work on "accessing it" and that I should go back and retrieve my bags from the Northwest counter. He also told me to hurry or I would miss the new Delta flight as well. I hiked back through the snow and found my bewildered father waiting with questions. He was a good sport about my own stupidity, and we made it onto an inter-concourse bus and found our way back to the Delta counter. Apparently, the man behind the counter found the icon labeled "Magic Seat Release" and so was able to find a spot for me. My bags were checked, I said good-bye to my father, and I got on an airplane, resolving to pay close attention to itineraries sent my way in the future.

When flying over oceans, first class is the way to go. Actually, I should write "business class." My seatmate felt the need to correct me repeatedly on the issue. I know this: the only people in front of my section were the pilots. The food was exquisite and the legroom was extravagant. I love first, er, business class.

I arrived in Barcelona somewhat dazed. I would best liken the condition after an all-day travel schedule to the feeling one has when one wakes up from the anesthetic after surgery—that is, like one wants to shoot oneself. Personally, in both cases, I seem to be unable to remember that I ever previously felt normal . . . or even human.

I was met at the airport by several Spaniards, including the woman to whom I had spoken on the phone. Others in the contingent were carrying cameras and microphones. I was surprised; I had not known that my arrival was going to be newsworthy. No mention was made of the flight scheduling mixup. (I had actually forgotten; it seemed like it had been a week since I had left Kansas.) (Okay, a week is an exaggeration. Two days, perhaps.) From the airport, I was whisked off to a hospital for a physical. It was the most in-depth physical ever experienced by man. I was at the hospital for six and a half hours. If the doctors missed something, that something is undetectable by current diagnostic devices and procedures. My day consisted of the following, as best as I can recall (there is no accounting for the time I was asleep in the MRI machine; who knows what really happened then): blood work, physical measurements down to the respective widths of my arms and legs, elbows and knees, wrists and ankles, and the diameter of my head; a treadmill test complete with a tube that measured oxygen consumption (I endured a Spaniard punching a hole in my earlobe every three minutes while I was running, from which he drew blood to measure lactic acid buildup); a shower; an echocardiogram; an electrocardiogram (I honestly did not know the difference until then); MRIs on both knees; a hearing test; a vision test with the *E*'s pointing in different directions, kindergarten-style; X-rays on every part of my body (no lie—like forty X-rays, starting at my toes and working up from there); a general physical examination by a doctor who spoke next to no English; and, of course, a drug test. During this extravaganza, I ate two meals at the hospital and became dangerously close to falling asleep on my feet. But it was all worth it when I was pronounced healthy and sent on my way. (It wasn't really worth it. It just seemed like a way out of the story.)

Next stop was the Joventut arena and offices. I was duly impressed by the fact that the offices were in the arena—in Greece my team's offices were set up in a makeshift office building accessible only by some secret elevator. (In fact, I never did know how to get to the Greek team's offices; I was always taken there as if I were a hostage who could not be allowed navigational knowledge. Minus the black hood, although that would have been awesome.) I signed a contract with Joventut after some rather tedious hassles with the federation known as USA Basketball. Apparently I was supposed to get clearance from the organization before signing a contract in another country. Another way for a middleman to filch $100 from athletes.

After we settled my eligibility, I was taken to my apartment. Not only was the bed made, but someone had actually stocked my kitchen with essentials—milk, bread, lunch meat, and the like. I was flabbergasted. It was a welcome change from Greece, where I'd spent the first five weeks of my time in a hotel room with only the selections at the restaurant downstairs available to me. (I'd never known that lamb could be used in an omelet.)

I dropped off my bags and learned about the workings of my domicile and then the team officials in charge of apartment orientation took me back to the gym for practice. I was working on two hours of sleep over the previous thirty-six, but I managed to survive without embarrassing myself completely. Afterward, I drove "my" car back to the apartment to collapse.

Before I passed out, I noticed that my apartment has three bedrooms—with a fourth that contained only an ironing board—along with two bathrooms, a kitchen, dining area and living room, and a balcony, from which I can observe the Mediterranean Sea, which is all of three-quarters of a mile from my apartment. The view is absolutely spectacular.

I also noticed that my car is a Neon. Can't win them all.

February 16

My washing machine and I had a little spat yesterday. I wanted it to (surprise) wash some clothes; it wanted to soak them for approximately twelve hours. The instructions on the dials are in Spanish, but one would assume that a reasonably intelligent person such as myself would be able to figure out the implication of phrases like "algodon blanco normal" or "centrifugo intensivo." I don't think the language barrier is the problem. The problem is possessiveness on the part of my washing machine. Once the clothes start, they cannot be coaxed out until they are finished. That is, until Mr., er, Señor Washing Machine decides they're finished. The washer is front-loading, with a round porthole of glass so I could see my clothes in all their immobility. I just couldn't do anything about their static state. I punched buttons and twirled knobs. Still they rested, marinating in the vile combination of their own filth and some foreign detergent I had purchased. The machine, of course, would not allow me to open the door;

to do so would have resulted in a minor flooding disaster in my kitchen. After a time, the machine randomly decided to accept the terms of my cease-fire and drained itself, allowing me to free my whites from its grasp. Unfortunately, they were never allowed the benefit of a spin cycle or a rinse. (Which is understandable—my clothes were in the machine for only half a day.) I was unfazed by the soap bubbles and dripping wetness and threw the clothes in the dryer for what turned out to be a 140-minute drying cycle. But, a day after I started, they smell okay and appear to be wearable. I need nothing more.

Unfortunately for me, while I was dealing with all of the clothes cleansing, someone broke into my apartment and replaced my legs with those of a fifty-five-year-old woman. The timing was unfortunate because the theft occurred the night before my first game with Joventut. During the game it truly felt like I was carrying around ten-kilogram weights in both shoes. I could barely move. (Okay, another exaggeration, I could move a little. More accurately, I could move, but only enough to be bad at most everything I tried.) I am not sure what the problem was. My team practices a lot more than I am used to in the CBA or NBA, but in those leagues we sometimes played four nights a week, so I cannot really point to overuse as the problem. Perhaps I am getting soft in my old age. Despite the condition of my legs, we managed to win. I contributed ten points, but only because our coach let me play through my blatant shoddiness.

At one point in the game, I participated in the following series of events: Receive the ball on the post, travel. Blow a defensive rotation on the other end. Receive the ball on the wing in an isolation play drawn up specifically for me and . . . travel. Next offensive possession, get fouled, and miss both free throws. Good times. As I mentioned, we did win, so I guess I should not be too worried. But in European basketball, one's status is always a little tenuous, especially at the beginning of one's stay. An American never really knows when he might have a Ricky Vaughn experience and find the proverbial pink slip in his locker.

After the game, I agreed to meet one of my teammates, a Croatian fellow named Nikola Radulovic, at a restaurant near our respective places of residence. He told me to go ahead, that he wasn't going to eat and would be along in half an hour or so.

(Side note: Because of my lifestyle, I now think nothing of walking into a restaurant and asking for a table for one. I find it to be an interesting sociological experiment. The other patrons don't quite know what to make of the solo act. "Hmm, what's that really tall guy doing here all alone? He doesn't look like a leper or anything. I wonder why he's speaking a different language. Oh well, back to my flan.") While in a relatively foul mood because of my earlier bastardization of the game of basketball, I managed to find the restaurant and placed an order. I ate; Nikola didn't show. I ordered dessert, to stall for time—I thought I had misunderstood his broken English. Maybe he had actually said he would be along in an hour. My dessert was an ice-cream-like substance covered with a chocolate shell—a shell that was of nearly the same Rockwell hardness as masonry. So, there I was, alone in a restaurant in a foreign country, futilely attacking some hateful dessert with all the weaponry available to me, waiting for a damned Croat, all the while observing the Spaniards around me as they made furtive glances my way. But since I couldn't give up and leave the restaurant in a disdainful sprint, I took a deep breath and called the waitress over for help with my dessert. She said, "Es muy frio." (It's very cold.) I smiled and thought, "Really, you nitwit?" She presented no solution, so I waited. It finally melted a little, my Slavic teammate finally showed his face, and everyone was happy.

Sometime before worrying about my companionship for dinner, I was the target of a racist comment. At least I think I was. It happened while I was on the court before the game, warming up by myself. (Me, alone: common theme.) One of the opposition's assistant coaches came over to say hello in semi-broken English. He asked me if I liked Spain and then said that last summer his team had considered signing me. They had even gone as far as taking a trip to Salt Lake City to watch me play in the NBA summer league there. I asked him why they had decided against the personnel move. He said, "In small town where we are, we must have black American. You know, dunking and exciting." (Most will find this hard to believe, but I'm fairly athletic and tend to have some rather impressive dunks in Europe—more than many of the "dunking and exciting" black Americans around.) His comments neither angered nor surprised me—even though he was telling me that his team had blatantly discriminated against me because of my skin color. While his words were new, the sentiment is not. Usually American coaches say things like "We need to upgrade our athleticism" or "We need to find an athlete." Both are part of a not-so-subtle code that white players all understand. We are viewed as physically inferior and so should be thankful that we are allowed to set foot on the court.

The coach's soliloquy was brutal. In those few sentences, he made it clear that I would always struggle to find basketball employment because I am white. Nonetheless, I appreciated his honesty, even if that honesty was brought about only by his unfamiliarity with English. It is hard to be anything but blunt with only a few words at one's disposal. Perhaps we should all speak in a foreign language. There might be more actual communication.

Actually, something of a language impasse exists in this part of Spain. (*Impasse* may be a bit strong. *Hurdle,* at least.) My Spanish is limited, but I did have two years of half-assed instruction in high school, so I know the numbers and how to ask where the bathroom is. Unfortunately, the average Joe (or José) in Barcelona does not speak Spanish primarily. He speaks Catalan. Barcelona is part of Catalonia, the northeastern segment of Spain that has a separate history than that of the rest of Spain. The people of Catalonia (Catalunya here) have a strong sense of their own identity, enough so that they speak an entirely different language among themselves. In fact, my sources tell me that a law passed a few years ago requires all public announcements, signs, et cetera to be posted in Catalan in order to promote the use of the language. And when I write language, I mean just that. Catalan is not a dialect—as I have been told about fifty thousand times already. It is a separate language—as different from Spanish as French, Italian, or Wookiee. The problem, where applied to my own interests, is this: if Juan Carlos the Spaniard walks up to me and begins talking, I assume that I might be able to understand a little of what he is saying—I had a whopping two years of Spanish, dammit. But since I don't even know what language he is speaking, how am I to begin to decipher what he is saying? Do I not understand because we never made it past *queso* and *leche* in Spanish class, or do I not understand because he is speaking some tribal language? I suppose I will stick with "Se habla inglés?"

My linguistic development is also being hampered by the attitude of the Spanish people. In Greece, when I would break down and attempt to ask for something in Greek, the person to whom I was speaking seemed truly grateful that I was making an effort, albeit a poor one, at speaking their jive. Then he would—with a pitiful look in his eyes—correct my mangled version of the language and say something in English, usually along the lines of "Nice try. Now tell me what you want." In Barcelona, when I leap into my best "Quiero un . . ." people look at me as though they would like to set me on fire. I usually stumble through a poor attempt at whatever request and receive as my response . . . silence. I generally return to the aforementioned, "Se habla inglés?" They respond, simply, "No." The listener then experiences the pleasure of being subjected to *español* American-style. Which probably sounds a lot like English Ignorant Southerner–style. Because at this point, I am quite confident that, a lot of the time, when I try to say, "I will now walk to the store in order that I might purchase a pound of bananas," it probably comes out as, "I be fixing to go to that there store to get me some of them bananas." I would have no idea.

In my second outing with Joventut, we played a team from Belgium in the final game in the round of sixteen for the ULEB cup. (ULEB stands for . . . I have no idea. Some organization governing international basketball.) Much like my Greek team last year, Joventut plays in a secondary European competition, with Spanish league games on the weekend and ULEB cup games during the week. Because my team had lost by eight to the same Belgian team the week before, we needed to win by nine to move on to the next round of the playoffs. Before the game, I managed to pick out of the Spanish our coach was letting fly that I would be in the starting lineup. (Spanish is spoken almost exclusively around the team—most of the players hail from various parts of Spain.) I was a little surprised, but I performed relatively well. We thrashed our foes by sixteen; I scored eleven, and played a solid game all around.

After the game, we retired to the locker room, and my teammates immediately began undressing and showering. I asked someone if it was standard protocol for us to shower and then listen to the coach's postgame talk, which seemed strange but reasonably acceptable. I was told that the coach would give no postgame talk; he only spoke to us after a game if he was really happy or extremely displeased. I shrugged at the new information and took my shower, but the situation felt very strange—like there had been no real wrap-up to the evening's work. Years of basketball brainwashing have left me easily bewildered.

After the triumph over the Belgians I went out to eat with Zan Tabak, a seven-foot Croatian who is one of my teammates. (I should have written "triumph over the naturalized Americans." Like most European leagues, the league in Belgium allows each team to employ only two Americans. The team we played had four, but two of them had European passports—a common move in Europe. If one can prove European ancestry or if he marries a European woman, dual citizenship can be granted. A European passport allows players to circumvent the two-American limit and, thus, to drive up their own salaries. I'm still searching for the European girl who will be open to that particular business arrangement.)

Zan played for seven years in the NBA, most notably with the Indiana Pacers. He is one of two Croatians on our team, the other being the aforementioned fellow who struggled to find his way to the restaurant after our most recent game. Like most of the Yugoslavians I have met, Zan is quite worldly and thoughtful. During our meal, I asked him why he had come back to Europe after so many years in the NBA, even when he had offers from the American league for future years. He said that, first, it was important for him to enjoy playing the game the right way. He noted how much more pride European players take in winning. He talked about his constant disappointment with American players and their selfish attitudes. But most important, he said, he grew tired of the American way of approaching life. His take on it was the following: "In America, the people are only interested in the things you can touch—the car, the house, the TV. In Europe, the people are interested in things you cannot touch—the friendships, the love, the relationships." It comes out sounding a little hokey, but I think there is something to be learned in that quote from a gigantic Croat who started playing professional basketball at age sixteen.

February 23

While on road trips, we eat nearly all of our meals as a team, as provided to us by the hotel in which we are staying. Positive aspect of that arrangement: free food. Negative aspect: rather eclectic food selections. During a recent meal, I was faced with the following scenario: I was served a bed of white rice with a six-inch piece of off-brown matter lying drably across it. When I inquired as to the identity of the object that was scarring my pleasant-looking hill of rice, I was informed that I was looking at a fried banana. On my rice. Before I knew what was happening, a waiter began dumping tomato sauce over the whole confabulation. Soon after, he piled two fried eggs on top of the cornucopia of food groups and left me to my own devices. I looked to a teammate across the table with eyes that asked, *Did that really just happen?* Receiving no sympathy from my compatriots, I followed along and mashed it all together as if it were some kind of jambalaya from hell and ate it. And . . . it wasn't bad. The taste balance was tenuous, though. As long as the fork corralled at least three of the four constituents, things were A-OK. It was when only two were present—perhaps a piece of egg combined with a piece of banana—that I had to make a spastic grab for my water glass.

Overall, I have been unimpressed with Spanish food. Spaniards seem to have a fascination with canned tuna, which is an initial mark against their culinary instincts. In my mind, canned tuna is a last-resort food item—something to be consumed only when the other remaining options are bologna or Long John Silver's. Here in Spain, I was faced with the tuna crisis within hours of arriving in the country. When I was subjected to the über-physical, my first meal in the hospital cafeteria was based around a goulash-like substance (pasta shells with meat sauce) that used tuna instead of ground beef or chicken. Since I felt like I had just put the wraps on my own personal Bataan death march and could not see that I had another option, I forced it down and chalked the experience up to a bad cafeteria day, like spoonburger day (completely obscure childhood reference) back in grade school.

Since then, every Spanish salad to which I have been exposed has been topped with nearly a pound of canned tuna. Does this not break some rule? I cannot imagine what would possess a person to willingly place slimy canned tuna on top of crisp, green lettuce and freshly chopped carrots. The solution, to an outsider's eye, would be to push the fish to the side and carry on with salad consumption. That outsider would be one who is not intimately familiar with the properties of tuna. Tuna will not be confined. Banish it to the side of the plate— it doesn't care. It knows it has effectively contaminated the salad with its permeating funk, making the use of oil and vinegar a futile exercise. I never thought a fish could be so powerful and so ubiquitous. The only possible explanation involves Spain's president, a bad day at the international bargaining table, and a poorly translated arms deal with Syria, wherein the term *tuna* was misused as slang for cash or biological weaponry. So because someone spent the night before the big negotiations with a few belly dancers and a hookah, the Spanish people are faced with a surplus of ten million tons of tuna.

A few days ago, I was playing some basketball, minding my own business while trying to get through the last half hour of practice, when I ran into Zan Tabak's chest. With my head. As I fell to the floor, I could not figure out what had just happened. By the time my body flopped limply to the floor, I had decided that I had separated my shoulder, broken either my collarbone or my back, or taken a bullet to the neck. It felt a lot like someone was actively pouring fire into the top of my spinal column, through my back, and straight down my right arm, all the way to my hand. I flopped around on the floor for a bit and tried to find a position that would not send awe-inspiring pain shooting through my body. I am sure that I looked—as my father would say—like I didn't know whether I was stabbed or shot. I have felt some pain in my life; this was the easily the worst. When I finally settled down, I found that my right arm and shoulder were completely numb. The team doctor/trainer/some guy who appeared to know what he was doing arrived on the scene and attempted to convince me to lay my head back. Which allowed me to revisit the feeling that my spinal column was being cauterized. At that point, I am unhappy to admit, I let out a healthy shriek. It was pretty girlish. (I write girlish, but that is a poor generalization. Most of the females I know have a much higher threshold for pain than most of the males I know. And we need only look to childbirth for further proof. So maybe I should say that it was a boyish shriek.) The point being that my teammates will probably not rate me highly on any manliness scales.

By the time I shuffled to the locker room to assess the damage, I could feel my arm and shoulder again, which was encouraging. I was nonplussed to find that movement of my head caused shooting electric sensations down my arm and back. The doctor gave me an anti-inflammatory shot, scheduled an MRI for the next morning, and sent me home. When I got to my apartment, my body had settled enough that I was left only with numbness and tingling in my right thumb and forefinger. But when I touched anything with either of those digits, shock waves coursed through my entire body. Which sounds like a lot more fun than it actually is. Also, if I moved my head the right (or wrong) way, I felt tingles up and down my back. I had not received a real diagnosis of the problem from the Spanish doctors as they (1) did not seem to know what was going on and (2) do not speak much English. Since I had no experience with nerve injuries, I was a little concerned with the situation. I kept wiggling my toes, just to make sure I could still feel them. I was very much afraid to go to sleep—I kept envisioning awakening to find that I was paralyzed from the waist down. (Ever the optimist. At least my mind didn't jump straight to quadriplegia. I must be making psychological progress.)

The MRI showed no spinal or disk injury, so I began physical ther-

apy and treatment. I have not practiced or played this week; my right
hand remains completely useless, and the slightest touch to my
thumb continues to bring to mind the grasping of an electric fence. As
a bonus, I was started on a program that results in three daily injections in my ass, which has been thoroughly pleasant.

Despite my injured state, I finally made my way down to the
beach. It is all of a five-minute walk from the door of my apartment, so
it is easy to see why it took me ten days to get that done. I live life at
a slower pace than the rest of humanity. "My" beach is rather nice.
Real sand—none of that half-gravel crap to which I had grown accus-
tomed in Athens. Quality-sized waves, seashells, sunbathers—it has
all the accoutrements. And I live in Kansas for what reason again?

My team took a break from regular-season games to play the Copa
del Rey (King's Cup) which matches the top eight teams in Spain in a
midseason tournament that takes place over four days. Because of the
injury to the wiring of my body, I merely observed our participation in
the tournament. Even without my electric presence on the court, the
Copa provided an amazing basketball atmosphere. It was reminiscent
of a collegiate conference tournament. The teams all stayed in the
same hotel, with agents, scouts, and fans all milling about, mingling
with players and the general populace. The games were played in a
sold-out nine-thousand-seat arena; fans traveled from all over Spain
to follow their chosen team. Because only the best teams in Spain
played, there were no soft games and the intensity remained high
throughout. It really was the best basketball I have seen since the
NCAA tournament. The games I watched were about twenty times
more compelling than the average NBA contest. I wish more people
from the United States could see good European basketball; it reminds a person of the beautiful thing the game can be.

European basketball is more interesting because everyone on the
court is a threat to score. It is rare to find players who cannot shoot,
pass, and handle the ball. Of course, as more and more Europeans
make their way into the NBA, the world will begin to understand how
advanced they are. I don't really know why the players here are so
much more well rounded; I think it can be explained by the culture of

basketball in which they were raised. One would think that the social-ist leanings of most European countries would produce mindless automatons who care little about their personal abilities—a valid hypothesis that seems to remain true only in the Far East. (See also the blank expression worn by Yao Ming at all times.) In fact, the laid-back attitude toward life that most Europeans embrace produces skilled players. Coaches breed an attitude of "Why not?" As in why not be seven feet tall and handle the ball? Why not learn every position?

European players are trained from an early age to see few limits to their skill sets. In the United States, coaches are anxious to pigeon-hole players, if only to make their own jobs easier. It is much less time-consuming to teach a particular player half of the skills needed to play the game. Then the player can work on his abilities alone, becoming the cog his coach needs, without the coach expending excessive energy.

My own team, Joventut, is famous for developing young players. In fact, the word Joventut means something to do with youth. (This fact brought to the reader via the explanation of several people I barely know. I do remember that *joven* means "young" in Spanish, so the theory seems plausible.) On my walk every day from the parking lot to the locker room, I see as many as five youth basketball teams practicing—all under the Joventut banner. Young coaches spend hours working with their pint-sized charges. Of course, they don't do it for free. They are paid by the club, which is paid by its primary sponsor, DKV Seguros. (*Seguros* = "insurance.") The result: my team's actual name is DKV Joventut. Fitting, I suppose—the name it-self is a microcosm for the state of European basketball. Leagues embrace sponsors, which finance teams and their coaches and, in turn, develop multitalented basketball players. It is a rather efficient system that—in an almost factory-like manner—churns out highly skilled young players year after year. I hope we catch on in the United States. If we don't, the NBA might have to move to Europe.

March 2

I had an EMG on Monday. I recommend that anyone with sado-masochistic tendencies schedule one. I did not know this going in, but an EMG consists of a doctor (non-English-speaking, preferably) stick-ing needles in muscles and then instructing the test subject to flex the very same muscles whilst the needle is embedded in the muscle fibers. This is all, theoretically, a way to determine if the nerves in the corresponding area are damaged. After I was subjected to the torture session, I chatted briefly with the doctor who had performed the pro-cedure. I told him about the injury in my best broken Spanish. When he learned that it had been only a week since the mishap, he chuckled heartily. It turns out that an EMG would not show anything so soon after a possible nerve injury. From what I could tell, it was his recom-mendation that I do nothing until another EMG could be performed at the appropriate time—three weeks from then. But I'm glad I had a trial run. My day would have been significantly less fun without some-one jamming needles into my biceps.

On Tuesday night, we had a ULEB Cup game against a team from Serbia. I, of course, did not play. Before the game, I was in the training room, receiving treatment on my neck/shoulder/arm. I was lying on my back as the physical therapist did some manipulation of my neck when one of the team's doctors entered the room. The team has an official team doctor and another, older, more arrogant doctor who magically appears on game days and in time for team pictures. (Meaning that two people who speak limited English are trying to tell me what is going on with my neurons, axons, and dendrites.) The latter individual was the one lurking near my shoulder. He had developed a new theory. He thought that I had broken my thumb, which would explain why that digit remained numb. He wanted an X-ray done the next day. Every-one in the room rolled his respective set of eyes, which was very con-fusing, since his spiel had not yet been translated for me. When it was, I was rendered speechless. I am fairly confident that I would have re-membered breaking my thumb. Next, in what must have been some sort of power play, Dr. Mephisto motioned the therapist working on me out of the way and took up a position at the head of the table on which I was lying. For a few seconds, he probed the muscles around my neck and then, without warning, jerked my head violently to the left. As a PG-13 version of the X-rated pain I had felt a week earlier again shot down my back and arm, I sort of curled up into the fetal position and let out a gasp. (I kept the yelping in this time—way to go, me.) As I lay in a ball, the doctor said something to everyone in the room and left. After collecting myself, I first told the therapist that I wanted the doctor's family murdered and then asked what he had said. I was told, "Well, no X-ray tomorrow. He's now convinced that there is definitely something wrong with the nerves." I was quite happy to be of service to his greater intellectual development. At some point in the evening, this same doctor was asked what he thought about my situation. (I think he is the wizened figurehead to whom people look for medical answers. The other doctor is the brains behind the operation.) He told the inquisitive reporter that he thought there was "an injury to the nerve" and that I "would be out for one to two months."

The truth is that no one really knows how long the recovery will take. First step: I need normalcy to return to my thumb. Second: I would like to recover some strength in my shoulder and neck. Third: I would like a jetpack. Then I will worry about any return to the court. For now, there is nothing to be done other than daily treatments and conditioning drills with the strength coach. (My legs are fine, which allows me to do exactly what I want to be doing this time of year— mindless running drills.)

I did find out some rather disconcerting news today. It seems that my team has secured the services of an American named Zendon Hamilton to replace me for a month. I am not sure how I feel about this. My agent assures me that my injured status will not preclude the team from paying me. He says that there is nothing to worry about— the Spanish league is a trustworthy one. I, being, well, me, am a little pessimistic after my play-for-no-pay experience in Greece. But I'm willing to be a sucker one more time.

March 10

My team lost by the appropriate margin in Serbia this week. (Again, in this ULEB Cup competition, advancement to the next round is based on the aggregate score of a two-game series—we won by fourteen the first game at home and lost by only nine in the second game in Belgrade, resulting in our advancement to the next round.) My replacement, Zendon Hamilton, has really played in only one game, our recent loss in Valencia. He is a passable basketball player but is not much of a talker. Each time I meet an American who plays over here it becomes evident why the European players come to resent us so easily. Most of us look down our respective noses at the leagues here, and it shows in the attitude displayed.

I learned that my new "teammate" in fact signed a contract through the end of the year. I was reassured, though, by the team president (through a translator) that I remained the team's first choice, that as soon as I returned I would be back in the lineup. But Zendon Hamilton's contract brings up an interesting question. If he starts playing well, would they truly send him home, or will they set up some sort of competition between us for the remaining spot? I should be in good shape for such a situation, coming off a month or more of layoff during which I could not use my right arm.

In medical news: my right thumb is almost back to normal. The very tip is the only remaining region that continues to feel strange. Also, the nail has started to grow again; my thumb's compatriots, the other nine fingers I possess, had lapped my thumb with regard to fingernail growth. My right shoulder is not in such good shape. It's a strange feeling. My brain tells the muscles to work; they blatantly disregard the message. My shoulder and back muscles are like the dreaded ten-to-twelve-year-old age group at a basketball camp—they hear the instruction to do ball-handling drills, but it's just more fun to continue the game of grab-ass.

March 23

I've decided to stop taking drugs. One of the unfortunate side effects of sport is that it often involves fast-moving objects (bats, balls, human bodies) that exert forces on one another in strange ways, sometimes resulting in injuries—especially when the objects (human bodies, most notably) are not actually designed to absorb those forces. When an athlete is injured, he often begins introducing strange chemicals into his body to abet the healing process. For instance—let us examine the case of a basketball player; we'll call him "me" (or "I", as grammatical rules may dictate):

When I first jammed my neck into another player about five weeks ago, I was immediately given an anti-inflammatory injection in the right ass cheek. After the medical staff with my team had decided on a course of treatment, they started throwing drugs my way. At first, I received daily anti-inflammatory injections, along with twice-daily injections of B vitamins—all in the gluteal region. (Around the same time, I began the Ass-Cheek Rotation Program, or ACRP, so as to minimize the discomfort felt by one side or the other.) I also took one anti-epilepsy medication, Neurontin, thrice daily, and another, Rivotril, once (at night, because of its impressive sleepiness-inducing effects). I chased these with a pill taken to help my stomach deal with the other foreign substances I was sending its way. I was like an AIDS patient—drugs for the symptoms, and drugs for the drugs. The trainers soon discontinued the anti-inflammatory shots, leaving me with only two injections a day; two or three weeks after the injury, though, they started me on an oral anti-inflammatory called Voltaren and instructed me to up the dosage on the Rivotril (the aforementioned knockout pill). Fast-forward to this week. The results of a second EMG showed the nerve to be normal, which is good news—assuming that I trust the analysis of a bunch of doctors who don't really speak the same language that I do. Apparently the nerve is healed. All that remains is to strengthen the rubber bands that currently make up my shoulder, neck, and back muscles: which might take a while—right now I can't even do a push-up.

I am quite thankful for the cessation of the shots in the ass. The track marks made me appear to be a very confused heroin addict. The new, almost-clean me appeared to be a step in the right direction—until I tried to go to sleep at night. I realized then that while the Rivotril did make it hard to wake up in the morning, it also made it really easy to fall asleep at night. So I have spent the last few days in withdrawal from my drowsiness-causing anti-epilepsy pill, staring at the ceiling until five A.M., and then existing in a zombie-like state during the day.

While contemplating these very strange-sounding medications over the last few weeks, I had an epiphany: why do drug names have to sound so evil? Names such as Voltaren and Neurontin really don't bring to mind pleasant thoughts. Go ahead, say them out loud. They don't exactly make one think of puppy dogs and apple pies. When are pharmaceutical companies going to get their collective acts together and think up slightly more benign names? I think it would be a good idea to veer in the direction of cologne names. Breeze, by Pfizer Pharmaceuticals. Whistle, by Parke-Davis. I can hear the conversations now: "Well, my doc's got me on Breeze for the incontinence and Whistle for the gout." They sound a little better than, say, Fecotrix and Goutarin, don't they? I think I'm onto something here.

March 30

On an off day this week, the training staff coaxed me onto the court to try a few basketball activities. This somehow evolved into me catching the ball on the post and making moves to the basket while a stationary defender stood behind me. I gave the strength coach the eye—the one that says, *I probably shouldn't be doing this, eh?*—but he missed it. I was not too excited about the level of activity; at this juncture, holding my right hand over my head for five seconds took real effort, but I played along. (All those drugs may have been affecting my reasoning abilities.) At one point, I turned to my right and started to dribble en route to the basket. The dribble was not completed because some part of my wasted upper body gave out. I lost control of the ball and then of my brain, yelling like an infant and going into my best impersonation of a pouting, spoiled athlete. I didn't actually hurt myself—I was displeased only because I was not healthy, I was doing something I shouldn't have been doing, and my musculature had performed badly. I transferred my aggression to the ball and booted it into the stands, which made my fellow off-day participants take note. No damage was done, but the incident scared me.

I think my little display of anger scared the coaches as well. Everyone was overly apologetic for the next few days. The strength coach and the trainer kept asking me if I thought they were doing a good job. The assistant coach even had this to say the next day: "The trainers called me and said you were a little sad yesterday about the injury situation. You should know that there's no hurry, so just take your time. The only reason that everyone keeps asking how you are doing is that we all love you." I would wager that no one attached to the Atlanta Hawks organization has or will ever say such a thing. I almost started crying.

Said assistant coach was speaking English, not his primary language. As I've mentioned before, a secondary language can be both hilarious and endearing. The unfamiliar usage results in a child-like state, wherein everyone uses words like *good* and *bad, love* and *hate,* and no one has the ability to make witty or sarcastic remarks. While a little boring, it can be—even to me, the most cynical person I know—rather pleasant.

It also serves as notice that I need to get my act together and learn Spanish so I can speak well enough that people won't know quite what I'm saying.

April 6

I am always game for a public appearance. So when Joventut's media director asked if I could go speak to some people, I enthusiastically agreed without actually inquiring about what I would be doing. I need to work on my gullibility. I showed up at the appointed time on a beautiful spring evening, and my three media relations escorts and I set off

in someone's car for what I thought was to be an appearance at a
school. After spending half an hour settling on a parking spot in the
local neighborhood, we ambled down to a barrio-quaint gathering
place in the area. I noticed that we were decidedly not at a school and
that most of the people milling about certainly looked too old to be
students. I was handed several "No a la guerra" (No to the war) stick-
ers and introduced to the organizer.

I was the celebrity guest at a war protest.

Someone handed me a piece of paper with lines written in Spanish. I rehearsed a little and tried to calculate accent placement. By my
rudimentary translation, it was something with which I agreed, so I
didn't feel the need to make editorial changes. I was set for my first
act of civil disobedience. Sometime between a Spanish version of
"Imagine" by John Lennon and the simulation of war-like noises
played at 120 decibels over the gigantic speakers set up for the event,
I was pushed toward the microphone. The crowd of at least seventy-
five waited in hushed silence. I delivered my manifesto and the
masses erupted into polite applause. Before I knew it, I was whisked
off the stage by my handlers, and my Bill Waltonesque experience was
over before I had time to enjoy it properly. Next time, I'm requesting
either looting or tear gas. A demonstration ought to involve some kind
of disobedience, whether civil or otherwise.

We recently took a trip to Slovenia for a game. I didn't play, but accompanied the team because . . . the coach told me to. Generally, ours
was an uneventful journey. I was glad I got to make the trip since I did
get to fly across a large portion of Europe in a very small plane. I found
the quarters to be cramped, but they were hell for our head coach,
who has something of a nicotine addiction. (He smokes at practice occasionally.) At one point during the trip, I thought I could smell cigarette smoke, but when I remembered I was on a plane I said to myself,
There's no smoking on airplanes. Then I turned around and took
stock of the situation in the seat behind me. There was our head
coach, with a look on his face that portrayed a mixture of guilt, relief,
and absolute glee, happily puffing away. At least one of us could be
happy, I suppose.

Slovenia is a beautiful country. It reminded me a lot of Colorado—clean air and forested mountains, with houses scattered here and there. We (they) were in the country to play a game, of course. We (they) did that poorly and managed to be eliminated from the ULEB Cup semifinals. This leaves us with only one game a week—the Spanish league game.

While I watched the game in Slovenia in street clothes, I noticed our opposition's relatively docile supporters and had a flashback to Greece. I remembered the coins, rocks, and cell phones that would assault us on the court from time to time. After a game against one of the more well-financed teams in Athens, which we lost in heartbreaking fashion, a few of our fans ripped up a row of bleachers and threw them on the court. In another instance, we lost to Olympiacos, another of the big teams in the country. As I jogged off the court, I noticed a silver streak in the upper left quadrant of my vision. I ducked just in time to avoid being knocked flat by a rather large bottle of water. Ah, the good old days. True fans. The Slovenians have a long way to go.

When we got back from Slovenia, my next-youngest brother arrived in Spain. He just finished a mind-numbing job at a hospital in Kansas and has some time before medical school starts in the fall, so will live with me for the rest of my time in Barcelona. One of my most impressive early Spanish-language accomplishments was ordering pizza over the phone, in Spanish. I thought I would impress my brother Dan with my pizza-ordering skills on one of his first nights in town. I ordered two identical pies to simplify matters. When the doorbell rang, I thought, *I've done it again. Pizza's here, proving that I am indeed quite the linguist.* Then two things happened. The first changed my view of the world, the second of my Spanish skills. I handed the deliverer sixteen euros for a thirteen-euro bill. Pizzaboy said, "That's too much, isn't it?" I nearly fell down. He had just refused a tip—the exact opposite reaction to the glares I got in college, back when I had no money and thought that sixty cents was an acceptable tip. I assured him that it was okay and closed the door, and we turned to the pizza, delighted at the prospect of hot food. As we opened the boxes,

I quickly realized by the smell assaulting my nose that my linguistic overconfidence was going to haunt us. The scent was familiar. In fact, it was the smell of the food that has become my palate's nemesis in Spain. I had managed to procure for us two *tuna* pizzas. My faith in my intelligence was destroyed. More important, Dan and I had to eat pizza with tuna on it. It was as bad as it sounds.

April 13

Our dance team is a constant source of amusement for me. I gather that they are something of a big deal—they dominate the team's Web site. The group does include some attractive girls, but they appear to only just be able to put a routine together, and once they do, they can barely perform it. In their defense, they dance in tight jeans and cowboy boots—part of an overall cowboy theme. Such an ensemble can't be the best outfit for dancing.

Interestingly, the dancing issue is not unique to our group; I have seen it wherever I have been in Europe. I thought at first that the population base must be to blame; perhaps there simply aren't enough good-looking girls who can also dance in Europe. I quickly saw the flaws in that hypothesis: (1) the respective populations of the various countries in which I have played are hardly small, and (2) the girls in Europe are better-looking than the ones in the United States, if only because they are generally thinner. After further analysis made possible by my recent injury and the subsequent abundance of time on the bench, I have developed the theory that Europeans suffer from a life bereft of songs with good rhythm. While the citizenry of the United States is now raised on the unpredictable beats of rock, rap, and R&B, Europeans cut their musical teeth on the facile rhythms of the latest traditional folk songs with only a smattering of simple pop songs and techno ditties to keep life semi-lively. The result: dance team participants who look the part, but who dance as if they were transported from the 1950s.

The lone male dancer in the Joventut group adds a special touch to each game. Unlike an American male dancer, who would be more of a prop, he does exactly the same dances as the girls. He even attempts the age-old, chest-out breast-shake that is nearly ubiquitous in dance routines. During our last game, he wore a midriff-baring shirt and some low-cut jeans, same as the girls. I nearly passed out due to laughter containment as I discreetly observed the action unfold during one of our time outs. Of course, I should note that our very gutsy hero is actually the best dancer on the floor. And he is at every game—notable because the girls seem to appear only when they want, making for a different number of participants each time, which can't possibly be easy to coordinate. (Incidentally, the routines are exactly the same—and done to the same songs, in the same order—at each game.)

Lending further credence to his claim of best-dancer honors is Julio's constant enthusiasm. Of course, he really appears enthusiastic only by comparison. I have learned that the girls all work at the same bar at night. It shows during the day. Most of them spend a good portion of their time mustering the energy to leave the bleachers they occupy during game action, and they rarely appear pleased about venturing onto the court. Not Julio. (I don't know his actual name. Julio seems appropriate, for some reason.) He lusts for the stage that is center court. And I say bravo Julio.

April 27

Good news: it appears that the members of the female population of Spain show even less inhibition regarding bikini removal at the beach than did the women in Greece. On a recent sunny day, my brother Dan and I made our nearly daily walk to the beach. As usual, we maintained a diligent watch for rampant toplessness. Our weekday trips are not always replete with quantity, but they do seem to inspire quality. Often, we will be two of only twenty or so people on a quarter-mile stretch of sand. Fortunately, a large proportion of that number is often of the lithe female contingent. At any rate, on the day in question, we were greeted by the sight of a very attractive woman of about twenty-five wading out of the water, hair wet and skin glistening, wearing only her swimsuit bottom. She walked from the sea to the showers used generally for sand removal—still topless, of course—and proceeded to rinse off in a manner reminiscent of the most scandalous shampoo commercial ever seen. It was a fine start to our day at the beach.

Sadly, I can't work the topless-girl angle. Spanish women have been unimpressed by my attempts at discourse; they seem impatient that I can't speak their language. This has been a mite confusing. In Greece, the girls thought it was cute when I tried to speak Greek. Of course, since Greek is a useless language in the rest of the world, they all spoke at least a modicum of English; I could always fall back on their knowledge. The Spaniards are more resistant to Westernization. Thus, I make little headway. I definitely cannot hold up under the pressure caused by the approach to a topless Spanish girl on the beach at one-thirty in the afternoon on a Tuesday. My chances of success are so low as to be nonexistent.

I did have a promising romantic encounter recently—but not with a Spanish girl. She was German.

A friend of mine visited during the spring break of his study-abroad university in Italy. Dan and I met him in one of the central train stations in Barcelona in order to escort him to my apartment, where he was going to stay for a few days. On the way home, I sat down on the train next to a gorgeous blond girl. Desperate for an icebreaker, I used an argument we had been having regarding the translation of some word to Spanish. I asked for her help. She was of no real assistance but seemed slightly amused. We talked for the remainder of the train ride—her English was quite impressive. Germans are smart. As we got farther from the city of Barcelona proper, the train became more and more empty, but my new friend stayed on. I began to get my hopes up; I thought maybe she lived near me, which would definitely make the relationship I was already planning more convenient.

She didn't just live near me. She lived about fifty paces from my front door, in an apartment above the grocery store at which we shopped on a daily basis. When we said our farewells, she gave me her number and I promised to take her to dinner sometime soon. She agreed that a date was a good idea. I was pleased with the prospect.

I waited a few days and called. She had given me a work number, which was curious, I thought. When I told her who I was, she brightened and then told me she would call back later.

She didn't call. I chalked it up to one of life's little disappointments. We left on a two-day road trip and I tried to forget about my new favorite German girl. Sometime after we returned home, I made a solo trip into the center of the city to buy some music. Then, lo and behold, as I boarded the same train for the trip back to the suburbs, there she was again. I asked her what had happened; she said that she had lost my number. We had a great train ride home. (I thought it was great anyway. Then again, she was gorgeous. It would have seemed great if she would have stabbed me in the leg.) She promised to call the next day.

She didn't call. Obviously, we were not headed to a grand future together. With that in mind, I took it upon myself to march over to her apartment one evening, if only to cause an awkward encounter, which I think is always warranted. When the door opened, there was a guy I had never seen standing on the other side of the threshold. My once-future girlfriend quickly appeared at his side and then introduced me to her live-in boyfriend. Not one to be daunted by an uncomfortable situation, I allowed myself to be ushered in. I sat down and had a fine conversation with said boyfriend, who seemed to be a fine fellow. After twenty minutes, I took my leave without anyone ever explaining exactly who I was. I haven't seen either of them since. I'd like to; I want to ask the girl why she was giving out her phone number to random guys if she was already living with one.

Unfortunately, I don't get paid to chase girls. With that in mind, I resumed my basketball career. Our head coach approached me after a weekend game and said that he had set up a lunch meeting for the next day. He, the trainer, the strength coach, the doctor, and I were going to discuss my return to the court. With little choice in the matter, I agreed to make an appearance. Before we set off, I had a feeling it would be an interesting meeting; the trainer and strength coach had warned me that the coach was going to try to convince me to agree to play again right away. They were a little apprehensive—my right arm remained only as strong as the average eight-year-old girl's.

We all shuffled into a local restaurant, and the coach ordered up some of their best shellfish-in-their-shells-floating-in-some-crappy-brine stew. While I wondered what possesses any human to willingly consume such a mess, we got down to business. The coach speaks only a little English, and while my Spanish has gotten better, I am certainly no Cervantes at this point. He asked me, "Cómo está tu hombro?" (How is your shoulder?) I thought about using the truth: "Well, each day is different. Some days I really feel like I am making progress; other days I want to retire from sports entirely and spend the remainder of my days on a fishing boat in the Barcelona harbor. Right now, the deltoid is gaining strength, but the pectoral muscle is almost nonexistent. And the bones are showing through my back where a trapezius muscle used to reside."

Instead, I said, "Mi hombro está así así y comiendo esta comida es muy similar a comiendo mis zapatos." (I think that means, "My shoulder is so-so and eating this food is like eating my own shoes." I may have left out the last part.) The coach then told me that he really would like me to play at whatever speed or ability I could muster. He next said that he would prefer me in any capacity to my American replacement. (I promise that I am not making this up to make myself seem like a Spanish basketball god.) He said I could practice as much as I wanted, play as long as I could, and generally dictate the situation for myself. My there's-something-fishy-going-on-here radar went off. Coaches don't usually make such statements to their players. Then again, they don't usually smoke at practice, either. The team doctor, in whom I have almost no faith, rang in with his belief that my lack of strength would probably increase my chances of a new injury by 5 percent or so. The trainer and strength coach (the only people here I trust) said that they thought I could start participating in more practice situations each day but that they did not know how quickly my recovery would progress. After more broken bilingual discussion, I agreed that I could probably start to do a little more but that I wouldn't know until the end of the week. A decision was not needed until that Friday night, so my proposal seemed acceptable to all parties. We finished our meal and went on our ways.

About six hours later, the filth I consumed exacted its revenge upon my digestive system. I have now given up on Spanish food entirely. Apparently they need to wash it or something.

On the Friday in question, we left Barcelona for a game in Granada, Spain; we had decided that I would play in three-to-four-minute bursts. The team was ferried to Granada on the second-smallest plane in which I have ever ridden. (The smallest was a two-passenger Piper that a friend of mine flew.) We usually take a smallish prop plane to our away games. That plane—the Concorde, as we will now call it—is of a similar size to the one we used in college. The new plane (new, meaning different)—the Mosquito, as my teammates call it—was not much bigger than some seventies-era Cadillacs.

On the way to the airport, we were all assigned seats, which I thought was a little strange. I was pleased, though. It appeared that someone had accounted for legroom needs. When we were told to board the plane, the officials in charge made us fill the plane from front to back. Because of said legroom constraints, we larger humans sat down first and then everyone duck-walked past us to their seats. I thought that the method was a mite inefficient, and said so. I learned that behind this plan lay very solid reasoning. Our comfort had been no one's motivation. As the biggest players on the team, we were being used as ballast. If we had been allowed to fill the plane at random large-body placement, starting in the rear, the craft would have tipped over backward. I'm not joking.

I started the game in Granada. Which makes sense—it had only been two months since I last played. I was a little surprised, but took the news as a vote of confidence. I began the game apprehensive about my assignment to play under control and to protect my shoulder, as caution on the court is impossible for me. I am like a lawn-mower blade; I am either whirring along at full speed, cutting grass, or I am just dead weight, along for the ride. (That was quite possibly the worst analogy I've ever used.) Surprisingly, the play-at-half-speed plan actually worked, if only because I was so rusty (not a lawn mower reference) that I had to plan my every move. We started the game badly but turned it around in the second half and came through with a much-needed road win. My performance could hardly be labeled transcendental, but all things considered, I played pretty well and finished with eleven points.

May 13

Tourism update:

There appears to be some sort of pollution situation affecting our beach. We're not entirely sure what is going on; my brother Dan reports unidentified dead life-forms washing up on the beach, and we have heard rumblings of contamination through our admittedly inefficient grapevine. I think we will wait for a satisfactory all-clear before making any further forays into the sea. While searching for information about our problem here in the Badalona/Barcelona area, we did come upon some news about another pollution situation somewhere in Spain. In a nearby coastal town, some mechanism went awry and thousands of liters of human excrement were released into the sea. Call me crazy, but I don't think it is outlandish to expect each seaport to be responsible for its human excrement disposal problem. In fact, it may be priority number one.

About a week ago (before the pollution talk), I finally had my first swim in the section of the Mediterranean Sea that serves as my backyard. It was pleasant enough, aside from the occasional mouthful of salt water. (It seems that one needs to be reminded by a swallow every fifteen minutes to keep one's mouth shut—one forgets how awful seawater tastes.) As some friends and I frolicked in the water like only kids from landlocked places can do, I noticed that my brother Dan had stopped and was holding his neck, where he thought one of us had slapped him. We left the water while reassuring him that we had not been abusing him for sport. As we did, an angry welt began to rise on his neck. He had been stung by a jellyfish. Fortunately, this story has a happy ending; we didn't have to consult any Spanish physicians, nor was a golden shower necessary. The welt faded away after a day. Unfortunately, Dan will never again swim in the Mediterranean Sea. Considering its high fecal count, his might not be the worst idea.

May 25

Prior to my team's last two regular-season games, we were ranked somewhere between seventh and twelfth in the league. The first eight teams would make the playoffs. By someone's calculations, even if we won our last two games, we would need some help from other teams if a DKV Joventut playoff appearance is to become a reality. That someone was not Stephen Hawking, but I believed him nonetheless.

My shoulder has held up relatively well through our playoff push. I've played in four games while in disabled status and have not yet been asked to quit and join the dance team. My defense and rebounding abilities are generally terrible—perhaps due to my severely impaired level of arm strength. (At time of writing I remain unable to do either a push-up or a pull-up.) I try to make up for my glaring weaknesses by taking many, many shots—which keeps me entertained.

While my shoulder has been improving, my general health has been . . . not great. I think someone in Spain wants me to die. A little melodramatic, perhaps, but I don't think it is inaccurate to write that my body has spewed forth its proverbial last gasp. It needs this season to end.

I'm a little ashamed at my thoughts—my team is currently playing in a first-round playoff series here in Spain. But, seriously, it's May 25. Basketball season is over. And my body tells me so.

My final descent began last weekend. We won the second-to-last game of the year and so entered the final regular-season game tied with something like forty-seven other teams for seventh place. (This on May 17, one month after the NBA's last regular-season game—and the NBA season is hardly brief.) We needed a win on the road in our final game to have any hope of qualifying for the playoffs. I spent the night before the deciding game alternating between sweating through my sheets and searching in vain for extra clothes and bedcovers to combat the chills coursing through my body. I managed about two hours of sleep. (Obviously, my body does not know how to deal with Spanish microbes. I haven't had so many fevers . . . ever.) On game day I felt relatively bad but did not mention my discomfort to anyone. (I have a theory that I am allowed to complain about one malady at a time. "Deconstructed shoulder" is the injury of record, so I feel compelled not to draw attention to my other failings.) We won the sloppily played game. I did not play very well. Nor did I feel very well. After the game, we found out that we had received the prescribed help from the other particular teams and we were playoff bound. The team was excited. As we rode back to the hotel, the mood on the bus was positively giddy. I couldn't muster much giddiness. I wanted nothing more than to return to my room and lie down.

I spent the next days moving slowly between the couch and the bathroom, as whatever organism was breeding inside me wreaked havoc on my GI tract. Good times. With the first game of our playoff series approaching on Thursday, I muddled my way through about five minutes of practice on Tuesday and then returned home for more work on my weight-loss program. On Wednesday morning, Dan and I ventured briefly out of the apartment. Upon return to the homestead, I stumbled to my bed, doubled over in pain, and didn't move for an hour. I resolved, as I was lying there, that I would call a medical professional as soon as I regained the ability to walk. I did not see how I was going to play very effectively the next day. I finally gathered the strength needed to walk to the phone and called the team trainer, hoping for some help.

I have described my other Spanish medical issues in excruciating detail. I will not do that here. To summarize, I spent nearly six hours of my day wandering around Barcelona's most ghetto medical facilities in order to confirm something that has been true all of my life—that I did not have appendicitis. In the interim, I didn't make any progress toward actually feeling better. When I got home from a day of examinations, I evaluated the situation. Because the quest for my health had taken longer than expected, the team had left for Valencia without me, but I could tell from what the team doctor had said that the coaches wanted me to come to Valencia that night for the next day's game.

When I finally tracked down the trainer at the hotel in Valencia he said that he thought it would be best for me to stay home and rest, with the hope that I could play in the following game. (I sometimes think he is the only one in the organization with a fully functional brain.) I asked him if Zendon Hamilton was in Valencia. (He has remained with the team, practicing in case he was needed.) Incredibly, he was. The solution seemed simple to me: call the league, change Americans, problem solved. I was flattered by their confidence in me. (Or their confidence in what remained of me.) But I was at half mast because of the shoulder fiasco. Meanwhile, my case of the plague and the accompanying lack of energy had me functioning at about 20 percent. I couldn't imagine how I was going to help my team win a basketball game. The trainer put the coach on the line. He said that if I could play the way I had the week before, it would be plenty. (He spoke of the last regular-season game, in which I had played like an eight-year-old girl with spina bifida.)

I hung up and discussed the situation with my brother Dan, who had enjoyed a festive day of untranslated Catalan television in the hospital waiting room. After some back-and-forth, he convinced me that it would probably be a better PR move to make an effort to play. Nonplussed that my little brother was probably right, I called the trainer and told him that I would go to Valencia.

I left Barcelona after ten that night. I was in fantastic shape when game time arrived the next day. I played minimally—most of my time on the court was spent wondering where I was. We lost badly. (At least, I think we lost. It all seems like some sort of horrible dream.) Our playoff run was off to a poor start.

While riding around in hazes caused by various maladies, I've been analyzing my thoughts on this playoff series and this season. Conclusion: I don't care anymore. I'm not sure what that says about me; probably nothing good. In my defense, I am anxious about the job of rehabilitating my shoulder. The addition of the events of the last week to an already taxing season has not been helpful to my attitude. My body is used up for the year, and it is time to move on. Ideally, I need to be ready to play by early July in order to begin the process of finding a job for next season.

It is a sad state of affairs that I am forced to look ahead so much, but that is the nature of my life. I suppose if I had a six-year, $14 million contract, I could afford a season that lasts until Independence Day. But I don't, so I am obligated to think in selfish terms.

The good news: while I can actively hope for my team to lose between game days, I cannot change my habits on the court. We played yesterday in the second game of the best-of-five against Valencia. I was still not in great shape. I didn't feel all that bad, but I was weak from the starvation of the last week. (I've probably lost about fifteen pounds since I arrived in Spain.) I did not play well, but I did play hard. Which, along with a quarter, might buy me a minute of international long distance. We were obliterated on our home court, losing by nearly twenty points, which left our advancement hopes in dire straits. So while injury, a really long year, and constant rejection at the hands of Spanish girls has eroded my desire for the season to continue, I know that while I am hoping for a loss this coming Thursday, I won't play like it when the day comes.

June 7

Extend-o-season is finally over. We lost in the third game of the series with Valencia. Overall, it was a rather poor playoff showing. Obviously. After the game, we boarded a plane bound for Barcelona. I was somewhat distraught. The end of each season always brings with it a panicked feeling. Even in college, I rarely dealt well with the prospect of starting over. My European counterparts were surprised by my gloom. To their way of thinking, we had made a good effort. Making the playoffs had been something of a heroic accomplishment considering our placement in the standings a few weeks earlier. In their minds, there was nothing about which we should be ashamed.

My contract with Joventut stated that I was bound to the team for three days past our final game. While we boarded the plane that would take us home to Barcelona, I heard—through my funk—talk of a postseason banquet a week from that day. I was in no mood to discuss a dinner, but knew that there was almost no way I would remain in Spain for another week. NBA summer leagues were looming; more important, I needed to go home for a few weeks of stability after the most chaotic year of my life.

When we got back to the arena where our cars waited, I asked the coach if there was any way to reschedule the banquet within the next few days so that I could attend and then leave the country. He said he would ask.

My team had something of a love affair with me since I arrived in Spain. I have never fully understood it. (Note to self: improve self-esteem so that affection does not come as a shock.) I do think I was a pleasant surprise. I played hard and was a better basketball player than they expected to find on short notice. Additionally, I embraced the Spanish culture, which is very important to these Mediterranean types. I didn't bristle at coaching and melded well with the team already in place. I gather that the player I replaced had been quite talented but had also been difficult to deal with. Because my stay went so well, there was talk of a contract extension for me. Barcelona is hardly the worst place in the world for a person to live, so I would have seriously considered another year with Joventut.

Unfortunately, I don't think that said talk will lead to any further employment by DKV Joventut. I became entirely too stubborn when the team informed me that there was no way that the date of the banquet could be moved. I took a stand and told them that I was going to leave the prescribed three days following our last game. It was not among my shining moments. Even when asked by the team president, who told me just how much such events mean to the Spanish people, I didn't back down. I felt panicked about wasting any more time in Spain. (As if sitting by the beach with no responsibilities is a waste.) I told him that I had to get back to the United States.

And so I left without any real closure. The team was disappointed by my admittedly immature decision, but I, in typical American fashion, felt I had to stick up for myself. Again, it wasn't among my better moves.

Now it is time to prepare for the next stage. The doctors I've seen since I've been back in the United States tell me that the nerve injury I sustained could have been worse . . . but that it certainly is not going to magically heal in three weeks. It will be a long summer of rehab. Hopefully I can rest my brain while I rest my body. I have to get ready for next year, which I'm sure will be smooth, worry-free, and filled with thoughts of bunny rabbits and butterflies. Whatever happens, I'm confident that I won't complain about it at all.

YEAR 2

October 5

I recently caught one of my teammates as he opened some mail at the arena. Along with his fan mail and other assorted posts, he had received a blank journal. Another player noticed his prize and asked him if he (gasp) actually kept a journal. The mail opener scoffed at the idea and said that he did not, as if that would be completely beneath him. When pressed with "Come on, man, I won't tell the guys," he said, "No, I really don't . . . but I do keep a prayer journal from time to time." Amazingly, the inquisitor assented that a prayer journal is cool, and went on his way. I wanted to jump up and say, "No, man, that isn't cool. I would say that it falls decidedly *not* under the category of 'cool,' and more under the category of 'boring,' 'extreme,' or, at the very least, 'really odd.' But, guys, as I am a habitual journal keeper myself, don't bother worrying about my opinion."

Because I am a lowly, un-guaranteed free agent trying to make his way at training camp with the New Orleans Hornets, I kept my mouth shut.

It seems that the obvious question, when presented with the factoid contained at the end of the previous paragraph, would be: "Why, Paul, when you have, not once, but twice before attended training camps under similar circumstances, would you subject yourself to it again?" If approached with this question immediately preceding the second practice of the day, the answer would be: "Because I'm a fucking idiot." If faced with the same question, but under better conditions (a situation in which I have yet to be placed since my arrival in New Orleans, unless one were to count the time I found out that the hotel gift shop sells little cartons of milk and packages of ready-to-eat Apple Jacks in plastic bowls), I would reply with: "I really feel like all the credit goes to God and to my offensive line." No, wait, wrong stock sports-related answer. Actually, I am here in New Orleans because I had offers to go overseas in August and September but they were unspectacular ones, because this summer my shoulder was still too broken to allow me to play in NBA summer leagues, and because I need to get my name back in the shuffle, so to speak. Most important, I am here because Tim Floyd is the head coach of the Hornets. Since things worked out pretty well for me the first time he asked me to play for him (back at Iowa State), I thought it was worth trying again. Dance with the one who brought you, and all that.

Theoretical reporter questioning Paul Shirley:

Theoretical reporter: Paul, tell me about your situation with the Hornets.

Paul Shirley: Well, here's the deal with the Hornets (yes, the Charlotte Hornets did move to New Orleans several years ago, which is something of a shock to many people, including some of the citizenry with whom I have conversed here in this fair Louisiana city). Continuing in a theme similar to that found at my training camp stints with the Lakers and Hawks, the Hornets have invited more players to camp than will be on the opening-day roster. As always, an NBA team is allowed only fifteen on that list. But there is no limit to the number of players invited to training camp. (Actually, there is probably a limit. It seems like 972 would be a few too many. Unfortunately, I don't want to admit my ignorance and let on that I don't know what that limit might be.) In camp here in New Orleans, we are seventeen.

TR: Sounds like pretty good odds, I would say. Fifteen out of seventeen make the team? How could you possibly screw this up?

PS: I would advise caution if anyone were tempted to fire up the Paul Shirley replica jersey looms. NBA teams, or more accurately their general managers, remain proponents of huge, guaranteed contracts given to players who do their jobs well. The Hornets currently have fourteen players who are guaranteed for the upcoming season.

TR: Okay, so that means there are three players fighting for that fifteenth roster spot. Those aren't bad odds, are they?

PS: Not so fast. The management of the New Orleans Hornets has made it quite clear to me that they will be keeping only fourteen players on the roster this year.

TR: What a bunch of tightwads.

PS: You said it.

TR: Why, then, did you come to New Orleans if you had no chance to make the team? Are you retarded?

PS: Both good questions. I came because this team will lose a bunch of players after this year and it is possible that those in management positions might see something they like out of me and my skinny white frame. When Coach Floyd called to ask what I was doing this fall, he told me that I had no chance to make the team, but if I had nothing better to do, I should come down and go through training camp with the Hornets. Since my agent could not come up with a better option, I made the trip. Plus, there is always the chance that half the team will fall prey to HIV because of some freak, previously unheard-of, homosexual locker room gang bang, and I will be around to fill one of the open roster spots.

TR: Fair enough. Our time is up. I need to go talk to someone more important.

A part of me was intrigued by the prospect of training camp with the Hornets just to see how Tim Floyd would go about coaching a professional basketball team. I played for Floyd for two years at Iowa State before he left Ames for the thankless job of replacing Phil Jackson as coach of the Chicago Bulls. I had heard from varied sources what Tim Floyd: Version 2.0 Pro was like, but was intrigued to judge for myself. (Most reports out of Chicago leaned toward a mellowing I thought to be impossible for one of the most intense coaches I have ever seen in action.)

Watching Coach Floyd do his open-the-season speech in New Orleans was surreal. It had never occurred to me that I would be on the receiving end of such an event again. The first time I was subjected to the experience, I had walked to the team meeting with absolutely no idea what to expect. It was my third day on campus at Iowa State. I could barely find my way to class each morning, so I was in no way prepared for the three-hour monstrosity that passed as our welcome meeting. I had never seen such intensity. To consider interrupting Coach Floyd as he stood at the front of the room going through the twenty-page booklet he had prepared for the occasion was seemingly to consider having one's person, along with one's basketball career, thrown out the nearest window. I left the meeting with sweat running down the inside of my shirt. I was scared.

Fast-forward to the Hornets' welcome meeting. The atmosphere was slightly more relaxed than it had been in college, not in small part because we were all seated at a swanky restaurant in the French Quarter and not in a dimly lit basketball office in Ames, Iowa. The proceedings with the Hornets were delayed about forty-five minutes while we all awaited Baron Davis' arrival. When he did grace us with his presence, he was neither frazzled by, nor apologetic for his tardiness. (I think his basketball upbringing might have been a mite different than mine.) Stacey Augmon drank five Heinekens through the course of the evening and seemed much more interested in the events in other areas of the restaurant than anything his coach was saying. Meanwhile, Coach Floyd seemed relieved just to get through his opening remarks without being shouted down from the microphone. It seems that coaching in the NBA takes a slight change in mind-set from coaching in college.

Practice is not exactly the same either. NBA players are not used to a lot of, shall we say, criticism, so Coach Floyd is forced to be a bit more positive than I remember. The famed intensity is still present, of course. But now after a defensive breakdown, instead of spewing forth a rant containing several unprintable expletives and an allusion to the fact that the player's mother was not known for her defensive ability either, he will say something like, "That wasn't really what I had in mind there, George, why don't you try it another way?" Which, of course, is hilarious to me, because I know exactly what is whizzing

around in his head. The player involved, having had no prior experience with the man, has no idea of the bullet he just dodged because
he plays for the New Orleans Hornets in 2003 and not the University
of New Orleans in 1992. (Floyd coached at UNO before taking the
Iowa State job. His New Orleans connections don't stop there. He was
raised in the city and returned after his stint in Chicago. He was then
in exactly the right place when the Hornets fired head coach Paul
Silas.)

The Hornets' organization is not known for being a particularly
well-run outfit. The owner is among the most penny-pinching in the
NBA and, because of its quick departure from Charlotte, the team
walks something of a thin line with the league. Coach Floyd knew all
of this when he took the job. While he did understand the risk, he is
not an idiot and would have been remiss to turn down a large, guaranteed contract when handed the opportunity. I, however, knew very little about the Hornets before getting to the Big Easy. For now, I am on
the fence in my judgment of the organization. I have observed a few
entertaining exchanges—perhaps a few more than in other places.
For example, at our opening meeting, the assistant to the general
manager attempted to lay out the guidelines for the year, while also
introducing the personnel involved with the team. His lack of prepa-
ration was quite apparent. He was unsure of the identities of several
of the people he was supposed to introduce and seemed confused regarding the exact point of his talk throughout. More telling—and
more entertaining to me—he completely sweated through the armpits
of the blue dress shirt he was wearing. It was as if he had never spoken
in front of more than three people in his life. The most disconcerting
aspect of the meeting, though, was that the first person introduced
by the sweat-stained wonder was not the head coach. Or a new
player. Or a team captain. It was the director of marketing. Priorities,
priorities.

NBA players are full of surprises. The Hornets are no exception.
When I think of Stacey Augmon, now of these Hornets, I think of the
University of Nevada–Las Vegas Runnin' Rebels. (I have always hated
that the word in their mascot's name was actually spelled Runnin'—

such purposive grammatical errors give me no hope for humanity. Yes, I am a dork.) I think of Larry Johnson, Greg Anthony, and Jerry Tarkanian. I think of scoring and Loyola Marymount. I think of casinos and gamblers and under-the-table payments made to spectacular athletes with questionable integrity and intellect. I do not, however, think of nice guys. But maybe I will now, because Stacey Augmon seems like a hell of a good dude. A little old, perhaps, and with a run-hard-put-up-wet look about him, but about as friendly a professional basketball player as I have seen. It throws off my whole value system. Dammit.

October 13

For me, a typical NBA game experience with the Hornets usually goes something like this . . .

Two separate team buses depart the hotel. One, the early bus, leaves about two and a half hours before the game. The late bus follows half an hour later. Since I have nothing better to do, I always take the earlier of the two. Upon arrival at the arena, I usually hang out in the locker room for a bit, partaking of as much of the available free food as is humanly possible for a person about to participate in a physical activity. After gorging myself on fresh fruit and Gatorade, I don my uniform. In my experience, the NBA game uniform is not exactly built for comfort. It feels like it weighs five pounds and the inner lining appears to be made from sandpaper—my skin often comes out of the evening red and blotchy. (I have a theory that the powers that be do not notice a locker room full of rosy backs and chests because of the rather one-sided racial makeup of most teams. I don't know what a black guy's skin does when it is irritated; whatever it is, it is not nearly as evident on his as it is mine.) NBA players are provided with about thirty-seven different shooting shirts and warm-up tops; most players do not put on their actual jerseys until right before the game. I, being deathly afraid of the scenario wherein the coach calls for me to join the game and I rip off my warm-up only to find that I forgot to adorn myself with my game jersey, always put on my jersey and the lightest of the warm-up tops for the pre-warm-up warm-up. Oh, and I put on shorts, too. Naked from the waist down is not encouraged in the National Basketball Association. At least not in games.

Once I have prepared myself for battle, I head out to the court to work out. I write "work out" instead of "warm up" because a workout is what my warm-up usually becomes. Since I know that I am unlikely to play meaningful minutes in the game that is to follow, I assume I ought to do as much ass kissing as I can and so stay on the court as long as possible. Plus, any scout watching would have to be impressed by my ability to simultaneously dodge announcers, cheerleaders, and rogue basketballs while participating in an hour-long individual workout.

When I am finished honing my game and/or talking to opposing players I know, I report back to the locker room. There, the usual pregame hoopla takes place. The coaches speak; the players do their best to tune it out. I mean, they are the best in the world, right? There is hardly anything that some little white guy wearing a suit could tell them that they don't already know. After waiting until the last possible moment, the team exits the locker room, usually to engage in complex warm-up rituals, such as when most everyone stands around under the basket and watches the three people with basketballs shoot until one of them misses, at which point the rebounder gets a chance to saunter out from under the basket to cast up a shot. Warm-up routines in the NBA are complicated.

After the introduction of the starting lineups, I scurry over to the end of the bench in order to secure a seat. In my experience, sitting on the floor for the two and a half hours that a professional basketball game consumes is neither comfortable nor enjoyable. I can usually find a chair at the beginning of the game. However, problems arise when the starters come off the floor. Because they are tired, they spread out all over the place and seem none too excited when I try to squeeze in my nonplaying ass, so I am sometimes relegated to the floor with the rest of my bench-warming contemporaries. (The number of available seats is too small because the benches are set up for regular-season games. Preseason rosters are, obviously, larger than regular-season ones.)

Once game play begins, my brain goes numb and I fall into a routine of clapping, getting up to congratulate players when they come out of the game, and trying to make it look like I am paying attention during time-outs, when all I really want to do is watch the dance team. I break out of my reverie about midway through the second quarter, when I could conceivably enter the game for semi-meaningful time. An NBA coach generally leaves his starters in the game for the first eight or nine minutes of the game. The second string, if the coach is blessed with a good one, usually plays the next six to seven minutes, depending on its success on the floor. In an early preseason game, the coach might call upon some of what would be his third string at this point in the game. (Me, for example.) During the season, it would be folly for the coach to throw so many players into the game, but during the preseason, when a team is trying to find out all it can about the players on its roster, the man in charge may do just that—hence my attention to the game. I also make sure the laces on my shoes are tied—any invitation to play that I might get would certainly fall under the category of "on short notice."

At halftime, we return to the locker room, where more talking and non-listening goes on. When the coaches are finished, we wander back to the court. Then the third quarter begins . . . and time slows down. NBA games are extraordinarily long; the third period is the worst. I would not advance the theory that it is actually longer; I think it just appears as such because the early-game excitement has worn off and the end-of-game excitement is still a quarter away. Both teams muddle their way through the third with what appears to be little care for the score, hoping mostly to pass the time until the end of the game.

If, at the onset of the fourth quarter, I have not appeared in the action, one of two things happens. If my team is ahead, I cheer for each addition to the lead and despair for each subtraction from it, but do both somewhat halfheartedly. If my team is behind, I am much more of a die-hard fan. I have no desire for any garbage time—that period after the moment everyone in the arena realizes that one team is lying on the canvas next to two front teeth and a pool of bloody snot. I want no part of cleanup, for two reasons. (Game cleanup, not bloody-snot-from-the-boxing-analogy cleanup.) First, it is a no-win situation. If I play badly when it doesn't matter, I must really be awful (e.g., "I can't put Shirley in the game in a meaningful situation, he couldn't even play well when we were up thirty"), but if I play well, then I only did it against tired players or fellow scrubs (e.g., "Well, sure, he scored ten points in five minutes, but the guy guarding him was dog-tired and only had one eye"). Second, after sitting around for two-plus hours, my body is in no condition to try to perform at its best level. It's like taking a rubber band out of the freezer.

If I am given mop-up duty, it is usually only for about two minutes, which doesn't sound like much. However, those often seem to be the most exhausting two minutes of all time. For whatever reason, be it the adrenaline or the two hours of ass-sitting, I am always nearly completely spent after a minute and a half. (Insert sexual prowess joke here.) I don't understand it; perhaps my body is trying to compress the thirty minutes of action most players get into the two that I get. Whatever the reason, by the time the buzzer sounds, I usually feel like I just played the whole forty-eight minutes. But, since I didn't, I have to appear calm and collected and act like whatever misdeed or heroic act I performed during my two minutes of glory was no big deal.

I was given an opportunity to consider this progression of an NBA game during a recent preseason game with the Dallas Mavericks, but this time, I had to balance all of my philosophizing with actual game play. (Warning: basketball-speak ahead.) With about three minutes to go in the first half, the two power forwards ahead of me on the depth chart were incapacitated, one due to foul trouble, the other because of fatigue. Coach Floyd started searching the bench for a replacement; I assumed he was looking for me. I was wrong. He, in fact, put one of my fellow bench warmers, a small forward, into the game. My brain would have accepted the move quietly if either of the following conditions could have been met: (1) said player actually knew that position in addition to his own, or (2) I thought I deserved to stay on the bench due to blatant inability on my part. I could not justify either condition in my mind, so I just sat on the bench (floor, actually; I had a poor round of seat stakeout in this particular game) and steamed about the fact that I played more in preseason games when I was fresh out of school and a temporary member of the two-time defending world champion Los Angeles Lakers than I had on a not-very-good team with my goddamn college coach at the helm. As the—to take it back to third grade—topic sentence of this paragraph indicated, I did in fact get in on the action . . . with six seconds to go in the first half. I even had time to make my mark on the game. With two seconds remaining in the half, we had the ball at the end opposite our basket. I was given the duty of heaving the ball to the opposite free-throw line, where our center was supposed to make some miraculous play or another. Because my right arm is still prone to noodle-like behavior due to a slow recovery from the injury of last spring, I wanted to make sure I didn't girl-toss the ball to half court. Result: I threw it out of bounds on the far end. Maybe I should have stayed on the bench after all.

Before practice sometime last week, I approached Coach Floyd to ask him if I could do anything better—if I was playing like I needed to be playing, et cetera. He said that I was doing great (but what's he going to say?) but that, as we knew going in, I wasn't going to make the team. In fact, he said, the general manager was going to cut me and another player the next day because the GM was worried about his financial responsibilities if we were to get injured. I was surprised; I had planned to be around for at least two or three weeks and had thought I would get to play in a couple of preseason games. (We hadn't played any at that point.) I quickly came to terms with my lame-duck status; I am a lover neither of organized practices nor of hanging out in cities I don't really like. And, since I had already proven to the Hornets that I have some basketball ability, I thought I could withstand the early rejection and prepare to move on. After practice, I asked if the next day was definitely going to be the day; Floyd told me he thought it would be Wednesday. Strangely enough, I was not particularly motivated for Tuesday's practices, but managed my disgust and got through the day. After the final practice on Tuesday, Coach Floyd told me that my doomsday would be delayed, but that he didn't know by how much. At that point, my mind was already halfway home and on to the next stop on the Career Tilt-a-Whirl. I didn't need further confusion in my addled brain.

We played a preseason game Wednesday in Baton Rouge. We won, I didn't play. We practiced back in New Orleans on Thursday and Friday. I walked around like a GI in a minefield wondering if, when I next saw the general manager, he was going to present me with a plane ticket. No news was forthcoming on either of those days, so I set off on a road trip with the team to Dallas (see action-packed description above), Houston, and my present location of Orlando. My guess is that I will be, er, fired sometime when we get back to Swamp City. (New Orleans. I have no idea how anyone thought building a city there was a good idea.)

October 19

I'm still a member of the Hornets, which I suppose is a good thing. I'm starting to wonder, though, why I put myself in these situations, because I usually just end up in my current state—frustrated and angry.

This state of limbo needs to end soon. Obviously, I knew coming into the Hornets' training camp that I was going to be cut at some point. It is not news to me that I will soon have to find another basketball job. But I don't particularly appreciate that I was told two weeks ago of my impending termination, only to have the guillotine suspended over my neck ever since. Consequently, I remain a little uptight around the team's management. Pursuant to my earlier minefield analogy, every time the GM says hello, I wonder if it is going to be followed by "Well, Paul, it's been great having you here, but . . ." or just the usual awkward silence. (The awkward silence occurs because he knows I'm not going to be around much longer, and I know I'm not going to be around much longer, so why should either of us engage in even the most inane small talk? It would simply be throwing away good material that could be better invested in a relationship with a future.)

But I soldier on. (Sorry. Official moratorium on wartime metaphors.)

I cannot see how I could ever be expected to speak to Tiny Archibald after what I heard him say. Archibald, a Hall of Famer with the Celtics in the sixties, seventies, or eighties (I don't really know—I wasn't alive for a good portion of his career) was in New Orleans to observe practice. He is an old friend of Coach Floyd's and so spent a fair amount of time talking to Floyd and hanging out in the locker room, ignoring the likes of me. One time, as I stood there in some state of undress or another, a teammate of mine asked Tiny if he had worked for the NBA at all after his playing career ended. He shrugged and murmured a no, with his body language suggesting that he had been wronged by the league. He paused for a few seconds and then said, "I saw that billboard out there in the arena—the lottery jackpot is up to $140 million. I'm going to win that thing and then buy the whole NBA. And then I'm going to turn it into the, well, I guess it will still be the NBA, it'll just stand for Negro Basketball Association." I have a few queries regarding the preceding statement. Tiny Archibald is black, obviously, and must feel that he has somehow been slighted out of a management position. Maybe he has been. But how much do you want, Tiny? The player pool in the NBA is something like 80 percent black (I checked it out one time a couple of years ago, just to see what my chances were). When I last looked, there was an average of two white, American-born players on each NBA team. It seems to me that his NBA is much more a reality than some imagined WBA. So, can't we have something? Are a few lonely management positions too much to ask? The denizens of the front office don't even make that much.

The preceding passage may seem a little inflammatory, but turn it around. Imagine a black person trying to break into a business in which whites are grossly overrepresented. His would then be considered a noble statement. Mine would probably be labeled as totally ignorant and insensitive.

I'm really glad I chose to pursue the one profession in which I am the distinct minority. (With the exception of lawn mowing, of course.)

On the lottery theme, the same jackpot billboard drew the attention of one of my teammates during our warm-up for practice the other day. He told me that he was going to stop at a gas station on the way home and buy $40 worth of tickets because, in his words, he would be "set for life if he won that thing." Bear in mind, of course, that this teammate was a first-round draft pick who is now under contract with the Hornets for the next three years to the tune of a little more than $1 million a year. Guaranteed. Let's do the math on that. Out of $3 million, he'll take home about $1.4 million. He buys a house for $250,000 and a car for $50,000, leaving $1.1 million. Because he has neither a mortgage nor a car payment, he should be able to easily live on $30,000 per year for the next three years, leaving $1 million in the bank. (I realize that my simulation is for that of a rather modest lifestyle.) Invested at a rather shoddy 4 percent, he clears $40,000 a year. Forever. And that's if he never plays basketball or works again—in his life. I am surrounded by imbeciles. I don't know how I make it through the day without punching someone in the throat.

Now, on to what's really angering me of late. I came to camp with the Hornets with the knowledge that I had no chance to make the team because fourteen players were already under guaranteed contract for the year, and the team was only going to keep fourteen around. I knew that I would be in camp with two other players in similar situations (unguaranteed and hopeless) as myself: a point guard who is four years out of college but who had never been to an NBA training camp, and the team's second-round draft pick, name of James Lang. Lang's story could be culled from the pages of the book called *Straight to the NBA Out of High School: Oops, I Wasn't Quite Good Enough and Slipped to the Second Round, So Now I Have Neither a Guaranteed NBA Contract nor the Opportunity to Return to College.* (No, I don't think that title will move many copies.)

He's big—really big, like six-ten, 290 pounds, but not particularly good. He can catch a basketball and moves relatively well, but he barely knows his ass from a hole in the ground and has no real chance to play in the NBA for a couple of years at least. However, I have recently heard rumblings that the Hornets are planning to keep this Lang fellow around for the year, and may have been planning to do so all along. I certainly have many faults, and may not be the totally modest, self-deprecating person I once was, but I think I do a pretty good job of analyzing when a player, especially one with whom I have been practicing for three weeks, is a better or worse basketball player than me. The individual in question definitely falls into the latter category. He may be better at age twenty-five than I am right now, but at present he is twenty and is not even close. (By the way, where does one go to high school that he graduates when he is nineteen years old?) My agent, Keith Glass, informed me that he was told that even though I might be a better player than Lang, the Hornets drafted him and don't want to look stupid for doing so, so they would prefer to keep him around instead of me. Self-fulfilling prophecy, anyone? Implied in this is the belief that since Lang is only twenty, he will, by default, improve as a basketball player over time. First, twenty isn't all that young. If he hasn't figured out some of it by now, it isn't going to get figured. I learned some of the skills he lacks when I was twelve. And, second, as if I plan to get worse. I can even remember where I am supposed to be during particular set plays. Truly irksome is the fact that because the Hornets have dedicated so much time and energy to this kid, they are going to make damn sure that he turns out to be a serviceable basketball player. Imagine if I had access to those resources. I might turn out to be something more than some skinny cracker fighting for a spot at the end of the bench.

How am I supposed to justify all of this information in my mind? If being the better basketball player is not the most important criterion upon which placement on a team is based, how am I to motivate myself? It seems that the idea would be to get the best available basketball players on your team at one time (with the exception, of course, of the really good ones who can't stop snorting cocaine and beating women). If that is not the case, what more can I do?

I don't know how the Hornets' personnel moves will transpire. But if what is supposed to happen actually does, I may soon be hard at work on my alibi so when the firebomb goes off in New Orleans, I can prove I was elsewhere.

November 2

I decided to take the high road. I engineered my release from the Hornets (read: they cut me). I thought the world would be better served if I let them keep the $660,000 they would have owed me for the year. And I felt it was time to move on to the next stage of my career—I mean, I had been there for nearly five weeks. Any more time than that and I would have been accused of having some stability in my life. The team brass didn't show much regret when I left them, but I did not react to their apathy. Instead of violent retaliation, I chose passive suppression and stored my vengeful feelings for use in a vitriolic rant at a later date.

The death knell for my hopes with the Hornets came on the plane ride home from a game in San Antonio. I was basking in the glow of another DNP-CD (Did Not Play—Coach's Decision) when the assistant to the general manager—or the Grim Reaper, as I now call him—tapped me on the shoulder. He informed me that I needed to stay on board after everyone else deplaned. I then launched into a rant that went something like the following:

"Okay, Allan, here's the deal. I'm not leaving. You are going to have to unbolt this unbelievably comfortable chair and use it to carry me off the plane. Look around—this is a 737 outfitted for thirty-five people. I could put a family of chimps between each of our seats. I can't leave this. Do you see that stewardess over there? If I asked, she would bring me an entire meal like the one I just ate, including the fresh-baked chocolate chip cookie, all over again, just because I wanted her to." At this point, I was gripping his shoulders and staring pleadingly into his eyes. "What if I beg? Would it help if I got on my knees right in the middle of this aisle right here, the one that is big enough for Tractor Traylor's Hummer, and begged?" I was then holding on to the cuff of his pants as he turned his heel and departed for the smorgasbord in the back of the plane. "Don't make me grovel, Allan. . . ." Then he kicked me in the head with one of his jackboots. Next thing I knew I was back in Kansas.

Strangely, none of that actually happened. Instead, upon our arrival back in the Big Easy at 1 A.M., I was given the usual "Thanks for playing, better luck next time" speech and told that a ticket for my flight home at 10:30 that morning would be waiting outside. (The nine hours they gave me to gather my things is what shows they cared.)

In retrospect, I suppose my time in New Orleans was well spent. I left home knowing I was not going to be on the team come November 1, so I shouldn't have had my hopes up. But hope is tricky like that. It sneaks up on a person from time to time. I find consolation because I played as well as I could have, and even got to hear the following quotes from a particular, not-to-be-named-here assistant coach: "If this were about winning and not about money, you'd be on this team" and "In our meeting the other day, I asked Coach Floyd if I could take a box cutter to [an also not-to-be-named player]'s Achilles so that you could have his spot."

So I have one fan, which is nice. (And no, I'm not making these statements up just to make myself look good.) Plus, I was fortunate enough to get to see a player—Baron Davis—participate in an NBA practice wearing sweatpants six sizes too big for him and shoes that were not even close to tied. Everyone should be so lucky.

After I arrived home from New Orleans, I spent a good portion of the next few days sleeping. I'm always amazed at how exhausting these little experiences are. Physically, they are somewhat difficult, but mostly they are a mental mountain climb. Trying to wend one's way through the ups and downs of training camp is a little hard on the psyche. Especially when the conversations are so taxing on one's brain: *So, what do you guys want to talk about tonight? Ah, sports, huh? Well, that should be stimulating. It has been at least half an hour since we last opined on how we think LeBron James will change the NBA.* When I spend any sustained time around basketball players, I find new respect for the people who are willing to tolerate my presence. We athletes are *boring.* I also remember why I almost always hang around with the trainers and other support staff. If one can ignore the thousand-yard stare they affect some of the time— brought on by the observation of way too much absurdity over the years—they are easily the most normal folks around.

My release from the Hornets meant that my basketball career was, once again, left to twist in the wind. But not for long, as it turned out. I had not been home a week when I received a call from an old coach. He inquired about my interest in playing with the EA Sports touring team—one of a few corporate-sponsored squads that plays exhibition games against college basketball teams. After a few days of cajoling by him, I relented. It may have been one of my worst decisions ever.

When initially approached with the idea, I gave an unequivocal no. But when I woke up last Monday morning and was faced with the prospect of going to the track and forcing myself to run, I realized that it might be easier to get paid to stay in shape while deciding what to do for the rest of the year. Plus, the folks at EA Sports (they make video games) were willing to make me the highest-paid player in the short history of their sponsorship of exhibition tours. They would send my way a whopping $4,000 for two weeks of basketball. It wasn't $660,000, but it beat the unemployment line.

Before I even got around to joining the exhibition team, I was given one last cruel hope. My agent called one night just after I had agreed to the exhibition tour. He told me that I needed to buy a ticket for a flight to Houston the next morning. It was a strange way to begin a conversation, to be sure, but I listened on, hoping for more details. Keith told me that the Houston Rockets had some doubts about some of the players on their roster and wanted to fly me down for a work-out. I had absorbed a few days of rest and felt I was recovered and recharged sufficiently to absorb another rejection, so I bought a plane ticket for the next day and readied myself for the trip. (I write "readied myself" as if I did something profound to prepare—maybe mixed up a good-luck potion or sacrificed a virgin . . . goat. The truth is much less glamorous. I think it involved some quick roster research and then some lying around while I worried about whether I would be able to play well under scrutiny.)

Going into the excursion, I was blessed with some very sparse information. I was under the impression that I would go down on Tuesday morning, work out for the team, and come home that night, unless the coach decided that I was absolutely the cat's meow (or something similarly positive and less gay), in which case the team could theoretically sign me. At the time, only two days remained before NBA teams had to submit final rosters the requisite forty-eight hours prior to the season's first game. My workout was part of a last-ditch effort by the Rockets to find better players just ahead of the deadline. At least, that's what I thought. Still, when an NBA team calls on the eve of the regular season, one gets a little excited. I didn't sleep a lot that night.

The next morning, I donned a sports coat and slacks (it's not every day that an NBA franchise calls with cryptic instructions for odd workouts) and rode down to Texas while trying to suppress fanciful visions of NBA contracts. I arrived at the arena at about two-thirty in the afternoon. The coach who met me outside the arena was appropriately impressed by my attire. I immediately realized my error. I could tell that my choice had painted me further into the nice white guy corner. I should have gone with the leather pants/eyepatch combo I had laid out. Dammit.

I was on the court an hour and a half later. Sans warm-up or even a trial jump shot, I was told to begin firing at the basket. It was rough going. My body, like everyone's, I think, does not do well after sitting on an airplane all day. I felt like the tin man during an oil shortage. The joints moved, just not very well. To make matters worse, the workout was *hard*. My partner in crime for the ordeal, Jason Hart, a guard from Syracuse, agreed wholeheartedly with my assessment through gasps for breath in our one water break. I spent an hour and a half running up and down, shooting, rebounding, and trying to guard not only Hart but also one Patrick Ewing, now an assistant coach for the Rockets. While big Pat has probably lost a step or two, he's definitely still a few ahead of me.

I left the court disheartened, thinking I had just junked any opportunity with the Rockets. My mood only worsened. After the workout, the Rockets' head coach, Jeff Van Gundy, informed Hart and me that the team had no open roster spots; that this was just a chance for him to "get to know us as players." (I love a good cliché.) It's a good thing I didn't get my hopes up or anything.

Wednesday dawned, and Keith told me over the phone that the Rockets had realized that the conditions surrounding my first workout—that my legs had not been fully functional, for example—had been less than ideal. Poor conditions notwithstanding, the team was pleased with the way I had played. Negativity, out; optimism, in.

Over breakfast, I read in the day's paper that the Rockets had signed a player named Scott Padgett the day before. Apparently, Van Gundy hadn't been lying. Pessimism snuck back in. Along with confusion regarding the point of all that exertion. That afternoon, I played well in our second scheduled workout. The NBA Hall of Famer gave me trouble again, but I did everything the coaches asked, and acquitted myself nicely. Afterward, Van Gundy retired to his chambers. Hart and I showered and then, unceremoniously, Van Gundy came into the locker room . . . and thanked us both for coming to Houston. He is supposedly a "straight shooter"—he does not "beat around the bush"—but the words coming out of his mouth sounded a lot like the ones coming out of everyone else's: ". . . surprised you're not in the NBA . . . would be comfortable with you on my team," et cetera, et cetera. He was carrying neither a contract nor a bag of cash, so I stopped listening around basketball cliché number four.

I still don't understand the point of my little two-day trip to Houston. I learned that I had never actually been in line for a spot on the roster; Scott Padgett is a player similar to me, and the team would never have signed him one day and me the next. He had become available the day I had been told to find a way to Houston, but at the time the Rockets did not know if they would be able to sign him. I think I

was a contingency plan. When they signed Padgett, I became unnecessary. I wonder if the workouts mattered at all. Or were they just part
of an audition for a role somewhere down the line? More important,
were the coat and tie too much? I may never know.

I did find out how I had caught the eye of the Rockets, via a post-
workout conversation with Van Gundy and one of his assistant coaches.
During one of my few preseason appearances with the Hornets—a
game in Houston against the Spaceships two weeks prior—I had made
a late appearance and had scored two straight baskets. At the time,
Van Gundy turned to an assistant and said, "Paul Shirley? Who the
fuck is Paul Shirley?" When I was cut by the Hornets, he called his
friend and my two-time former coach, Tim Floyd, to find out if I was
worth a damn. Coach Floyd told him of my vast basketball prowess,
and so I spent two days in Houston, participating in another hopes-
dashing experience, thus hastening my descent toward an emotional
breakdown. Fantastic.

November 9

My current residence is the Super 8 Motel in Hampton, Virginia. With
the exception of the Thrifty Inn, a fine establishment in St. Louis my
mother once naively booked for the Shirley family for a 1989 long
weekend in the Gateway City, this could be the worst hotel in which I
have ever had the pleasure of staying. This afternoon, when I arrived
"home" from my day's work, an EA Sports exhibition game with Old
Dominion University, I noticed two youths running into the motel.
One was apparently in charge of lookout; the other was carrying a
television. Both constantly cast furtive glances behind them as the
cord trailed limply across the parking lot. I may be a bit of a country
bumpkin, but even I know that when purchased, TVs usually come in
boxes and are usually taken to homes for viewing, not to hotels for
selling.

There are Non-Smoking Room signs on most of the doors in this
place. They should be amended to say Non-Cigarette-Smoking Room
because there is a pervasive herbal smell coming from about half of

them. This is good news for the teammate I just saw in the hallway. He related that he had called one of the rooms already, looking to make a purchase. Good times on the EA Sports All-Stars Exhibition Tour.

Why, oh why, would I subject myself to this misery (other than the fact that it makes for interesting stories)? Because, (1) I'm a sucker, and can't say no, (2) I'm a money-grubbing greedy bastard, and (3) It actually sounded like fun at the time. Silly me. (Actually, it's really not that bad. I'm just not good at writing from a positive-person view-point. Must work on that.)

The first game of my exhibition career took place about three hours after I got off a plane from Kansas City—the window of time in which, as I have noted before, we athletes are known for our best work. After I found my luggage, my escorts rushed me to the Holiday Inn in Roanoke, Virginia, introduced me to my roommate, Matt Houser, who, thankfully, is a hell of a guy, took me to a nearby Subway for some pregame nourishment, and then shuffled me off to the game at Virginia Tech.

When I left Kansas City after my return from thirty-six ill-fated hours of Rocketball, I was under the impression that my exhibition team wasn't going to take these games against college teams all that seriously. I thought it was a way to stay in shape, make a little money, and have some fun. My coach seems to think otherwise, which has been a source of constant amusement. Maz Trakh (yes, that is spelled correctly—his parents were Jordanian) was the assistant coach of my CBA team in Yakima last year and is the man who talked me into this gig. Unfortunately, Maz has decided that the EA Sports Exhibition Tour is a way for him to bolster his coaching resume. I gather that he thinks if he pulls off a big upset win at Kentucky, someone will notice and give him the reins to some glorious team somewhere. Meanwhile, I keep hoping we can institute a game plan in which we resolve to shoot nothing but three-pointers. There might be a conflict in philoso-phies here.

After a big victory in Blacksburg against Virginia Tech, the traveling road show set off for the city of Cincinnati and the Xavier whatever-the-hells. I can't remember the mascot because of the haze caused by lack of sleep. We arrived back at the hotel in Roanoke after the game with Virginia Tech at about eleven, got to sleep at midnight or so, and had a wake-up call at 4:15 A.M. We boarded a plane in Roanoke at 6 A.M. with the idea that we would get to the hotel in Cincinnati by midmorning, leaving us with a few hours of sleep before we engaged in a 2 P.M. tip-off. Obstacle number one in our path was presented by the smoke that began spewing from the vents on our thirty-passenger puddle jumper while we sat on the runway awaiting takeoff from Roanoke. At first, the stewardess calmly suggested we vacate our seats; she quickly changed her message to "Everyone leave everything and get off the plane! Now!" We took note of her tone and, even at the ass-crack of dawn, were inspired to get the hell off the plane. We soon learned that the air conditioner had malfunctioned (but isn't that what they always say?), so they shuffled most of us back onto the vessel. I say most of us because two of my teammates were spooked by the malfunction and opted not to rejoin us on that particular death trap and took a later flight. We arrived in Cincinnati battered and cramped only to find that the airline had managed to leave behind half the team's bags, which knowledge took only an hour and a half to ascertain. The remaining thirty minutes of rest time was insufficient— Xavier obliterated us.

Even though we're no juggernaut, I feel some pity for the teams we play. I vividly remember playing exhibition games as a collegian. I was usually totally exhausted from two weeks of hellish practices and hoped only that whatever washed-up pro I was guarding did not feel like playing too hard, because I was certainly not going to be able to muster much energy to stop him. In fact, I'm pretty sure I resolved then that if the roles were ever reversed, I would have mercy on my college brethren and take it easy on them. Unfortunately, I am not the humanitarian I once aspired to be. Back then, I thought that if I were on the other side, playing for a team that was loosely organized by some shoe company (or video game company), I would relax and kick it down into neutral once in a while. Apparently, that is impossible. Once the lights go on and the fans start screaming, we basketball players undergo a Pavlovian transformation and begin to play hard in spite of ourselves. In some cases on this tour, I have actually cared more than I have about some of the professional games in which I have played over the last few years. My emotional investment stems from our underdog nature as an exhibition team. Everyone—referees, the opposing team, their fans—is wholly disdainful of a bunch of guys who are apparently not good enough to play in the NBA but who cannot let go of that dream.

It should be noted that the makeup of the average exhibition team has evolved over the years. Instead of a washed-up World B. Free and a forty-five-year-old Paul Mokeski (players I saw on exhibition teams we played in college), the teams are filled with young players who are between an NBA training camp and a trip to the minor leagues, or who are waiting on a basketball job in Europe. Someone noticed that college coaches were none too interested in obliterating a bunch of local God-squadders and would rather have their teams actually tested by their opponents. (That's a dig on Athletes in Action, an exhibition team that reportedly passes out copies of the Good Book at games and leads halftime Bible question-and-answer sessions.) Sports-related companies seized on the idea as a way to make a dollar and began outfitting teams in their gear, figuring the five thousand students in college arenas across the country were a ripe marketing demographic. And so I find myself wearing a T-shirt bearing the EA Sports video gaming logo, playing in basketball games on college campuses once again.

What will be the last half of the Goat Show, as we have come to call it for no particular reason except that it sounds kind of funny, has been marred by a near-catastrophic blow to my face. As I lay on the court at Freedom Hall in Louisville, I analyzed the situation. There was a lot of blood on the floor immediately in front of my eyes, the world was spinning, and my head hurt a lot. I used my full mental capacity to trace it all back to the arms I had seen flying toward me a few seconds earlier. My deduction was correct: I had taken a pretty good shot to the melon. I was escorted back to the training room for some facial embroidery, and I am confident the trainers took fine care of me and did their best to repair my face. Random players on opposing exhibition teams get nothing but the best care. Fortunately, I was never going to be a model anyway, so one scar above my upper lip and another on my cheekbone probably will not cost me any future royalties. But shaving will be tricky for a while. Upon further review, it turns out that when the player I was guarding turned to face the basket, he caught me with both elbows—one for each wound. This means two things. First, I obviously need to work on my reaction time. Second, next time I see that guy, I am definitely going to de-accept his apology. Two elbows to the face seems a bit much.

My head felt a little fuzzy after the blow to the noggin, and as I am totally into being able to speak in complete sentences when I am sixty—and because I am a sissy—I took the next night (versus the University of Tennessee) off. I don't think the guy who's in charge of this traveling circus appreciated that too much (again with the over-seriousness—come on, they're exhibition games), but it was not his brain in the balance. (I totally overdramatize these events.)

November 17

Seventeen thousand turned out in Rupp Arena for our long-awaited matchup with Kentucky. (Long awaited by our coach, who still thought he was going to be recognized as exhibition coach of the year if he kept it respectable against the Wildcats. No, I don't know why.) In my time at Iowa State, we rarely filled the bottom section of Hilton Coliseum for an exhibition game. Perhaps Kentuckians are as die-hard about their basketball as they claim to be. We stayed with the Wildcats for the first half and were down only one at the break. When the dust settled in the locker room at halftime, the team's manager, an executive at Adidas (one of the sponsors of the team), made his way into the locker room and offered us each a $100 bonus if we somehow pulled out a victory over Kentucky. It was quite a contrast. Had I, by some strange turn of events, made the New Orleans Hornets, I would have been paid a little over $3,000 that day. Instead, a $100 incentive to win a basketball game legitimately piqued my interest. Not that it mattered: we lost. By a lot. Kentucky's full-court press wore us down and we turned the ball over to them more times than I can remember. The bad news: we lost to Kentucky. The good news: $100 is not enough to convince me to lead my exhibition team to victory. Yet.

The better news: I had my own room for the night. We have roommates in most cities. But because we have an odd number of players on the team, we each rotate through sleeping alone. (We do get two beds when we have roommates. Perhaps I should have made that more clear.) I scheduled my turn specifically for our night in Lexington.

I don't write much about my love life, in part because it is not all that exciting, but in part because it is not really relevant. It is impossible to develop anything approaching a normal relationship while living my current lifestyle. End of story. This time I am going to make an exception, because I feel like it.

When we played Western Kentucky early on in the Goat Show, I looked pretty rough. I had just had my face beaten up in Louisville and hadn't shaved in a week. Despite my ragged appearance, I played well in our loss to the Hilltoppers and, afterward, was feeling good about life. (Note alarming trend toward apathy regarding the actual result of our exhibition games.) When we emerged from the locker room after showering, I saw a young woman I had noticed during the game. She was easily the best-looking girl in the gym and had been sitting courtside, so it was no surprise that she had caught my eye. She stood with another girl near the door in the lobby of the arena; they looked to be contemplating plans for the evening. I realized that I would never again be in Bowling Green, Kentucky, so I marched up and asked the two girls if anything exciting was happening in their city that night. I felt like I did a fine job of involving both girls in the conversation while making it clear that I was interested in the more attractive of the pair—always a tough task. By the midpoint of our brief conversation, my usual exhibition tour roommate, Matt Houser, had made his way over. The four of us put the finishing touches on a relatively benign conversation, and Matt and I promised to meet the two girls at a bar later.

We talked our coach out of one of the team's rental minivans and toured the streets of Bowling Green until we found the right place. When we arrived, I confirmed that I hadn't been hallucinating—the girl in whom I was interested was the best-looking female in the bar as well. We all sat around a table and discussed the game, life in Kentucky, and the other semi-intimate details that people relate when learning about each other over malted adult beverages. It was pleasant—a welcome break from the madness of an exhibition tour. Matt did a fine job of wing-manning, keeping the conversation going when it lagged and isolating the friend when I needed his help. When the bar closed, we continued the night at someone's apartment. The four of us sat around and watched TV as if we were thirteen. I don't really remember what was on. I do remember that I was quite taken with the girl from the game. (Her name is not important. Well, it is—I'm just not going to divulge it.) She was smart, funny, well read, well spoken, and beautiful. I couldn't find much wrong with her. She was even tall. I could tell that we would get along famously if given the opportunity. I just couldn't figure out when that opportunity might arise—I was leaving in the morning.

At the end of the night, my new friend and I exchanged a chaste kiss and said our good-byes. We were scheduled to return to Kentucky later in the week to play the University of, so I asked her to come to Lexington to see the game. We exchanged numbers and she said she would make an effort, but I have endured enough disappointment in my life to know how unlikely her trip was. (Goddamn pessimism. Seriously. I need to work on this.)

She surprised me, though, and made the journey. I arranged things with the coach of our team and, as I mentioned, secured lone-wolf status for the night. She came straight to the game from her job in Bowling Green. Afterward, we retired to my palatial room at the Ramada and had a fine post-game evening. We spoke of nothing of consequence and lay around watching bad television. She spent the night. I was happy to have her there. When she left at five-thirty in the morning in order to drive back in time for work, I was actually sad. (Rare for me.) I could tell that in a different life, she would have become my girlfriend very soon. As it was, that could never be. She has a fine job in the Western Kentucky athletic department and I have a sometimes-tolerable job wandering the world in search of people willing to pay me to play a game.

It is possible that I read more into the situation than was justified. It could be that I liked the girl for what she represented (i.e., everything I haven't had with regard to women, relationships, and even the vaguest sense of stability). My gut feeling tells me otherwise, but unfortunately, I won't ever know. I do know that if I were John Fogerty, I would have written a song about her by now.

November 30

I had forgotten what a great holiday Thanksgiving is. I was seventeen the last time I was with my family for Thanksgiving dinner. Since then, I have had turkey in interesting places such as Hawaii, where the main course wasn't turkey at all and was roasted all day in an underground pit, and not-so-interesting places such as an Indian casino in Yakima, where the turkey was harvested from a can. These stops along the way have had one overriding effect—they made me anticipate a return to my grandmother's Thanksgiving table in Wichita, Kansas, with what is probably an unhealthy level of expectation. My grandmother is an excellent cook. (As is her daughter, my mother.) Thanksgiving dinner at Grandma's house is no mere meal; it is an event, replete with candles, china, and crystal. And place cards. Which is really strange considering that there are rarely more than a dozen people at the table. Perhaps there is more to the family dynamic than I understand. Or maybe my grandmother just wants to keep me on the opposite side of the table from her.

With the EA Sports Wandering Minstrel Tour finally finished, I was determined to put off whatever next destination to which my basketball life/roller coaster was taking me until after this most gorgeful of holidays. It took some work, but I was able to hold out; I think even the most coldhearted of the interested coaches took note when I said that it had been nearly a decade since I was last at home for Thanksgiving. With a little time cleared, I anxiously anticipated a few days of coddling under the culinary care of my grandmother.

When I settled in, I noticed that a few things had changed since 1995. My grandfather got selfish and died on us, my youngest brother drank way too much milk and grew up on us, and my grandmother . . . actually, amazingly, she didn't change a bit. She gets caught in repetitive story mode a bit more often, but generally is as spry as one could expect an eighty-two-year-old woman to be. I simply hope to be able to remember my own name at that age, so I am quite impressed by her steady-state appearance.

I think the great thing about Thanksgiving is the lack of responsibility involved. (Unless, of course, one is in charge of the dinner proceedings—then the pressure is on.) For those of us with limited turkey-cooking skills, it is an opportunity to master the most American of pastimes, consumption without regard to consequence. Followed by napping. Followed by a groggy return to the kitchen in search of pies, cakes, and maybe even the odd choice cut of turkey that would look splendid on a leftover dinner roll. It is truly an amazing holiday. Also, I realize that I am not the first to write such things about Thanksgiving. Forgive me—it has been a while.

It is most important that I got to be there for it all. I may miss the next seven or eight, so I needed one to refresh my memories of what a Thanksgiving is like.

December 4

While I've been sitting around becoming more American (fatter), the basketball season has been moving right along. With that in mind, I set about deciding what to do with myself for the rest of the year. I was due; it had been at least three weeks since my last life-altering decision.

I have not yet received any earth-shattering offers from teams in Europe, so I am considering staying in the United States with the hope that someone currently playing in the NBA will rupture his scrotum and have to miss some time, causing his team to need a replacement, thus leading to a job for me. While I wait around for this turn of events, I need to find a place to play in the States. The ABA is the early leader.

The ABA is similar to the CBA, the league in which I played last year. It is just another minor league—a holding ground for players hoping to make it back to the NBA at some point. The ABA is intriguing because there is a team in Kansas City. I find this attractive because I own a bed, a couch, and the walls that surround them in that city. My agent and I researched whether NBA personnel care whether a marginally talented white guy like me plays in the ABA, CBA, or NBDL (another minor league). The overwhelming consensus was that (1) it did not—good news for my hopes of playing in my home area, and (2) they were tired of Keith and me asking them intelligent questions.

Unfortunately, the ABA (stands for American Basketball Association, I think) is inherently unstable. When the league was hatched three years ago, the plan was to pay players decent salaries (read: $60,000–100,000 annually) in order to keep them in the United States. The hurdle encountered en route to fulfillment of this plan was that revenues were not nearly enough to support such high wages, so several teams went belly up and many players never got the money promised them. (Basically, it was like playing in Greece.) As a result, the ABA was not able to complete a full season in either of its first two years. But now the league is back, economics lesson learned, paying crappy salaries just like the CBA and NBDL, and hoping to get through an entire year.

My agent has not been too excited about the ABA plan. He is rather set in his ways—he has been finding tall white guys basketball jobs for a long time. In his experience, the CBA is the best choice among the minor leagues. I cannot argue with his logic, as the CBA certainly worked well for me; note last year's call-up from the Yakima Sun Kings to the Atlanta Hawks as evidence. As it turns out, though, I could have been playing in the Alabama Correctional League for all they cared; they knew what I was like as a player because I had participated in their training camp. They weren't sending scouts to

Yakima and Bismarck to find contingency players. That being said, my experience in Yakima was tolerable enough that I would not have been opposed to going back and playing for Coach Bill Bayno and the Sun Kings. (Tolerable on the basketball front, that is. On the having-a-life front, not as much. I could count the number of dates I had in Yakima on zero fingers.)

Unfortunately, a return to the state of Washington is not a possibility. The CBA has banned me from playing for Bayno for one year.

Yes, banned for one year. It all happened like this. The owner of the Sun Kings had this beautiful daughter. I could have sworn she was twenty-three, but it turns out she was only seventeen. Just kidding. Actually, the problem was a monetary one. The CBA did not like when Coach Bayno held up his end of the bargain and waived the team's half of the buyout, resulting in my Pete Rose–like status in the league.

Without any loyalty to a particular team in the CBA, I couldn't get too excited about the idea of starting afresh with a new one when I could easily be playing in my home city. But, like in life, there are intricacies to the politics of basketball. My agent also represents the coach of the CBA team in Boise, Idaho. He would like that coach to have success. He has a player, me, who did well in that league a year ago and would conceivably do that again. Why not bring the two together? So I've had to fight off a bit of inner politicking in order to decide which plan is actually in my own best interest.

Leading into Thanksgiving, it seemed to me that I would soon become a Kansas City Knight (the ABA team). But then, in a phone call with the coach of the Knights, Scott Wedman, of Boston Celtics and Kansas City Kings fame, I listened incredulously as he told me he wanted to "work me out" so he could "get a feel for me as a player." (I realize that those quotes imply that he made flaming advances toward me, but in this case, I use them only to preserve his actual statements.) The younger, humbler version of me would never have had a problem with that request. Unfortunately, that version has been replaced my current, somewhat arrogant, slightly prima-donna-ish self, and that entity was a bit insulted by the idea. But I suppressed my ego and agreed to get worked out. (Sorry.)

When I showed up at the gym, it seemed as if the coach did not really know what to do with me. His orders, as I got started: "Why don't you just do what you would do if you were by yourself? We'll just jump in and add some stuff as we go." (Which, incidentally, could also be the instructions given to a porn star at the start of the day's shoot.) Afterward, he somewhat grudgingly admitted, "You're, uh, pretty good. I think you could help us." Unfortunately, he has been treading on thin ice with my agent and with me; a coach called from an ABA team in Long Beach with a guarantee of a starting job, a lack of any contractual buyout, and a higher salary than in Kansas City. It sounded okay to me. But, the one thing he cannot offer is access to my own bed.

As with most of my life, we'll see what tomorrow brings. Maybe it will be Kansas City. Or Long Beach. Or Boise. Or maybe I'll just move in with my grandmother and eat turkey.

December 8

As it turned out, the prospect of sleeping in my own bed won and I became a Kansas City Knight. After my first game I had to wash my own uniform. As I stood over the sink in my basement, trying to scrub out the bloodstains caused by someone's leaky elbow, I was forced to question my decision to stay in the United States this year. I think the exact thought process involved some math work, like this: "Hmm, last spring I was making $20,000 after taxes a month to play two basketball games a week and live in an apartment overlooking the Mediterranean. Now I'm in my basement, washing my jersey by hand so that it will be ready for tomorrow's game—all for an astounding $2,400 a month before taxes. It would appear that those four calculus classes I took in college are going to waste."

I was washing my jersey in the sink not because it is some sort of initiation after my first game with the team but as part of standard team operating procedure. We have since remedied that situation.

I was using the sink instead of my washing machine because I don't have a washing machine. And since the old folks in my condominium association decided that we all needed new roofs, it would appear that my trips to the Laundromat will not be ending anytime soon. It would seem that I, as a professional basketball player, should be able to weather such financial hits without flinching. The truth is that I haven't exactly climbed to the top of any fiduciary mountains just yet.

Speaking of Laundromats, I recently visited one. After I'd gotten the business of laundering started, I settled down to contemplate how many days I could tolerate as a Laundromat operator before I would go on a killing spree. When I looked up from my reverie, I realized that I had just finished running three loads of laundry *without adding detergent*. My clothes were thoroughly rinsed and prepared for a real washing, and I was $3.75 and a half hour poorer. An engineering degree does not a genius make. Perhaps my limited exposure to life in the NBA has left me bereft of even the most basic instincts of self-preservation. Apparently, when I started letting people carry my bags, I lost my ability to function as a human being. Whatever the case, someone should assign a monkey to the video recording of my life—I need a way to prove that these instances of knee-buckling stupidity do actually happen.

It appears that the Kansas City Knights have a religious bent. One of the first team officials I met, even before the trainer, was the team chaplain. My first reaction was to wonder if he can get called up to the NBA like a player would. If the San Antonio Spurs' team chaplain dies, does our chaplain call his agent and tell him to get to work on a ten-day, word-of-honor-only contract?

At some point in my first day, someone mentioned that two years ago the team occasionally conducted a Bible study class. It is very possible that I am living in an alternate universe. I just don't understand how religion and athletic competition are supposed to mix. I somehow doubt that Wilt Chamberlain ever went to Bible study. Or Magic Johnson. Or Bill Laimbeer. Or anyone else with any sort of killer instinct on the basketball court. Two of the players on my new team are serious Jesus freaks. They both played an exhibition tour this fall with Athletes in Action, which, as previously mentioned, is a cultish group that during halftime of its games with college teams attempts to convert the paying audience to Christianity. I actually know one of these guys pretty well. He went to training camp with the Lakers with me a couple of years ago. I was amazed then that a professional basketball player would read the Bible on our flight to Hawaii for training camp. I mention that tidbit because, due to my earlier experiences with him, I should have known better than to ask him how the exhibition tour with AIA went. (Actually I should have known better than to ask him anything at all.) He said it was great, both from a basketball perspective and from a spiritual perspective. After I threw up in my mouth, I said, "That's great. Want some cocaine?"

My first few games with the Knights were each followed by an autograph session. Sinners like myself signed "Paul Shirley, #11" and moved on to the next white-trash kid in line. God-boys one and two signed every autograph with a Bible quotation attached, as in "Bob Johnson, #24, Acts 12:5." Every single time. Granted, it was not necessary for them to do it too many times; our attendance averaged out at around three hundred for the first three nights. Consistent with my brother's suggestion, I began combating their ploy with a bit of sabotage of my own and started signing made-up Bible verses, as in "Paul Shirley, #11, Larry 33:86."

We (the Kansas City Knights) have won all three of the games in which I have played. We played those games on back-to-back-to-back nights, which is good for the knees, I hear. I would like to say that we won those games because of my presence, but a more appropriate description of the situation would be that we won them mostly because the other teams were so bad. The first opponent in the Paul Shirley epoch was from New Jersey and might have been the worst basketball team I have ever seen assembled at any level at which I have played. We were up by thirty at the half and won by forty. The next two nights at Hale Arena in Kansas City (which normally hosts rodeos) were spent dueling with the Juarez Gallos. As in Juarez, Mexico. I believe this means that the first *A* in *ABA,* for *American,* is used in the more general North American sense. Before the games with Juarez, all in attendance were treated to the Mexican national anthem. At least that's what the public address guy said the piece of music was. I became suspicious when the same melody played over and over, until someone finally manually faded it out after about five minutes. It was a little awkward.

December 21

Good news—my basketball reappeared.

I should explain.

Part of my responsibility as a member of the Kansas City Knights is to keep track of the whereabouts of the basketball and jump rope that were issued to me at the beginning of my tenure with the team. I use both at practice. When we are finished for the day I put them in my bag and take them home with me. We practice at a college gym; we do not have our own facilities. We don't have a locker room, aside from the public one used by staff and students. We don't even have a training room—taping and treatment take place on a folding table near the end of one of the courts. As the trend of not-haves would suggest, to expect racks of basketballs awaiting us each day would be folly. So we each cart our own ball to practice, to games, and on road trips. Coach Wedman tells us that the process is good for our general mind-set, as we get "closer" to our balls since we carry them around all day. Which is true—I always like my balls better if I take them with me instead of leaving them on the bedside table. (Yes, it was a cheap gag. It was right there, though.)

Back to the story of my reacquisition . . . During a recent home game with the Juarez Gallos, I meandered over near the opposing bench while waiting for a time-out to end. There, nestled in a ball bag with several others of its kind, was a basketball with my initials on it. It was like finding the last Easter egg back behind the couch. After the game, I explained as best I could to their non-English-speaking coach, first, that our team was so small-time that each player is required to transport his own basketball and, second, that they had taken my ball with them the last time we had played. He could not argue with the overwhelming evidence provided by the *PS* on one of the basketballs, and allowed me to take back my ball. It looked no worse for the wear after its trip to Juarez and back. More important, I will no longer be ostracized from the team and left out of pregame shooting drills because I don't have a basketball to play with.

December 31

Keith called on a recent Wednesday night. It was about 11:30. Since my agent rarely calls to read me bedtime stories anymore, my curiosity was aroused. Over the course of the phone call, he explained that he had spoken that day with Scott Skiles, the coach of the Chicago Bulls (whom, incidentally, he also advises). The Bulls had recently found out that one of their players, Eddy Curry, was going to be out of commission for a few weeks due to a bone bruise in his knee. (Remember this diagnosis, it will be important later. Bone bruise.) This, of course, was only interesting to someone like me insofar as Curry's potential hiatus would cause the Bulls' roster to shrink to just nine healthy players.

At the time of Curry's injury, the Bulls had a full roster of fifteen players but also had recently experienced a raft of injuries. Because of this, Keith told me, the team would petition the league the following Monday for a special exemption that would allow them to sign another player.

The Bulls had some interest in my limited basketball talents last summer and I had always been loosely tracked by whomever operates their basketball radar. The recent hiring of Skiles, with whom Keith claims to have some measure of influence, seemed to indicate that the time was nearly right for me to join the Chicago Bulls. In summary, Keith told me, *if* the Bulls got their exemption, there was a good chance I would go to Chicago. (Keep in mind, I'm only telling it how I heard it. Keith could have been blowing sunshine. For all I know, none of this ever happened and he created a story just to keep me on the hook and make me think he is diligently doing his job. But since we have now had at least five face-to-face meetings, I think I can trust him.) After all the background about the Bulls, Keith asked me if I was healthy. I told him, "Well, yeah, I'm doing fairly well. My knee has been bothering me a little, but I think it will be okay." The preceding state-ment was made with my heart aflutter, because the actual truthful translation of that sentence would have been: *Well, yeah, I'm doing fairly well . . . except that my knee has been bothering me ever since I started playing with the Knights. It doesn't hurt enough that I would consider not playing, but it has felt better at other times in my life. I've been taking prescription anti-inflammatories for two weeks. In fact, I had an MRI just yesterday; I'm waiting on the results. So yeah, I'm great.*

So much for a truthful agent-player relationship.

Actually, at the time, the MRI was done only to rule out anything severe, so I was not all that concerned. I did find it humorous that knee pain in Eddy Curry's world equals a two-week hiatus, whereas in my world it rates only extra ice and the odd anti-inflammatory. He and I live in two very different worlds right now.

I spent the next few days in a sort of high-alert mode, wondering if I would be spending Christmas at home or in Chicago, with my mind making all sorts of ludicrous leaps: *Maybe I'll get there and be unbe-lievable. Then they'll keep me all year. Then they'll want me to stick around and will sign me to a multiyear contract. That would be amazing. What's the first thing I will buy when I'm a millionaire? . . . Truck for Dad? Porsche for Mom? Oversized key-board like Tom Hanks in* Big*? . . . Wait. What if I'm terrible? What if this is my one chance this year and they send me home after one day? What if that is my last chance ever?*

I really should be on some kind of medication.

Monday arrived with no call from Keith. On Tuesday morning, he did call, but it was to say that the team doctor could not certify that Curry would be out more than the league-required two weeks, and so no petition could be granted. I thought about saying, "Uh, duh, Keith, he only has a bone bruise, and since the MRI I had last week showed that I have one too, I could have told you he wouldn't be out two weeks. If he was in the ABA, he would be out there doing dribble re-lays like the rest of us."

I'm going to give Keith the go-ahead on not telling me about these if-and-when scenarios. I think my emotional state will improve after such a plan is implemented.

While I'd rather be in Chicago, it is great to play near my home for a change. I sleep in my own bed most nights and I drive my own car to practice. (And not a 1980 Malibu. *See also* Yakima, Washington.) More important, I was able to have a real Christmas and didn't have to worry about traveling on Christmas Day in order to make a long journey back to a place I don't really like in the first place. Good times. I enjoyed the hell out of it.

Of course, playing near home does have its disadvantages. Well, one, at least. It is great to be near friends and family. But when people I know attend games, I feel pressure to at least try to play well, for their sake, if not for my own. It was not really a problem at Iowa State (the last place I actually knew enough people to need to deal with making ticket requests), since there were fourteen thousand other souls in the stands to mix up the scenery. Here in Hale Arena in Kansas City, where our attendance jumped to a new high of 892 on a recent winter's eve, I can pick out faces and watch their reactions. Don't get me wrong—I love having people about whom I care at my games. It's just hard to face them after a particularly badly played game. Faced with such a situation, I always want to apologize: "I really didn't know the other team was going to bring high school players and you were going to have to sit through that" and "Please don't judge me on that performance. I'm better than that. Really. It's like a Monet. You have to blur the lines a little to see the beauty."

January 8

Time loses meaning in the Mojave Desert. Especially on a bus. In my world right now, there is only sand, the scrub, and the highway, un-changing for miles and miles. I know all this, and am inspired to write hokey, bad-author-y phrases about it, because I am on a rather lengthy trip from Fresno, California, to Las Vegas. It appears that it may be a never-ending journey. We are on this bus because of a bit of a scheduling mixup—the type that makes me want to put a gun to someone's head. My own might suffice. Then again, it could be that no one would care. In fact, the disappearance of the usual barrage of complaints coming from the mid-left section of the bus might be a welcome change for my teammates.

Originally, the well-thought-out road trip itinerary called for an early-morning Fresno wake-up followed by a direct flight to Vegas before a 7 P.M. game. Sometime in the last few days, the brain trust in Las Vegas decided that a change was necessary and settled instead on a 5 P.M. start time. I've gathered that this meant that our direct flight would not get us to the city of neon lights in time, so a new flight—one that would have us connecting through Phoenix—was scheduled. Of course, this new plan would absorb most of the day, so Coach Wedman called a bus company and set up our current arrangement, which required a 5:30 A.M. wake-up and a six-hour trek through the desert, at which point we would "rest" for about the amount of time it takes to build up the appropriate lethargy that would allow us to be completely ill-prepared for another ABA matchup.

The coaching staff's excitement about this plan was a bit undue. Our assistant came up to us with a smile on his face last night and said, "Boy, have we got a deal for you guys. Instead of leaving at the godforsaken time of 5 A.M., we're going to let you have a whole extra hour and leave at 6, since we're taking the bus." Easy there, fearless semi-leader—I'm not quite ready to break out the party hats. The twist, one that I should have expected, having participated in my own life for over two and a half decades now, is that Wedman received a call about an hour ago (somewhere near Bakersfield) that the game was being moved back to 7:30 P.M. Which means, of course, that this bus ride, along with the thought behind it, was completely unnecessary.

Our journey through this hellish terrain comes near the midpoint of what has been a relatively calm West Coast swing. (When I write "West Coast swing," I can almost make myself believe that I am a part of something well organized. It brings to mind a smoothly run process scheduled by executives in New York. The truth is probably closer to that found in a VFW on bingo night.) Our trip began with two games in Long Beach. We followed those with a forgettable off day in southern California.

For the start to the day's entertainment, we were shuttled to a local YMCA for a quick workout. We lifted in a shoddy little weight room and then found our way to the locker room. There were, of course, no towels in the building. (I don't know why I was surprised.) Which is how I came to find myself drying off with paper towels and one of my T-shirts in a YMCA locker room in Long Beach, contemplating why it is that old men have no shame when it comes to walking around with their genitals hanging out. And also reflecting on the fact that while I did look pretty stupid drying myself with paper towels, at least I wasn't the fat guy whose belly was hanging over his balls.

Soon our trip will be over. I will be happier then.

January 18

When we finally arrived back in Kansas City after our twelve-day tour of the West, I was completely spent—and in just the right mood to hear, as I walked in the door of my place, "Hey, Paul, the furnace is broken." I try not to subject myself to situations that involve extreme mental fatigue; I got enough of that in college. I had forgotten what it feels like. It is a good thing my brother/roommate/tenant was around to walk me through the steps of furnace repair (calling the heater people) or I might have bundled up in three sweatsuits and gone to sleep in the cold. I have an engineering degree, yet could barely figure out how to remove the access panel so I could stare blankly at the innards of my heating system—I was that far gone. Fortunately, the nice repairman who came fixed everything without a problem and we were quickly returned to the blissful state of an artificially created interior atmosphere. The experience, though, left me pondering how people are able to balance a job, a spouse, kids, home ownership, car ownership, credit card debt, two mistresses, and a drinking habit. I don't know if I am cut out for that lifestyle. I'm going to start concentrating on avoiding career-ending injuries so I can continue to put off any flirtation with that whole real-world thing as long as possible.

Happily, I have a job that allows little time for contemplation of the concept of settling down. It pays well, the travel is comfortable, and the lodging on the road is luxurious. And sometimes hard to come by.

When we arrived in Las Vegas sometime after our bus ride across the land of Steinbeck, we were informed that the home team had not, in fact, reserved rooms for us at the entirely full Super 8. I said, "Cool, let's go to the Bellagio." My advice was not heeded. Because the Consumer Electronics Show was in town, it was difficult to find rooms, so we settled into the lobby for a wait. (Keep in mind that we were coming off a six-hour bus ride from Fresno. No one was in a wait-and-see mood. Also, game time was rapidly approaching—four hours and counting at this point.) Amazingly, after only an hour or so, it was determined that the Super 8 was big enough to hold us after all (I think somebody was paid off), and we settled into our fabulously spacious, pristine, used-by-who-knows-whom-for-who-knows-what rooms for some rest.

Shockingly, there was some miscommunication between the Las Vegas Rattlers and the van rental company and the team was not able to secure transportation for us, so we rode to the UNLV recreational center in taxis. The Rattlers do not usually play their games in the UNLV student rec center but, because the porn convention in town had outbid the team for the use of their usual facility, we played there that night. (I'm not joking.) The rec center was a fine venue for a professional basketball game: seating for eight hundred, no lockers, no towels. It was also, I think, the fourth place we were told we would play. Which is a good method for hiding the location of a meth lab, but is ineffective if the goal is to attract fans to a basketball game. Actually, we have played in front of fewer, but all the secrecy did make it difficult for me to communicate where we were playing to the people who were trying to come and watch me play. One made it, one did not. We lost to a motley group of players masquerading as an organized basketball team. (Not all that surprising, considering our day to that point.) Afterward, we wanted to leave as fast as possible. The one friend who did make it to the game met me afterward, and I introduced him to our coach as we were standing around waiting for word on transportation back to the Super 8. I was amazed at how interested our coach was in hearing about my friend's acquaintance to me . . . until he asked him how many people he could fit in his car. Turns out he was just being nice so he could save cab fare.

The Las Vegas team employs/is financed by one Master P (aka Percy Miller), the ex-rapper-turned-producer who is worth millions. (At least that's what people say. I'm not sure how rappers like him— those with no discernible talent—become so wealthy.) In the same way that he aspires to be a decent rapper and produce quality music, he aspires to be a basketball player—that is, he isn't very good at any of the three. He didn't play in our game in Las Vegas but did make an appearance in a recent game in Kansas City. He is not a truly awful basketball player—it's not like he is retarded—but he doesn't really have any business being on the court. Of course, I'm not opposed to him playing; he donates a lot of money to the pockets of his "team-mates" and brings in fans, along with providing us, the opposition, the opportunity to play five-on-four whenever he is on the court. I was amazed, in both games, with the lust of the average person for a brush with fame. (He walked in to cheers midway through the second quarter of our game in Nevada and signed hundreds of autographs in Kansas City. Well, dozens, anyway.) I mean, the guy could hardly be considered cool; his fame passed years ago, but that doesn't stop people from clamoring to be in his presence.

That we do not have a team trainer becomes especially evident on road trips. The obvious rebuttal to this is "Well, Paul, don't get hurt," which is advice that is as good as most I have heard. It does pose problems, though, should a Knights player actually have the gall to sustain an injury. I mentioned at some point that I have been dealing with a bone bruise on my knee this season. It doesn't bother me much—as long as I take care of it. Treatment usually involves ultrasound before activity and ice after. Simple enough, right? With no trainer, it's not that easy. For our trip out West, my vaginitis called for me to lug around a secondhand ultrasound machine that the girl who is the training staff for our home games bought from a former employer for $10. Before we left, she taught me how to use the thing. "The intensity read-out is broken, so to get the right level of energy you have to look for the flickering 888 on the LED screen and line up the marker on the dial with the first *T* in *INTENSITY.* Treatment time is five minutes. Don't use too much gel, and if you start to feel something burning, turn it off."

It was a reassuring lesson.

I did a fine job of self-administering ulstrasound on the trip, but I was hampered somewhat by the apparatus' systematic breakdown. A couple of days into the trip, the intensity light itself burnt out (no 888 to find), but the tip of the ultrasound wand seemed to remain warm, so I continued to self-treat. After a few more days (and a few more jarring impacts with other bags in airplane cargo holds) it was necessary to hold down a button in order for the timer to count down. By the end of the trip, the timer readout was totally shot and the complexity of the machine's operation was on a level with that of a flashlight: there was on and there was off. I'd say there is a fifty-fifty chance I now have some sort of tumor in my knee.

After Las Vegas, we traveled to Juarez, Mexico. The team ran out of money, so we were forced to hitchhike there. (Not really, but that would have been an amazing story: Kerouac meets Feinstein. I think I could have pulled off the story and nobody would have been the wiser. Opportunity lost.)

I approached our trip to the land of sombreros with some trepidation. I had never been to Mexico, but the place does not inspire my mind to visions of cleanliness, safety, or comfort. My intuition was correct on two of the three—strangely, our hotel in Juarez was actually the best on the trip. (Not that the competition was all that stiff.) I was amazed. The room I shared with Derek Grimm (my best friend on the team) did lack hot water, but the surroundings were generally pleasant and the food was decent, so I couldn't complain too much. (Check that. That should have read: "A normal person couldn't complain too much." I could. And did.) The arena was another matter. It was absolutely frigid inside, both baskets were crooked, and the locker room appeared to serve the secondary purpose of being a breeding ground for cockroaches of unusual size. ("La Cucaracha" indeed.)

We won the first game of a back-to-back in Juarez. It was a foulfest. My team shot fifty free throws (I shot fourteen myself), which is unheard of in an ABA game; the referees in the league do their best to keep the action going, and free throws would not be considered action.

We won the second game as well, but it was kept close by some rather subpar officiating. At some point in the fourth quarter of game two, I noticed that one of the referees was repeatedly making peculiar calls. This official had been assigned to several of our previous games, so I had gotten to know him relatively well. I even knew his name. (Darrell. Poor decision by his parents.) I didn't think he was prone to consistent lapses in judgment, but I was beginning to question my analysis. Near the end of the game, he called two phantom fouls on me; after the second I inquired, in my most polite manner, what the hell game he was watching. He replied, "I know, Paul, I know." To which I said, "Well, if you know, then make the right call." Our point guard, Joe Crispin, intercepted me and told me to settle down, saying that he would explain it all after the game.

Once we were tucked safely away in the filthy locker room, he explained. Darrell the Referee had told Joe early in the game that one of the Mexican team's officials was continually threatening his life, saying that if Darrell didn't make most of his calls in favor of Juarez, he was going to kill him. The ref took the man at his word and told Crispin early on that he was scared enough that he was going to screw us on some calls. Joe told Darrell to do what he had to do (and rightly so—it was only a minor-league basketball game), and so Darrell proceeded to work us over for the rest of the game. I was amazed at the story, and more than a little incredulous, but Joe (who is not one to exaggerate) assured me that our friend Darrell had looked truly scared on the court. I thought it over on the way back to the hotel and came to the conclusion that the guy probably had been pretty fright-

ened. Intimidation comes fairly easily when one is in a completely foreign place. However, I did think the claims of death threats were a little much. I attributed the story to some overreaction on his part, and
possibly a shade of storytelling on Crispin's part. That is, until Darrell
the Referee walked into the hotel restaurant that night. He was visibly
shaken and looked completely bedraggled and said the following to
those of us sitting there: "Guys, I'm sorry. I cheated you out there
tonight. But I was scared. I'm going to try to get out of town tonight
because I don't know what might happen if I stay here." He then sort
of wandered over to the lobby desk in a state of confusion, got his
bags, and left. Upon final analysis, I probably would have done the
same.

January 27

Since the last time we played them, the Long Beach team added one
Dennis Rodman to their roster. It all seemed like an ill-fated publicity
stunt and I never actually thought he would take the court, so I was
surprised to see his name in the box score after a couple of their recent games. Not surprisingly, it was next to a line including "0–0 FG,
14 RB." I'm not easily starstruck at this point in my basketball career;
I've played with and against many well-known players. It would be
folly to allow their notoriety to affect the way I play. But, I will admit
that I was anxious to see Rodman in action.

Unfortunately, my curiosity would have to wait—he did not play
against us. He was at the game, though, conservatively attired in a
white T-shirt and jeans, wearing orange shoes, an orange hat, and a
matching bandana that precluded me from seeing if his hair was dyed
interesting hues. The official word is that he is still injured. The other
word, and this is just hearsay, is that he played so badly in his first
game back that he was found in tears in the bathroom after the game.
Which could be dampening his excitement to get back on the court.
The man is forty-three and has had more substances pumped through
him than a Willy Wonka factory, so it would be surprising if he were
able to fall back into old ways and perform at a high level without at

least a few months' training. At any rate, he looked to be the consum-mate teammate during our game with Long Beach—he was on the court congratulating his teammates and generally behaving like one of the guys. In fact, he may have blended in too well. After the game, two of my teammates asked me if Rodman had been in attendance. I replied with only a furrowed brow. The man did do a pretty good job of remaining inconspicuous, but he remains Dennis Rodman. It's kind of interesting that he's around. I think it's allowed in the basketball code to take a gander at the opposition's bench to see if Dennis damned Rodman is sitting there. I nearly blurted out, "You know, there are people in the stands, too, as well as reporters, scouts, and even cheerleaders from time to time. In fact, you may want to look over their way once in a while. You might see something you like." In-stead, I politely explained what had happened. I'm such a nice guy.

From Long Beach, we meandered back up through the heart of California to Fresno. If it appears that we are always either in Kansas City or out west, then everyone is paying attention, because that is in fact the case. At this point, there are seven semi-viable ABA teams: Tijuana, Juarez, Long Beach, Las Vegas, Fresno, Kansas City, and New Jersey. Since the last of the group is the least organized, we rarely venture east for games with that team and so are often wandering about the West Coast looking for hot basketball action. Also, it should be noted that being the least-organized ABA team, as I called the team from New Jersey, is like being called the sluttiest prostitute in Amsterdam—it's not exactly an honor.

Our game in Fresno was quite a spectacle. When we arrived at the gym, I asked a janitor if he could find a wet mop (for the uninitiated, a wet mop is a dust mop with damp towels wrapped around it, used on a gym floor to pick up dust and unwanted detritus). I told him that if he could find one, I would be willing to mop their sorry excuse for a basketball court. I didn't actually expect him to make me do the mop-ping; my sarcastic remark was meant to imply that someone ought to get that done. After a wait of entirely too long, he reappeared with a mop-and-bucket combo of the sort used to clean up vomit trails in ele-mentary lunch rooms. I told him I didn't think we actually needed to disinfect the wood, but he didn't really understand me. With no other option availed me, I set about sweeping the filthy floor myself, with only a large dust mop I found in a corner at my disposal. (Reason #487 I'd Rather Be In the NBA: no sweeping of the floor by participating players prior to the game.)

About halfway through my janitorial internship, I noticed one of the opposing players shooting around in street clothes. After admonishing him for befouling my freshly cleaned area, I asked if he would be playing that evening, thinking he was perhaps injured. He misunderstood and replied that he didn't know; it looked like there might be a players' strike, as no one on his team had been paid for five weeks. I told him I supported his socialist-leaning tendencies, and went about my work.

At about 6:15 P.M. (tip-off set for 7), we took a uniformed, on-court appearance by the opposition to mean that the strike had been broken. (I learned that most of the players had chickened out when the coach asked their intentions in the locker room.) A few minutes later, we were told that the game would be moved back to 7:30 because the referees would be late. Eventually, the officials appeared and, magically, tip-off was reset for 7 P.M., to the joy of the fifty-five impatient souls in the stands. We went about performing a quick warm-up for the game. With four minutes still remaining on the time-until-the-game clock, while we were doing layups as a team, we heard, "Ladies and gentlemen, would you please rise for the national anthem," which sent us scurrying for the sidelines, a bit less warmed up than we would have liked. The game was played, but with a few minor hiccups. For example, every time he scored, one of Fresno's players, a guy named Randy Holcomb, was announced as Ray Holcomb. Also, it was brought to my attention late in the game that a runner had been sent from the scorer's table to the home team's bench in order to find out another player's last name. We lost to the Heatwave, but at least the floor was clean.

February 1

I will now set about destroying any and all remaining credibility I ever had as a basketball player, or even as a human being.

On a recent wintry evening in Kansas City, we played a game against our ABA arch rival, the Long Beach Jam. The game was highly anticipated because Dennis Rodman was to suit up and play for Long Beach. For a change, the attendance register tipped out at over a thousand. In fact, Hale Arena was sold out.

I was not as excited about the matchup as were our fans. I was tired from our recent road trip. I am bored with the ABA and am beginning to wonder if I will ever get back to the NBA. The night's events did nothing to bolster my self-confidence.

I air-balled the first free throw I ever attempted in interscholastic competition. Seventh grade. Oskaloosa Middle School. I listened to Vanilla Ice on the bus en route. I was excited and nervous about my first "real" basketball game; I had looked forward to the day for months. When I stepped to the free-throw line for the first time, I did so with confidence. That confidence quickly dissipated when I tossed up a shot that found no rim, net, or backboard—the dreaded air ball.

I hadn't air-balled a free throw since. That is, until the game with Long Beach, when I did it three times. Out of four attempts. In one game. The probability of such an event is ridiculous. I would say, conservatively, that I have attempted 1,500–2,000 free throws in competition in my basketball career. Meaning that—prior to this late meltdown— the chances of me sending up an air ball on a free throw were something like 1 in 1,500.

I don't know that I can even describe how it all happened, but I will try. It was late in the game and I was tired, but that is hardly an excuse. I had played fairly well considering the long road trip we had finished only the day before. It was a close game when I stepped to the line late in the fourth quarter for my first free throw of the game. (An odd occurrence, actually—I spend a fair amount of time of my ABA experience getting hacked and chopped near the basket.) I took my customary two dribbles, bent slightly at the knees, and then watched with dismay as the shot I had just released fell well short of the basket. I looked around to check for another sign of the impending apocalypse, took a deep breath, and prepared for my second shot. Determined not to repeat the event, I launched that effort with gusto. It missed off the back of the rim and I jogged back on defense, ready to forget the entire thing had happened.

I found myself back at the line soon after. It should be noted that I have had some struggles with free-throw shooting this year. Free throws have never caused me a great amount of stress in the past; throughout my career I've been an average-to-decent free-throw shooter. This year has been different. The lingering effects of the bizarre shoulder injury I suffered last spring caused my shot to develop an undesired in-motion hitch. That, combined with a recent ability to obsess in a Howard Hughes–like way over the possible repercussions of a few missed shots, has twisted my mental view regarding the difficulty of a free throw. My mind seems to be convinced that it is a very challenging shot, which is simply not the case. (Seriously, free throws aren't that difficult. Professional basketball players do not air-ball free throws. If I randomly selected a child with Down syndrome, blindfolded him, sent him to the free-throw line, and told him to really try to make four free throws, I would wager that he would do better than to air-ball three of them. If I were to add a wheelchair and subtract an arm, we might be discussing three air balls out of four attempts.) However, my unstable little brain's skewed view of the relative difficulty of an unguarded basketball shot hardly justifies air-balled free throws.

The previous paragraph played through my mind just prior to my second pair of free throws. I told myself to relax and shoot the ball as I normally would. Result: another wounded duck that traced a smooth arc ending well short of the basket. I didn't know what to do. The crowd had forgiven one transgression; now the rumblings of disbelief were becoming noticeable. I tried to block out the external chaos and concentrated, simply, on making a goddamned free throw. I was unsuccessful. Yet another air ball.

Whatever the cause of my complete loss of motor ability, I was not pleased with myself afterward. One would think that I, as a semi-functional adult, would be well equipped to deal with an air-balled free throw at this stage—at least better equipped than the thirteen-year-old version of me who last violated the aesthetics of the game so wantonly. However, I do not recall bursting into tears after that seventh-grade game.

I could be wrong, but I think my inability to shake off an air ball points to a larger problem. It is a game, after all. But perhaps I take this game, and myself, a little too seriously. I feel like I should have been able to laugh off the first occurrence in that game against Long Beach. Maybe, to show I was a good sport, I could have shot the next one with my left hand. I didn't. I actively tried to recover. In doing so, I became more uptight about the fact that I had just air-balled a free throw, which obviously didn't help me make the next few. I think there's a lesson in there somewhere.

I woke up the next morning legitimately thinking that I had dreamed the whole thing. I wish that were true; instead I will just treat it as such. The good news, as I told several people, is that I now have a new benchmark for a bad night. Even after the worst game I ever play, at least, I can say that I . . . am not a one-armed kid with Down syndrome.

February 12
Day 1. Location: Fresno, California.

My phone rang at 6:30 A.M. My first thought was, "Shit. I forgot to turn off my phone last night." My second was, "Keith must have something important to say to call this early." (Actually, that was a lie. My second thought was, "I have to pee," but nobody wants to hear about my bodily function needs.) Keith was calling because my former team in Spain, Joventut, wanted to inquire about potentially purchasing my basketball-playing services again.

It may seem counterintuitive that I would consider leaving the country to take a basketball job in Europe. After all, I have dedicated most of this year to the hope that an NBA team would find room on its roster for me. To give up on that now might seem folly. However, since I haven't been called up yet, it is possible that it isn't going to happen. The $700 a week I am making here in the ABA is not going to provide much justification for this lifestyle. At some point, I probably need to make some money playing basketball.

As we pulled out of the Fresno Holiday Inn parking lot for the last time this year, my brain was already in high gear. I was happy that we would have no further contact with the Fresno Heatwave; we had played them four times in the previous two weeks and I was getting entirely too familiar with their personnel. Our encounters were becoming near-intrasquad scrimmages. (I should note that I will miss the baskets at their gym. My last two nights there netted thirty-one- and thirty-two-point outings, respectively.)

Keith called again as we set out on our bisecting journey of California, final destination the U.S.-Mexico border and a game the following night in Tijuana. He told me that Joventut was willing to offer $15,000 for one month of gainful basketball employment. Last year, it was $20,000 a month, guaranteed for a four-month stint. This year's offer was insultingly low. Of course, I was half an hour into a seven-hour bus ride through the desert, so I probably would have seriously considered indentured servitude to be a viable option. In the end, I told Keith to take a harder line with regard to my salary.

By somewhere north of Los Angeles, I resolved to go to Spain if the team was willing to guarantee three months at $20,000 per. Some of the impetus for my decision came from Tim Floyd, who told me that the Hornets were not likely to sign anyone else this season. I knew that my best chance for a contract was probably with the team with which I had gone to training camp. If that team had no interest, my NBA fate might be sealed for the year. Because I like to maintain the illusion of being a stand-up guy, I walked to the front of the bus and told Coach Wedman of my dilemma. He became appropriately flustered but was supportive of any decision I had to make.

We stopped somewhere between LA and San Diego for a practice at a Boys and Girls Club. After our brief workout, we worked with some kids to give back to the community or whatever the appropriate cliché is. While we played with some of the ragtag bunch, our most, um, aggressive (some would say "dirty"—not me) player, my good friend Derek Grimm, managed to unwittingly knock down an eight-year-old who had just shot the ball. The poor kid left the court in tears. It had no bearing at all on my decision-making process.

When we got back on the bus, I called Keith once more. He had not learned much else; by this time, it was nearing two in the morning in Spain, so we resolved to pick up the matter in the morning. While we spoke, I wondered how much of the information I was receiving got from the Spanish team to me in correct form. They probably were actually offering me a two-year deal worth $14.

Day 2. Location: Very Near Mexico, California.

My day began, not with a conversation with my mother or my girl-friend, but with a talk with my agent. (Of course, that comparison is an invalid one due to my complete lack of a dating life at this point. What a glamorous lifestyle I lead.) Keith informed me that Joventut had counteroffered with a two-month guarantee—exactly what I had feared. Since I had resolved to go to Spain if offered a three-month contract and to stay if offered only one, it was fitting that Joventut had offered two.

What followed was a day of flux. (Derek's term, not mine. I'm not that creative.) I waffled back and forth. By the afternoon, I was shop-ping online for a flight back to Kansas City that night before being reined in by, of course, Keith. I do not know what I would do without him, although the term "nervous breakdown" comes to mind. He told me to relax, to play in the night's game with Tijuana, and to quit wor-rying so much, as the decision would become easier as we gained more information. Seriously, he's a good agent.

Our game with Tijuana was rather thrilling. I accomplished my main goal of remaining injury-free. (A blown-out knee would have removed the Spanish option for sure.) After the requisite controversial call by the referees, Ryan Sears hit the game-winning jump shot, and we managed to get out of Mexico with all of our possessions. It was a good night.

Day 3. Location: see Day 2.

Coach Wedman woke me at 7:30 with a knock on my door. He asked me to join him in the hotel lobby for breakfast. I donned some clothes and moseyed down as I wondered why the world is united against my quest for sleep. Wedman proceeded to tell me that my confusion had made him realize that it was time for me to get called up to the NBA. He had risen at 5 A.M. and had begun making calls to NBA teams. He had finished six, and promised to get to the remaining twenty-four later in the day. I was taken aback. I was a little disappointed that it had taken my impending departure to light an inspirational fire under him, but I was glad he'd had the revelation, whatever the cause. My only motivation to play in the minor leagues stemmed from a need to get back to the NBA. I certainly wasn't doing it for the paycheck or the cushy travel schedule. I left breakfast somewhat touched by his kindness.

When I got back to my room, I called Keith. He told me that Joventut was not going to budge from their two-month offer. I said that I would think it all over and get back to him with a decision fairly soon.

I wasn't going to leave for Spain. The team's reluctance to meet my demands didn't help its cause, but the real impetus behind my desire to stay was Coach Wedman's efforts. I don't want to get too melodramatic, but I will say this: not many people have really believed in my basketball ability over the years. I mean, *really* believed in it. I'd say the list contains my parents, a few coaches along the way—most notably in high school and AAU—and Keith. Finding another person to add to the list means a lot to me.

I waited until we arrived back in Kansas City to tell Coach Wedman that I would finish the year in the United States, one way or another. He looked really happy, which sort of made me want to cry. (There is no limit to just how emotionally screwed up I am, by the way.) He promised to do all he could to assist in my quest to get back to the NBA.

February 17

After confirmation that Scott Wedman was to be my fairy godmother, we traveled to New Jersey for a game in the cavernous Hoop Zone of East Englewood. When I took note of our locker room accommodations, I realized that I was going to be lying when I later used the term "cavernous" to describe the Hoop Zone. Coach Wedman's pregame talk in the eight-by-eight-foot room we were provided was interrupted when a woman knocked on the door to request use of the bathroom facilities for her daughter. He looked around, said, "Sure, nobody's going in there," and held the door for the two of them as they passed through to the next room. Madison Square Garden it was not.

Our trip to New Jersey began with my team in fine shape. We had just played a back-to-back home set with the Las Vegas Rattlers, so were rather fatigued when we boarded a plane bound for Newark at 11 A.M. on game day. We had won both of the games against a somewhat depleted Las Vegas squad. The Rattlers' main protagonist and financier, the rapper Master P, had recently departed the scene, taking several of the team's players with him after learning that a team manager had been embezzling the money he was supposed to be routing to the players. Fittingly, the team's uniforms had also disappeared. To combat this, we were instructed to bring both our home and away jerseys to the first game of the pair; in case the opposition couldn't drum up some apparel, they would wear whatever we did not, which would have—I'm confident—really upped their professionalism in the eyes of those spectating. The Rattlers were able to secure uniforms of some sort, so the intrasquad-scrimmage look never came to be, thankfully. After two games under those dubious circumstances, we were looking forward to a relaxing and problem-free journey to New Jersey. (The previous was, of course, meant to be sarcastic. However, we did have cause for some optimism. Supposedly, the team in New Jersey had signed two NBA veterans who were hoping to keep the dream alive, so it at least seemed that the team still existed, which, in the ABA, is reason for a rose-colored worldview.)

After we got off the bus at the Hoop Zone, I resisted the urge to try out the attached batting cages and followed my teammates inside. I noted the broomball game going on behind the check-in desk while we were guided to the gym by, well, no one. With an hour to go before tip-off, I took in a few minutes of a pickup game that was pitting some Jews against some Gentiles. (I can only assume that the ones without the little beanies were Gentiles; they wore no identifying headgear.) After gorging myself on bad basketball, I took note of the court on which we would be playing.

I have seen an impressive number of YMCA and rec-league basketball courts in my time; this one was a conglomeration of all the stereotypes I have come to expect from the format. Our court was separated from the aforementioned interfaith scrimmage by a curtain that dropped from the ceiling. Between the curtain and the lines denoting out-of-bounds were several chairs that served as the teams' benches and as the scorer's table. On the opposite side of a court just barely wide enough to support a full three-point arc were two sets of metal bleachers, each with three rows of seats. The three-point lines did not intersect with half-court, but it was close—the distance from the top of the key to the midline was about twelve feet. The floor itself looked a lot like wood but gripped more like ice. Other than that, it was a fine place to hold a professional basketball game.

My teammates and I resigned ourselves to our fate, shrugged, and found our way to the locker room/family restroom. (At least, my teammates did—I was still harboring doubts as to whether I would be able to muster the chutzpah to actually participate in what looked to be an injury festival waiting to happen.) With about thirty-five minutes remaining before tip-off, we made a halfhearted effort at a warm-up and then walked the eleven paces to the locker room for the pregame talk that was destined to be interrupted by a daughter's full bladder.

As the game began, I was concerned. Appalled, really. I wondered, for the nine thousandth time this year, if I could be any further away from my intended career arc. But then I found the rhythm of the game and everything turned out okay. Sure, the only shot clock available was a stopwatch at the scorer's table and the referees' best judgment . . . and there was a game between two teams of twelve-year-olds going on ten feet from ours . . . and the other team appeared to consist of Zach Marbury (brother of Stephon) and a bunch of guys who looked to be straight out of the state penitentiary, none of whom were on the team three weeks ago when we played. (Because of the jail time.) But it was still basketball. And for all my bluster, I do kind of like the game.

Plus, since the court was a scale model of a real one, it was impossible to get tired. In fact, it was damn near leisurely. I think we need to request a pint-sized arena in Kansas City.

February 25

The age of the cellular phone and the accompanying automatic caller identification removes some of the shock of anyone's opening salvo on the telephone. For instance, I was playing some poker at my house with some friends on a recent night when my phone rang. I looked down and saw "Scott Wedman" displayed. Thus, I was able to prepare myself for whatever piece of knowledge he would soon be spewing forth. In the olden days, I would have answered the phone blindly, without any forewarning as to the identity of the caller, and would not have been able to prevent an expression of shock at hearing my head coach's voice at nine o'clock, the night prior to my team's departure for Tijuana. In our current, advanced state, I had time to say, before actually answering, "Hmmm . . . I wonder what Coach Wedman wants at nine o'clock, the night prior to our departure for Tijuana." And since I knew it was Wedman calling, which was strange in the first place, I was prepared for him to say just about anything. Therefore, when he said that our game in Tijuana had been canceled because that team wanted to save money so it could play in the playoffs, I was

not surprised. Much. Sure, I found it alarming that a professional basketball league would ever cancel a game to save money, but because I
was able to come about the information gradually, thanks to the tech-
nology we take for granted every day, the impact was minimized.

Receiving the above news was something like learning that school
would be canceled due to snow, in that it was great. The news cast the
poker game in an extremely cheery light—my personal level of responsibility for the next day had dropped significantly. And I didn't
have to go back to Tijuana. Of course, the ABA, and my participation
in it, was sullied slightly. But fuck it: no school.

The news, whether it was good or bad, certainly did not stop the
card game. In fact, it allowed us to play longer. But on a forest-for-the-
trees level, the development did give me pause. The ABA season is
limping to the finish line; we have only two regular-season games remaining before the playoffs, which will be of questionable viability in
their own right. No one attached to the Kansas City Knights knows
exactly where said playoffs will occur or even the format in which
they will be played. It is doubtful that every team in the league will
participate—most of the organizations are running their operations
on fumes and it is rumored that several of the teams are canceling
games with alarming frequency. (There is no real way for anyone to
know exactly what is going on; ABA scores are not running underneath the regularly scheduled programming on ESPN.) Even if the
season does linger on and concludes at its scheduled date sometime
in mid-March, what will I have accomplished? It is not as if the NBA
season is never-ending. And since I have not yet been called up, it
would stand to reason that my chances drop with each day that brings
nearer mid-April and the end of the regular season schedule. Maybe I
should have gone to Spain after all; those NBA calls that Coach Wedman made were nice, but I'm not seeing a real effect. I'm still making
$700 a week to play in a rodeo arena. And I'm shitty at cards, so life as
a professional poker player is out.

March 11

I've played my last game with the Kansas City Knights. Strangely, I'm not the least bit sad that I'll never again play in an arena that smells like cow manure. Or have to carry my own ball to practice. Or have to brush my teeth with bottled water because our road game is being played in a third-world country.

I won't even miss my own bed. It would stand to reason that while I no longer play for the Knights, I do own a house in Kansas City, and so should sleep there. But I can't.

Because I now play for the Chicago Bulls. Of the NBA.

That's *the* Chicago Bulls—the team with the red-and-black uniforms. In the best basketball league in the world. I should explain how this happened.

I knew before what would be my last ABA game in Kansas City that there was a good chance I would soon travel to Chicago for a workout with the Bulls. We beat the Jersey team that Saturday, but I can't say my heart was in the game. Keith had told me the day before that the Bulls were fed up with a few of their players and were searching for a dignified way to end the season while sending a message to some of their, er, employees. I found out the day after our game that I would, in fact, leave on Monday for Chicago and a Tuesday morning workout, with a possible ten-day contract as the most favorable outcome of my trip. On the way to the airport, I stopped by a Knights practice to say farewell. While there, I quashed the rumors that something had been guaranteed to me in Chicago. I have experienced enough of these very bizarre scenarios firsthand to understand just how easy it is for the entire process to derail. Ever optimistic that one of their own would finally make it big, my teammates assured me that I would not be back in Kansas City. I did not share their confidence.

I arrived in Chicago nervous but excited about the opportunity at hand, even though that opportunity would result in a missed trip to fabulous Juarez, Mexico, and the ABA playoffs. When I checked into the Residence Inn the night prior to my workout, I noticed—in addition to my own—a few other names listed under "Chicago Bulls," so I

asked the desk jockey if anyone else was staying at his fine establishment at the behest of the team. When he told me the names of three
fellow hopefuls, I came to the conclusion that unless the team was
going to run four separate workouts, this would not be the individual
workout I had been led to believe would take place. I was correct;
three other guys showed up at 7:30 the next morning. (I'm a genius,
really.)

As we warmed up/eyed each other, I noticed something about my
competition. They looked much more scared and apprehensive than I
felt. My brain told me, "If they *look* scared, imagine what is going on
inside those noggins of theirs." I note this because my ability to per-
ceive others' feelings is usually on the level of that of a kitchen table,
so I was impressed with my awareness. It was the first time I had ever
known, not felt, that I had an edge over my contemporaries.

The workout went quite well for me, at least by my reckoning. I
was under the impression that there would be some post-workout
consideration by the Bulls management and staff before any decision
was made regarding my future, so it was with much confusion that I
listened to a manager-type inquire, immediately after the workout,
"Paul, is your flight back to Kansas City this afternoon or tomorrow?"
I reeled internally, recovered, and then replied that I didn't have a
flight home. I told the fellow that arrangements were to be made for
me when I was finished. I walked to the locker room in confusion. His
question made me assume that either the workout had gone badly or
something had changed within the team. Either way, I assumed I
would return to Kansas City soon.

Once safely inside the locker room—in the comfortable surroundings created by the communal nakedness of four complete strangers—
my fellow workout partners and I commiserated. I learned that they all
had pre-planned flights for later that morning. (Probably an indication
that they had never really been in the running for a roster spot as
much as for future consideration.) We all parted ways after a nice
shower together.

Still befuddled, I wandered up to the office of Gar Forman, the
Bulls' director of player personnel, for clarification. Forman was an as-

sistant for Tim Floyd at Iowa State and had followed Floyd to Chicago. After his departure, Forman made his way up the baskocorporate ladder and was my tie-in to the Bulls. Coach Forman (now Gar to me, I suppose) told me I had done a great job (but they always do) and asked if I could go back to the hotel to hang out until some decisions were made. He told me that, as of then, the Bulls had no roster spots available; in order to make any moves they would have to waive someone. I had nothing pressing to do in Chicago, so I made my way back to the Residence Inn and waited for news of my fate. In the meantime, I had several phone conversations with Keith. The backstory began to take shape. The Bulls were going to waive a player named Corie Blount and sign someone. That person's identity would remain a mystery for a while, though. The Bulls were hoping that Lonny Baxter, a player they had traded to Toronto early in the year, would clear the waivers on which the Raptors had put him a day earlier. If that happened, the Bulls would sign him. (When a player is put on waivers, or released, by a team, the other teams in the NBA have forty-eight hours to claim him—with the stipulation that the new team has to pay his salary for the rest of the year. If no team claims the player, he is said to have cleared waivers. If Baxter cleared, the Bulls could sign him to a ten-day contract and would not be forced to pay him for the remainder of the season.) Baxter would theoretically clear waivers at 10 A.M. the next day. If he was available at that point, I would most likely be SOL. (That's Shit Out of Luck for those not acquainted with semi-lewd abbreviations.) With my anxious head about to explode, I headed to bed, and tried not to dream of myself in a Bulls uniform.

I awoke the next day to a *Chicago Sun-Times* sports page splattered with stories containing my name. Because the Bulls had cut Blount and I'd had a workout the day before with Chicago's only professional basketball team, it had not taken much of a leap of faith to come up with the tag line "Bulls Cut Popular Blount to Make Room for Shirley." Unfortunately, there is only one modifier in that headline, and it's not one that makes me look good. If Blount was popular, then I by implication became unpopular, which is fine—I get paid the same either way. However, it wasn't a great starting place with my future teammates, especially when the headline was not entirely accurate. It should have read, "Bulls Cut Popular Blount to Make Room for Player Jettisoned Earlier This Year; If Deal Falls Through, Team May Be Forced to Sign ABA Player Shirley." But when it comes to news, brevity sells. In the article, Kirk Hinrich, with whom I had several run-ins when he played at Kansas and I played at Iowa State, was asked about me. He said, "He killed us. He's just a scrapper." This could, of course, be interpreted in two ways: "That Paul Shirley can play the game. He does more with less than anyone I've seen. He's just a scrapper." Or, "Yeah, he's nearly worthless, can't shoot, can't defend. He's just a scrapper." And yes, I think too much.

After absorbing a slight media hit, I did find out some very good news. The Washington Wizards had claimed Lonny Baxter from waivers, and the Chicago Bulls would sign me to a ten-day contract. Of course, they never mentioned the Baxter thing; they just said it had taken some time to get some roster changes made. (Incidentally, when they signed me they were forced to put a player on the injured list to make room for me on the active roster; Blount had been on that list when he was released. Their choice? My teammate for three years at Iowa State, a former college player of the year, the fourth pick in the 2000 NBA draft, and a genuine nut job—one Marcus Fizer.)

The Bulls practice north of Chicago in Deerfield, Illinois. My hotel adjoins the practice facility. The Bulls' arena, on the other hand, is in downtown Chicago. When it came time for me to play in my first home game as a Bull, I needed some transportation. And so it came to pass that I was delivered to my first game in the United Center in a stretch limousine. While I was riding downtown, I had to keep telling myself, "You can do this. Just try to look like you ride in limos to basketball games all the time." I felt a little pretentious. But who am I to have denied that limo driver his chance to drive me to my first Bulls game?

My only regret from my first NBA experience—the ten-day contract in Atlanta last year—was that I did not score in a game. It certainly wasn't for lack of trying; I think I averaged a shot per minute in the whopping five minutes I played while a Hawk. Because of my regret, I was absolutely thrilled when the eighteen-foot jumper I launched midway through the second quarter in my Bulls debut against Philadelphia nestled itself into the bottom of the net. Of course, I did not let on that I had just made my first NBA basket. I jogged back on defense as calmly as I could, but the goose bumps were probably visible from the top row. It's not a huge step, but I can say I was proud of my then-career high of two. (I topped that by scoring a whole four points on the subsequent evening.) We all have to start somewhere.

I may not have made this entirely clear: my first-ever NBA points actually came during meaningful game time. I can't adequately express how happy I am about that fact. (The reader will have to take me at my word—I don't do jubilation well.) I have had some very good practices with this team. My work in practice, combined with the fact that the Bulls are truly dreadful and are searching for answers anywhere they can find them, meant that the coaches actually see me as a viable member of their basketball organization. I entered the game against the 76ers midway through the second quarter with my team still very much in the mix of the game. I probably played only a total of ten minutes on the night, but they were meaningful minutes and, as I may have mentioned, that is important to me. Even more telling than my early-ish entry into the game was the fact that Coach Skiles actually drew up what would prove to be the last play of the game for me. I had been on the team for all of four days, yet he had the confidence to, with a straight face, sketch a play that ended with me in the right corner, shooting a three-pointer that, if made, would have drawn us within one with about three seconds remaining. I didn't make the shot; in fact, the other team saw the whole thing developing about nine years ahead of time, and I was lucky to get the ball over the outstretched hands of what seemed like the entire Philadelphia 76ers basketball team as I fell toward the out-of-bounds line, so I didn't exactly have a clean look, as they say. But I still appreciated the opportunity—two weeks ago, I was playing basketball in a rodeo arena in Kansas City and was beginning to wonder if my short stint with the Atlanta Hawks had been merely a figment of my imagination. My basketball career was rapidly becoming nearly pathetic. Perhaps I am making too much of this, but there is a significant difference between that state of mind and the one that results after the head coach of the Chicago Bulls drew up a last-second play for me. I'm not yet going to ready myself for a retired jersey, but this is good news.

March 14

I realize that I am hardly in a position to complain. Two weeks ago, I was staring down the barrel of a complete disaster of a basketball season. Right now, I am playing in the best basketball league in the world. It would seem that nothing could get me down. I forgot something, though, and this turns out to be kind of important: I hate most professional basketball players.

I was sent down a path to remembrance by a particular incident on the Bulls' airplane: Kendall Gill told me to carry his bag. I think his exact words were, "Hey, rook, grab that for me." When he said it, the probability of me obeying his command stood at about 52 percent—meaning that 48 percent of me was on board for saying, "Go fuck yourself," and punching him in the jaw. Luckily, the majority continues to rule in my brain, and thus my NBA career rambles slowly on.

It is true that I should be able to deal with someone telling me to carry his bag. In fact, it is hardly worth discussing. But the frustration buildup caused by constant proximity to a bunch of . . . well, people whose company I don't necessarily enjoy is a subject into which I should delve. And so I will. There is a reason the Bulls have won only about 30 percent of their games this year—this team has the worst chemistry I've observed in my rocky basketball career. I understand completely why the team's management would want to shake things up by bringing in some new blood. (Especially when they had the chance to add someone as jovial as me.) My time with the Bulls hasn't been the honeymoon most people would probably envision—mainly because my time here has been spent mostly surrounded by people I cannot stand. (There are exceptions, of course. The trainers are good dudes. I suppose that a couple of the players aren't too bad. And the dance team seems nice.) Again, I understand that I should be thankful for my current status. I am. I could be contemplating a post-ABA trip to Venezuela to pick up some extra cash for the year. Instead, I am playing for the Chicago Bulls. But would it be too much to ask for me to have some colleagues with whom I can have the occasional conversation? A current point of contention with me, the one that led to Gill having the power to tell me to act as his camel, is that I have somehow been classified as a rookie by the powers that be. I've had my fill of the rookie treatment. I was a rookie when I went to training camp with the Lakers, so I got to air up balls and unload bags. By league standards, because I did not make the team in LA, I was a rookie when I went to camp with the Hawks the next year and so got to sing the national anthem for the team at team functions and, again, unload bags. I did not like it, but I did it because I understood the tradition, however asinine that tradition is. Plus, in both situations, I was around players I generally respected, and it was the beginning of the season, so there was a certain sense of playful optimism in the air. My rookie status remained the same when I got called up by the Hawks, and so I continued to play porter and schlepped luggage from plane to bus, bus to hotel. But all that changed when I went to New Orleans for camp. Because I had been "in the NBA" during the last year, a magical little number 1 appeared next to my name under "Years of Experience," exempting me from the demeaning life of a rookie for all eternity. Or so I thought. On my first road trip with the Bulls, a veteran player (read: he's all of four years my senior) asked me if I was indeed a rookie. He had to ask because few here had any idea who I was before I arrived. I told him proudly that I was not. (See above for justification.) He felt that my story was a bit wishy-washy and appealed to the head coach, Scott Skiles, who in one fell swoop tore down the whole system and relegated me back to rookie status under the grounds that I hadn't played enough actual games in the NBA. With that, I was sunk and Kendall Gill can rightfully tell me what to do whenever he wants.

Only four players who travel with the team are older than me. The Bulls have drafted some chronologically challenged players in the last few years, leaving them with a raft of players who are just above legal drinking age. I can't claim to be all that young—at least not in the world of professional sports—but twenty-six hardly seems old. These guys who were drafted three or four years ago remain younger than me but obviously are no longer rookies, so they sit on the bus while I and the other "rookies" haul their bags around. Under normal circumstances, if someone four-fifths my age told me to do something as menial as carry his bag, I wouldn't even have to consider it a valid request. In fact, I wouldn't even have to speak. I could give a quick cock of the eyebrow and he would rethink his query.

A person with a small capacity for imagination would now probably say something like, "Well, Paul, what are you going to do when you someday have a boss that is younger than you?" First, I would reply that there is about a 75 percent chance that the questioner would receive the GFY treatment mentioned earlier in this entry. If not, I would respond to the actual question with the following: if I were ever in a position where it was contained in my job description to carry another human's bags, it would mean one of two things: (1) I had sustained a massive brain injury and was lucky to get work release from the mental institution in order to work as a bellman for Embassy Suites, or (2) I had said to hell with it all and had begun a life as a Sherpa somewhere in the Himalayas.

Really, though, the main issue is not so much whether I am a rookie or whether I have to cart bags around. I resent the imperious looks from players who I know to be complete losers, both in the literal, basketball sense and in the more general, parlance-of-our-time sense. I think it speaks to the reason the Bulls are so bad that the players on the team actually have the gall to ask another human being to carry their bags. A large portion of me wants to tell Tyson Chandler the following: "Look, Tyson, I know you think you hung the moon because you are seven foot one and can jump. But you didn't work hard to gain that ability. You were given that. Up to now, it seems to me, you have squandered it. You don't know how to play basketball, and you certainly have no idea how to help your team win. Until you do understand either of those things, you hold nothing over me. I know, I know. I have not played much in the NBA. But check out my past. I do understand the game. I know what it takes to win basketball games. I can't move like you, and I'll never be able to, but I will always know that I earned this, while it was given to you."

But I don't say it, because I am on a ten-day contract and Tyson Chandler could easily make it known that he doesn't want me around, and off I would go.

It should be evident that I am questioning the reasoning behind this NBA commitment of mine. Am I really enjoying myself? I am making $3,750 a day to play a game. Adjectives used to describe that pay scale include *exorbitant, absurd,* and *ludicrous.* The money I have made playing basketball is going to give me a nice jump start on life. And let's not forget that I will receive this jump start based on my ability to play a game. I know of few people who would refuse such a gig. My "job" is a better one than the jobs held by most everyone I know. I think, though, that certain things remain true, no matter what one's station in life. I hear from almost everyone that one's colleagues make a job tolerable. I don't like most of my colleagues much. This isn't quite how I envisioned life in the professional ranks.

When I was a kid, the highlight of any trip to "town" (Topeka, which was all of fifteen miles from my childhood home) was an excursion to the library. My brothers and I weren't allowed to watch a lot of television, so much of our entertainment was provided by books. At some point, I got hooked on biographies. I loved baseball, so the natural progression led me to the section of biographies about baseball players. As I mowed through books about Cobb, Mantle, and DiMaggio, I took note of their lifestyle. At the time, I was sure that I would one day play professional baseball and assumed that my life would be like theirs had been—filled with postgame dinners with teammates who, like me, loved baseball more than anything else. I think this colored my view of the life of a professional athlete. My affinity for baseball was lost at around the same time as my face's first encounter with a pitched ball; as I improved at basketball, I began to dream about the NBA. When I thought of life in the pros, I assumed that when I got there I would find people just like me—whatever that means. I thought we would play games, congratulate one another after triumphs, console one another after defeats . . . and then all go out to dinner. Instead, I found a bunch of angry guys interested in dumb girls, jewelry, and the advancement of their own careers. The '49 Yankees this ain't.

March 17

With my time in Chicago off to a rousing 0–5 start, the Bulls management decided they were thirsty for more of my brand of applause, ass-slappage, and random jump shots, so they signed me to another ten-day contract. This only means more money for all the illegitimate Shirleys roaming the earth. And if they're happy, I'm happy.

When the Bulls signed me to a second ten-day contract they also signed a point guard named Jannero Pargo to bolster the backcourt. When we left on a trip to (editorial comment: picture me sitting at my computer, face screwed up in concentration as I attempt to remember what city was our destination, when a cramp in my hamstring sends me bolting out of my chair—hilarious to be sure, so long as you're not me, stretching and furiously trying to rub the rear of my left leg. Then, not so funny. The cramp, I'm sure, was a direct result of the practice I endured earlier today, but more on that later) Cleveland, Pargo asked me for a ride to the airport. I groaned inwardly, having been through the routine before, but couldn't come up with a legitimate excuse fast enough and was relegated to taxi duty.

As I sat in my car outside his room at the Residence Inn, preparing for honk number three, I was reminded of another reason I dislike basketball players so much. They're so goddamned unreliable. If I weren't one myself, I would recommend against ever putting oneself in a position wherein one has to deal with them. Eventually, my charge showed himself and we set off for the airport, already behind schedule. The conversation was a dull one; at first it dealt mainly with what we thought of our respective lots with the Bulls, but the lack of material with which we had to work made the ride a long one. I made a valiant effort, though, and we kept up the sparse discourse until we arrived at the terminal where our 727 waited.

The ride back to the hotel the next night was another matter. I had been dreading the trip since fifteen minutes prior to landing—the moment when I recalled that uncomfortable conversational work remained ahead of me. I had little time to prepare, but I did come up with some material I thought I could work in if things got stale. We had exhausted both "What do you think of Coach Skiles?" and "What problems do you see with the team?" by the time we got on the highway, so I knew the next twenty minutes would be long ones.

I'm not above giving someone the cold shoulder. If I'm on an airplane next to some mustachioed, 250-pound woman, I feel no obligation to carry on a conversation. But if I am in the car with a teammate, someone with whom I probably ought to develop some kind of bond in order to make travel at least tolerable, I feel I should make some sort of effort. Unfortunately, we had developed fully the obvious hometown and college inquiries on the ride to the airport. (Pargo was from Arkansas. I was not.) I had to stretch the imagination a bit. We passed a massive car accident, so I asked him if he had ever been in a wreck. His reply: "Yeah." *Okay, press on, Paul, he just needs prompting.* "Really? When?" "A while back." *Right, that narrows it down. I was beginning to wonder if you had a time machine. Which would have been amazing. It's good that we verified that this mishap did in fact occur in the past.* Me: "Oh yeah?" Him: "It was back in high school." *Good, good, now we're going places. We've reached back into the memory banks. Keep him warm.* "So did anyone get hurt?" "Naw, man, nothing really." Damnable seat belts! Killing my potential conversation. If only someone had been thrown through the windshield, we would have easily had ninety seconds of material. But his car accident had to be boring, so I let the matter die. Johnny Carson I am not. Later, though, Pargo rallied and tried to begin a conversation on his own. His opening volley: "You got any kids?" Not "Are you married?" or "Do you have a girlfriend?" Just "You got any kids?"

I reached a new career high last night, scoring six whole points in our loss at Cleveland. I say *loss,* but I mean *drubbing.* It was ugly. I played a little in the first quarter but came out quickly because of an early missed box-out. After the game got out of hand, I was inserted to do cleanup. Good times. I actually played pretty well in my garbage time, and my mates and I kept the score at about the twenty-seven-point deficit at which it stood when we took the reins. Mission accomplished. In addition to my NBA scoring high, I also dished out my first ever NBA assist. Good job, me.

When I was informed that I would get to stay in Chicago for a second ten-day session, I was told that if I wanted the team to extend my contract through the end of the season (after two ten-days, their only recourse, other than sending me home), I would have to start making more shots. When given the above message, I was coming off a game in New Jersey in which I had played about six minutes and managed to get off three long jumpers, none of which felt the need to go where they were intended to go. It's not cool to tell a basketball player, "Your future is dependent on whether you make jump shots." The statement may be true; it just is not said. It's similar to telling a bowler, "You really just have to roll a strike here." He would say, "Well, dude, I'm going to try, but I can't guarantee success." I would say the same. As in, believe it or not, I never try to miss—sometimes it just happens.

If someone who watched me play in college were to read this, he would be confused. When I was at Iowa State, I rarely—if ever—shot the ball from outside the lane. My team had plenty of players casting up shots from everywhere on the floor; we didn't need one more. I'd always been a good shooter, so my new role was a change for me, but I was willing to accept my new station in life, if only as a way to get in the game. As an unheralded non-recruit coming out of high school, I had to be creative; it seemed to be that playing really hard did the trick, so I stuck with that, maybe for too long. When I decided to attempt this professional basketball thing, I decided that I would do it only if it was fun for me. A big part of that newfound philosophy was playing the game the way I wanted to play it, which included shooting the ball from the outside more. A lot more. Turns out I am pretty good at it. However, I am not necessarily a shooter, in the basketball sense of the word. I don't stand around on the perimeter hoping for the ball to come my way so I can chuck it at the rim. I do shoot if I am open, but I think I have a good feel for when that is the best thing for the team's chances. It can't be every time; I think (or used to think) that there exist situations that call for suppression of one's own glory for the good of the team. It turns out that not everyone agrees with me. Even Coach Skiles tells me to shoot more. I'm still learning about this shooter's mentality; if I miss a couple from the outside, I usually think I ought to make a layup before resuming the exterior onslaught. Again, I don't find much acceptance of this theory. "Zero for fifteen from there? Shoot the sixteenth one." And so with nothing to lose and everything to gain, I have decided on a new approach: to hell with it, it's going up. The only way to make more is to shoot more.

I mentioned that we Chicago Bulls (still has a nice ring to it, even at 18–49 for the year) had a rough practice today. I don't know if I have been as tired after a basketball practice since college. Skiles was irked by our performance the night before and displayed it with his choice of a practice plan. Rebounding drills, running, scrimmages, more running. Fun stuff. Due to the regimen of psychological and physical torture I was fed in college, I thrive in such a situation. It is as if I've been in the Marines. We survivors of the Floyd-Eustachy regimes all had our own personal four-year course of basic training (five for me), and nothing we could encounter at this point could possibly be as hard as what we endured then. It's an empowering feeling. I just hate that those coaches were right when they said we would thank them later.

Eventually, the Bulls' practice devolved into multiple short scrimmages sandwiched around sprints for the losing team. It worked out that I was put on the day's first team, which was chosen not so much because of its aggregate talent as much as for its capacity to listen and play according to the wishes of Coach Skiles. My teammates were Kirk Hinrich, fellow newbies Ronald Dupree and Linton Johnson, and Antonio Davis. We were opposed by all comers—Jannero Pargo, Eddie Robinson, Marcus Fizer (who was practicing with something of a chip on his shoulder, obviously, as he had been told he had played his last game as a Bull), along with Tyson Chandler and Eddy Curry. Their team had about six times the talent of ours, but it could not overcome the adversity of the tough practice and the infighting caused by blame being thrown about within the team. We kept beating them. I played quite well, even making a buzzer beater from way out to win one for my team. It was intoxicating. On one hand, I was exhausted and wanted to retire to the showers ASAP. On the other, I never wanted the practice to end. I had almost forgotten the feeling could exist.

It should be remembered that I am talking about feeling invigorated about the basketball I was playing with one of the worst teams in the NBA, in a practice, on an intrasquad team that was something of a false first string, with less than a month left in a disaster of a season. Some would say that it is refreshing that I can still find a basketball high under those circumstances; others would say that I need to find some perspective and then call them when it actually matters. I'm not sure who would be right. But it's important to remember that I have never really been a part of an NBA team before. I've been marginally involved—as little more than practice fodder with possible candidacy for occasional mop-up duty—but never to the point where the coaches on the sidelines said things to me with their eyes actually focused on mine and not on the wall behind me. It's kind of nice.

April 2

Soon after my feel-good practice in Chicago we played a game in Indianapolis against the Pacers. I was inserted into the game early, but my involvement did little to stop a twenty-point deficit from building throughout the contest. In the second half, Coach Skiles became disenchanted with the effort of his main charges and threw several of us non-starters into the fray with around nine minutes remaining in the third quarter. At that point, we were down by around thirty; our insertion was Skiles' way of proving a point to his thoroughbreds. I played the next sixteen or so minutes without incident. I didn't necessarily play well, but I didn't look completely overwhelmed—which is about two-thirds of the battle, in my mind. I scored a basket or two and got a rebound now and then, but did nothing spectacular, other than guard

Ron Artest well a few times. (For some reason, my ability to do so came as a surprise to the coaching staff. Sometimes I wonder if NBA coaches even watch practice.)

With about five minutes remaining in the game and my team on defense, I noticed that the Pacers' Austin Croshere was going to have an unimpeded path to the basket. He had just set a screen for a guard on his team and was in the midst of rolling, uncovered, toward the lane. I was defending someone on the opposite side of the lane from Croshere and rushed over to attempt to provide assistance through taking a charge, blocking a shot, or some other heroic maneuver. By the time I found my way to his area of the court, he had caught the ball and was well on his way to laying the ball in the basket. Unfortunately, I arrived late on the scene. I managed only to impede Croshere's path enough to force a terrific collision between his knee and the left side of my torso. I went down in a heap immediately, sprawled in fairly significant pain. My first thought was, *Wow, that hurt. But at least I won't be expected to participate in this bloodbath any longer. This seems like a fairly honorable way out of the extreme fatigue that has been plaguing me for the last five minutes while I tried to make it look like I cared whether we lost by twenty or forty.* Next, I had flashbacks to time spent watching sporting events with my father and remembered how idiotic players seem when they roll around on the ground for minutes at a time, only to realize that they had merely had the wind knocked out of them or had twisted an ankle. So I told myself, *Pull it together and let the trainer get you off the floor. Don't make a big deal out of what is probably just a bruised rib.* I allowed the trainers to help me to the locker room, where X-rays were taken of my midsection. Initial indications were that no fracture was evident. Because of this, when people in the locker room asked, I attempted to shrug off any concern for my well-being. I said things like, "I'll be okay, they think it's just a bruised rib." In a fair amount of pain, I showered and then found a spot on a training table where I could lie down until it was time for the team to leave the arena for the bus to the airport. I was moving around without any major discomfort, and all my vital signs were good, so there seemed to be no reason for extreme concern.

When we got to the bus, my comfort level took a turn for the worse. The general closeness and the smell of my teammates' post-game meals made me nauseous. When the bus began moving I broke into a cold sweat. But when we arrived at the airport, the fresh air of the out-of-doors seemed to revive me and so I got on the plane. The Bulls trainers, Fred Tedeschi and his assistant Eric Waters, had been concerned enough about my condition that they had called ahead in order to have the flight attendants convert one of the plane's cabins into a bed. If my brain would have been functioning correctly, I prob-ably would have thought, "Hmm, this seems like a lot of trouble for a guy with a bruised rib." But I was not in a mood to argue. Lying down seemed like a perfectly reasonable idea.

After confirming that I was comfortable in my little cabin, the trainers found their seats for taxi and takeoff, meaning that I was alone when the night's fun began. Each bump on the runway elicited a little whimper from me and the general movement had me squeez-ing my eyes shut. The takeoff was no better; I began gasping as pain moved in stabbing waves from my side. It seemed that I could find no position that would make it more tolerable. As my condition worsened during the plane's ascent, I called out to Scottie Pippen, who hap-pened to be sitting in the adjoining cabin playing poker, and told him that I needed Fred Tedeschi. By the time Fred arrived on the scene, I was in bad shape. I was sweating like a whore in church. One side of my body was absolutely pounding. He asked me what was wrong; I told him that I was hurting a lot and could not seem to manage the pain. He informed me that there was not much they could do, as it was not a good idea to give me any pain medication until someone deter-mined what was wrong with me. So I resigned myself to my fate and tried to deal with the situation. As the plane leveled, I hit the eye of my pain storm and my general discomfort subsided slightly. Unfor-tunately, when we began to descend toward Chicago (fortunately, Indianapolis-Chicago is not a long flight), the pain reintensified, and I began to near the brink of my tolerance. A few minutes into our approach, I went over the edge and began, well, screaming. It wasn't so much a sustained woman-is-attacked-by-killer-zombie-in-a-movie scream as much as it was a man-watches-as-own-toenails-are-pulled-out scream. The pain seemed to take short breaks, redouble its efforts, and hit me from a slightly new spot every few seconds. The worst of it, as I mentioned earlier, was that I could not find a position that would help. Lying on my back, lying on my side, lying on my stomach, curling into a ball, raising my legs, lowering my legs—nothing helped. I knew at the time that I would later regret my childlike behavior, but I couldn't stop screaming/crying/blubbering. I kept asking Fred if there was any chance I was going to pass out, because I wanted to. Sadly, he kept saying no. At one point, my face and fingers began to tingle, which only added to my confusion. I learned that the bizarre sensation was a result of my hyperventilation. Apparently, such behavior causes one's body to expel too much carbon dioxide. I was given a paper sack into which, conceivably, I could either breathe, which was somehow supposed to help me get my carbon dioxide balance back to normal, or vomit, which would have at least given me something to do. At the time, my functional IQ was down to about 65, so I could hardly grasp the intricacies of my blood-gas levels. Consequently, the breathing bag did very little good. As we grew ever closer to the earth, I settled into a position lying on my stomach, my feet in the aisle, my face mashed against the side of the plane, and a paper bag poised under my mouth. I found a method of panting and moaning that seemed to give me the best chance of enduring and stuck with it as long as I could.

I found out later that the pilots had been informed of my state; they had subsequently radioed ahead to the Chicago airport to request landing priority. I was told that an ambulance had been called from the air and would be waiting for us at the end of the runway. I still had enough brain function to realize the absurdity of that scenario but was too wracked with hurt to care. And, I thought, at least I had something to look forward to. Fred gave me constant updates regarding our proximity to the emergency vehicle, and I tried to maintain my pant-and-moan technique as long as I could. Upon cessation of the plane's movement, everyone else was hustled off the plane while several EMTs were hustled on. I incredulously received the news that I would be expected to somehow heave myself from my prone position into some sort of seat with which they would carry me from the plane. I told them to wait a few seconds; the plane's new-found non-movement found me, if not pain-free, at least in better shape than I had been in for some time. They informed me that it would not help much to wait, at which point I thought, *Easy for you to say.* (A thought that would be repeated many, many times through-out the ordeal.) On the count of three, I gave it a go and fell, shriek-ing, back to my same position. It felt as if someone had stabbed me in the side with a bowie knife. After some consideration, I made another effort and, with the help of everyone standing around, made it into the stretcher thing, but certainly not silently.

My first-ever ambulance ride was another pain-filled extrava-ganza. To me, it felt like the ambulance had the shock absorbers of a 1952 Ford truck. The EMTs started intravenous morphine, but it didn't make much of an impact. Fortunately, the hospital was not far away. At least, that's what people kept telling me. I disagreed. When we finally arrived, it was necessary to transfer me to a hospital bed. It was less than fun—in fact, as soon as they managed it, I flipped back onto my stomach with another yell and hoped I would never have to move again. A nurse came in and said they needed to remove my shirt; she asked if I minded if they cut it off. Again, I was struck with the absurdity of such an action, but was in no mood to voice my reser-vations. So a long-sleeved blue-and-black-checked shirt—size XL tall—met its demise at the hands of an ER nurse in Chicago. I was just happy that I didn't have to move. At this point, the various parties in-volved had pumped a rather impressive amount of morphine into my system, with little result. Whether this speaks to the amount of pain I was feeling, the fact that I have the pain tolerance of a five-year-old, or just the sheer largeness that is me, I do not know. I was very thank-ful when they switched over to a wonder drug called Dilaudid. It did ten times the work of morphine. Heavenly. If I ever meet its inventor I will offer him fellatio. The Dilaudid finally took effect sometime after my CT scan (another uncomfortable experience—being moved from my bed to the CT machine and back again), and I was finally able to take stock of the situation. It was not a good one. The results of the hurried CT scan suggested that something inside me was bleeding rather spectacularly. It could not be determined whether it was my left kidney, the involved renal artery, or my spleen. The correct course of action, apparently, was to monitor my vital signs and wait. I was grateful that our trainer, Fred, was with me. Dealing with the situation with him around was hard enough; it would have been nearly impossible on my own. Fred stayed with me until six in the morning, and remained calm throughout. He called my parents with updates all through the night and kept the ER staff informed about my state as often as was needed. He did not, however, have an elixir that would stop the bleeding, so it was decided that I would be transferred to another hospital, one where the doctors under the team's employ worked, so that I could be kept for observation. Fortunately, my blood pressure remained stable, so there did not seem to be any immediate need for surgery, although the idea was bandied about. I was told that if the bleeding did not stop on its own and/or my blood pressure dropped significantly, it would be time for an emergency surgery to remove part or all of one kidney and/or my spleen. So overall, my prospects were pretty good. Twenty-six years old, one kidney, no spleen. Fantastic. When I was sent by ambulance to the second hospital, Fred left to go home and I was finally able to try to get my bearings. I was shipped to intensive care and, as the Dilaudid finally started to take effect, went to sleep.

April 5

The impact of Austin Croshere's knee with my side resulted in a lacerated spleen and a fractured left kidney. (I learned that it is termed *fractured* because the kidney is brittle and thus cracks more than tears.) The force carried by his knee drove both organs into my backbone, which opened up their respective backsides, spilling copious amounts of blood (a liter and a half, I was told) into my retroperitoneal cavity. The bleeding stopped because the cavity filled with blood and, in essence, dammed the leak—there was no place for more blood to go. It turns out that millions of years of evolution are good for something after all.

Fred had been concerned that I had ruptured something almost immediately after the incident in Indiana. At one point in his career Fred was on the training staff of the San Francisco 49ers and had observed a similar injury occur during one of the team's football games. Because of his experience, he knew that standard protocol was to monitor the athlete's blood pressure; if he were losing too much blood internally, his blood pressure would drop. (Which explains to me why they kept taking my blood pressure immediately after the incident. I was not smart enough to be suspicious of the fact that they were telling me I had a bruised rib yet kept measuring my blood pressure.) Given it all to do over again, I think Fred would have kept me in Indianapolis and would not have risked the flight back to Chicago. Luckily, I did not bleed out on the plane. Someone probably would have felt bad.

The final diagnosis was not given to me until after the bleeding had slowed down enough that the doctors could pinpoint exactly what was going on. As I mentioned above, their first concern had been that the renal artery had been severed. If that had been the case, they would have operated in order to cauterize that artery and stop the bleeding. When they eliminated that scenario as a possibility and realized that my kidney and spleen were doing the bloodletting, they decided that I needed to stay in the hospital until they were sure the bleeding had stopped. The early discussion of the possible removal of either or both of the two organs in question remained theoretical; I was told that such barbarity was unlikely unless the bleeding did not cease on its own.

Once it was determined, by the battery of doctors under the watch of the Bulls' team doctor, Jeff Weinberg, that I was going to live, the next step was to control the substantial pain I was feeling and get me out of the hospital. The agony I was suppressing with massive doses of painkillers was being caused by the blood that had escaped its normal habitat and settled in a very abnormal place—outside, instead of inside, my spleen and left kidney. As blood filled the area around my spleen and kidney, that part of my body became similar to a very large bruise. A bruise is simply a collection of blood that leaks out in a particular site on the body. In my case, there was a whole bunch of blood in a place it was not supposed to be. Consequently, it exerted a fair amount of pressure on parts of my body not equipped to deal with that pressure. Of course, that same pressure will not subside until the blood is gone. (Eventually, it will be absorbed by my body. Which is both gross and comforting at the same time.) Until that process begins, there is no real reason for the pain to subside. Therefore, I take lots and lots of drugs.

April 10

I would like to discuss the Foley catheter now. Doctor's orders included nothing but bed rest for the first few days of my hospitalization. Unfortunately, when a person is pumped full of fluid intravenously but cannot leave his bed to visit the bathroom, a bladderific logistical problem arises. Enter the Foley catheter. And when I write *enter*, I mean it both figuratively and literally.

When the word *catheter* is spoken, I think small. I think of a tube that could fit in a vein or artery. I do not think of the length of hosing the nurse held up as she described how my logistical problem would be solved. If I were instructed to describe the particular piece of machinery they held in my best layman's terms, I would say something like, "That there looks like some quarter-inch or three-eighths-inch industrial hosing." (That was in layman's terms . . . and white trash's terms. I am familiar with both dialects.) I would not think immediately of a conduit between my bladder and the outside world. Unfortunately, there is no gentlemanly way of putting the next part. In order to get said catheter (and I'm not kidding about it being at least a quarter-inch in diameter) into my bladder, it was necessary to insert it. Into my urethra. I had always thought there was something in there that did not allow for wrong-way passage, like one of those spiked speed bumps in parking garages that result in flat tires if navigated going the wrong direction. Apparently I was wrong. The doctor did ease the transition by lubing the catheter. He then attempted to, er, straighten his target and next, gave everything a good shove. It was not the worst pain in the world, but it certainly ranks up there with the strangest. Women always like to blather on and on about the difficulty of pushing the head and shoulders of a baby out into the world—"imagine pushing a watermelon out of a hole the size of a quarter." Bullshit. That's supposed to happen. It is a biological norm. However, pushing a tube the wrong way down a tiny one-way hole is not meant to occur. Ever.

They had to leave the catheter in for three days. The first twenty-four hours were the most difficult. Words fail to express the feeling; every movement caused chafing in a place I didn't even know I could feel. It was not comfortable. But after a day, things seemed to work themselves out (or maybe the nurses finally got the tube taped to my thigh tightly enough that it couldn't move around anymore) and I settled into the blissful existence of an infant . . . if said infant were on heavy pain medication and had the ability to complain about his situation.

As I mentioned, I was subjected to the catheter for only a few days, which meant, of course, that at some point they had to take the thing out. I was none too keen on the plan, as I could not imagine how ripping something back out of the aforementioned hole could possibly be even remotely comfortable, but I was anxious to get back to the very male activity of vaguely taking aim in the direction of a toilet, so I relented. Again, the process was not as painful as I expected, but it was very odd. Indescribable, really. But I was safe in the knowledge that I wouldn't have to do it again anytime soon. . . .

Wrong. They had to put it back in.

Warning: the following is quite disgusting. Stop reading if the above was offensive—this will be worse.

The pain "specialists" had come in on my case a few days after my arrival. My reliance on the wonder drug Dilaudid (or, as I liked to call it, heaven) was becoming a concern. It was the only drug that allowed me to sleep, but it is also a highly addictive narcotic. People in the know tell me it is bad to get addicted to drugs. I was all for ending my dependence on Dilaudid, but I could not seem to effectively express that all the Vicodin, morphine, Toradol, and Darvocet was about as effective as Children's Tylenol. The solution was to put me on as many different things as possible and then hope for the best. I probably was not actually on that many drugs; I just remember taking a myriad of different pills and then, if I wanted to get some rest, asking for some Dilaudid. The upshot of all of these various medications was that they are very constipating. (As I noted earlier, it may be time to go read something else.) Five days into my hospital stay, I was not only loopy from the painkillers but couldn't poop either. This eventuality led to another fun little hospital game I like to call Put a Foreign Object in Paul's Ass—also known as Suppository Time. (Fortunately, I was spared the enema bag, but only by about twelve hours.)

One night, post-suppository, I went on what was then a very long walk—probably about fifty yards. When I got back, I figured maybe I had loosened things up enough that I needed to make a seated entry into the bathroom log. So I sat down and had a go. Strange thing, though—I could not urinate. When I finally did force something out, it was little droplets of blood. This concerned me. I called out to my mother and sent her in search of a doctor. The resident on call came and, after some consultation with the bladder sensor, which told him I was full up, decided I needed the Foley treatment once again in order to relieve the pressure in there. I was overjoyed at the prospect. He repeated the catherization . . . to almost no avail. He used a syringe to pump saline in and out with the hopes of breaking something loose, but no real results were had. After some consultation with his sidekick, he decided that he had inserted the Foley catheter incorrectly and would have to take it out and put in a new one. Again, splendid news for me. As he pulled that one out, I felt something give way and called for the bedside jug. Out poured about 500 milliliters of a cranberry-juice-like substance that was somewhere between blood and urine. (I know, this is repulsive.) Unfortunately, the flow abruptly stopped, leaving me still half full according to the bladder sensor. At this point, he scared me a little by saying that my little walk might have shaken something lose in the kidney region, thereby restarting the bleeding. He inserted the second catheter without difficulty and did his pumping move again. His second try worked, and little clots of blood began to flow down the clear tube. It was as beautiful a sight as something so disgusting can be. Relief was at hand.

It turned out that my straining had caused my prostate gland to bleed. How the resulting blood found its way into my bladder I do not know or understand, but things cleared up nicely by morning and the resident's doomsday words were pushed to the back of our minds.

I have used the words *us* and *we* a lot because my mother was intimately (too much so, at least for her own sanity) involved in my stay in the hospital. She flew to Chicago the morning after the injury, with plans to stay as long as I needed her to. Aren't mothers (especially mine) wonderful? It's great that she's here; I don't know how a person would survive a hospital stay without an advocate watching over the situation. I know a reasonable amount about health care because of my mom's nursing background and my own frequent encounters with doctors and trainers, but I would have been totally lost if left to my own devices. I was drugged up and sleep-deprived and in no condition to make decisions about my own future. I could barely choose between the chicken salad sandwich and the meat loaf for lunch, let alone make any decision about what was best for my body. I recommend no trips to the hospital without my mom at one's side.

April 13

The best part of the hospital experience was getting out. The idea of spending nine straight days indoors is claustrophobic in and of itself; doing so without spending more than about half an hour out of a prone position is truly disgusting. When I was finally escorted out of the infirmary, I was amazed by the sights, sounds, and smells of the outside. The sky appears especially bright after staring at the product of fluorescent lighting for more than a week. The smells . . . oh, the smells. After nine days inside a totally antiseptic environment, one's nose is absolutely assaulted with smells from the out-of-doors. I would not really be able to put a label on a particular scent; it was more an onslaught of all the aromas and odors that are a part of our lives on a regular basis without our knowledge. An earthy smell, maybe—just the way the world smells.

That was the hokiest paragraph I've ever written.

To say that I am getting a little stir-crazy would be something of an understatement. My room at the Residence Inn is starting to close in around me. Thankfully, I get to go home soon; then I can close the book on this fiasco.

I neglected to mention that the Bulls did sign me through the end of this season. Prior to my kidney/spleen event, the general manager, John Paxson, told me that he was happy with how I had been playing and would extend my contract through the end of the year. When I found out the extent of my injury, some doubt crept into my brain regarding the team's plan for me. It was apparent that I would not be able to play at any point this season, so the Bulls would have been well within their rights to conveniently forget their promise and not sign me for the remaining four weeks of the season. But Paxson honored his end of the deal. He bucks the NBA trend; he's a stand-up guy and a man of his word. The contract was brought to the hospital, where I signed it as it sat next to my liquid breakfast of Jell-O and juice. Or, at least I think I did. At that point, I literally could not read a line of text; it all swam before my eyes, so for all I know it was an elaborate hoax. I will have to check my bank account frequently to find out if my drug-addled memory is correct.

Along those same lines, I had several visitors during my time in the hospital. I remember none of them. As I mentioned, my mother was around most of the time. She was able to remind me later who had been in my room and what they had said. One of the assistant coaches, Ron Adams, made at least one appearance, and Fred Tedeschi and Eric Waters were constant visitors/caretakers. I really appreciated when the entire team showed . . . ha. No one from the team made a visit, which is not shocking because (1) I had only played with the Bulls for around three weeks and (2) most basketball players are

completely out of tune with the customs/behaviors shared by the rest
of mankind. I did receive a phone call from Antonio Davis, who is
easily one of the classier pros with whom I have spent any time. I, of
course, cannot remember what was said, but it is doubtful that he told
me to die.

My release from the hospital set in motion a very predictable routine. Because of my depleted state during those first few days back in
the world, I was usually only able to muster enough energy for a walk
from my hotel room to my car, at which point my mother would take
me for a drive through the über-wealthy northern suburbs of Chicago.
I was of less use than the family dog—at least it looks cute from time
to time.

When I first got "home" from the hospital, I was faced with quite
an obstacle. My room at the Residence Inn is on the second floor, so I
needed to navigate some stairs in order to get to a bed so that I could
take a nap. It should be remembered that, to that point, a walk of
about a hundred paces was enough to necessitate bed rest for the
next two hours. I, of course, made it up the set of twelve stairs, but I
was struck with the fact that not two weeks earlier I had been playing
in an NBA game but now nearly needed an oxygen tank in order to
successfully conquer a set of stairs on my own.

I finally made it to a Bulls game—my first since the incident, and
our last of the home schedule. It was strikingly boring, just like any NBA
game I have ever witnessed from the standpoint of a non-participant.
I cannot believe that people are willing to pay, and pay handsomely, to
watch such inanity. I really think the only reason some people make
the trip is to root for a particular bagel in the animated race on the
scoreboard screen. That event seems to bring the loudest cheers. I
must admit that it was fun to have total access and complete freedom.
I sat behind the bench, so I was not expected to actively participate in
the up and down of team huddles and other assorted activities. When
I got bored in the third quarter, it was well within my prerogative to go
back into the locker room to rest and see what the trainers were
doing. It was like being invisible. My attendance was by far the most

strenuous activity in which I have participated in the last few weeks, and my body let me know it the next morning. I literally felt as if I had played the night before. This lack of energy is going to seriously hinder any advances I had hoped to make on the home improvement front when I get back to Kansas City.

My doctors convened with me today for a roundtable regarding my progress. It seems that my body is responding as well as could be hoped, with more knowledge to be gained after tomorrow's CT scan. I did have an odd encounter with the main team doctor, Jeff Weinberg, after everyone else had left. He asked me how anxious I was to return to the court. To this point, my return to basketball has been a very ephemeral concept; I thought of it only in the abstract terms of "Well, when I regain the ability to climb a flight of stairs without feeling the need to lie down for half an hour, I will then begin to consider my basketball future." Unfortunately, I have not yet conquered that very impressive feat, so I had not really thought about when I would be able to play again. My only prediction has been, "Sometime this summer." I think this apathy toward a return to the court is born of some degree of disgust for the game—my last experience with basketball resulted in a tremendous amount of pain and the longest stay in the hospital of my young life. In fact, truth be told, at this very moment I have absolutely no need to play basketball ever again. I think I will soon regain the desire; I just do not have it currently.

There is some chance, however small, that I will not play professional basketball again. I would repeat that such is probably not the case, but there is always that chance. With each passing year (and each new freakish injury), the chance that I will quit becomes higher. Last year, it was probably 4 percent. This year, it might be 7 percent. At some point, the odds will be such that I will not play the following year. As far as I can tell, I am still below that 50 percent marker, but I guess I won't know for sure until it actually happens.

So when I told the doctor that I really was not all that juiced about the idea of playing basketball anytime soon, he reacted incredulously: "Well, that surprises me. I thought you would be raring to get back on the court." Hold on there, Chico, let's review my last ten months. Last June, I got back from Spain and took all of ten days off so that I could begin rehabilitating the atrophied right side of my upper body. I finally did a push-up in July and had to work hard just to get back to a level of strength of which I would have previously been completely ashamed in order to go to training camp. At that point, I got cut from an NBA team, headed off on an exhibition tour to have my face permanently rearranged, and returned home only to have to try out for my local minor-league basketball team, with which I traveled all over the desert Southwest in, shall we say, less-than-stellar conditions in order to play games in rec centers and high school gyms. I seriously considered an offer to head back to the scene of my nearly catastrophic nerve injury before deciding to stick it out in the ABA, pinning my hopes on my coach's ability to find me a job in the NBA. Sure, I had a couple weeks of glory. I did get called up and when I did, more than held my own in what were, for the second-worst team in the league, some relatively meaningful minutes—all before being knocked back down to size by a knee to the flank, reducing my activity level to that of a stroke victim. So no, I am not all that excited about getting back on the court. Right now, I want to get out of the goddamn Residence Inn, go home, enjoy the fact that I have two kidneys and one spleen, and relax for a little bit. If that's too much to ask, I'll find another profession.

My return to the court is an issue to the Bulls because the contract I signed while in a hospital bed contains a team option for next year. In my case, Chicago must decide by August 20 of this year whether they will guarantee my salary for next season. This sounds better than it really is. It does allow me to work out with the team for the summer, the benefits of which are slightly negated by the fact that I will be expected to, well, work out with the team for the summer. Again, I should probably be happy about this opportunity, but at this point my tolerance for people telling me what to do is—as was probably evident in the preceding paragraph—severely limited. One of the main reasons the Bulls wanted to sign me to this "deal" is that they will have more trading flexibility. This does not mean that someone would trade for me; I am certainly not that hot a commodity. But if the salaries of a possible trade did not match, I and therefore my salary could be thrown in as filler so that the accounting would work. Under normal circumstances, after working out with the team, I would play in the six-game NBA summer league in Utah, and then wait for a decision on my future in Chicago. The circumstances in which I currently exist are obviously not normal. I have no idea what will happen. But I have to assume that some of it will be terrible and that some of it will be great, with very little in between.

YEAR 3

August 20

After much hope to the contrary, it would appear that I will be staying in Kansas for a while. The Chicago Bulls recently made it very clear that they will not need my basketball prowess in the coming season. Since I'm not sure if my period of employment ended when the season did or if it ends when the team declines to exercise the option on my contract, I don't know whether I am soon to be newly unemployed or if I have been for several months now.

I returned to Chicago for two reasons. First, it was time for what was hoped would be the final CT scan and subsequent doctors' appointments regarding my innards. Second, the magical date on which the Bulls were forced, by the terms of the contract I signed last spring, to decide my fate was rapidly approaching. To paraphrase my contract: if, by August 20, the Chicago Bulls do not waive the undersigned (that's me), the player will be entitled to a guaranteed contract for the 2004–2005 season in the amount of the minimum salary for a player of his experience. To paraphrase further: if I could convince the Bulls to keep me on the payroll, or if I could kidnap GM John Paxson for a few weeks, I would be paid something in the neighborhood of $740,000, guaranteed, for the upcoming season. So obviously, it has been a day I have been anticipating for some time. If I owned a calendar, I might even have circled it . . . and maybe put a cute star next to it.

When I left Chicago in April, I thought there was a good chance that I would be ready for some level of activity by June 1. It was an erroneous assumption. I'm not sure why I was so optimistic—it's not my usual game. Perhaps the living of my life's dream has softened me. When the NBA season ended for the Bulls on April 18 and I flew home to Kansas City in a drug-induced stupor, I could barely do a load of laundry. I'm not sure why I thought I would be running around on tracks and basketball courts a mere six weeks later. (Example #459 supporting the theory that I am not, in fact, a doctor.)

On my original target date, June 1, a CT showed that my kidney and spleen were healed nicely (good news). It also showed that the hematoma, or in layman's terms the mass of blood surrounded by a squishy capsule, that had resulted from my kidney's encounter with Austin Croshere's knee was still about the size of my fist. (Not such good news.) Of course, my fist is not really all that big. However, the process of natural selection in humans did not result in enough extra space within our body cavities for an object the size of my fist to simply hang out somewhere near my left kidney. The extra material I was carrying around prevented other pieces of matter from occupying their normal environs, leaving them vulnerable to injury by way of the jarring and jostling that an oversized person such as myself would undergo during strenuous exercise.

I was allowed to start riding a stationary bike. Splendid.

A mid-July CT showed that the hematoma had shrunk to the size of an egg. The doctor in Kansas City recommended that I continue life without running but was overruled by the Bulls' team doctor, who said, "What the hell, let's give it a shot." Which, really, is exactly the level of confidence one wants to hear from the doctor to whom one has entrusted the care of one's basketball career. But run I did. The first day was a little rough—I survived six hundred yards on the track before retreating to my bedroom to consider the feasibility of a career in farm implement sales.

Some good has come out of this otherwise wasted summer. (Wasted from a basketball perspective. I did get a pretty nice tan. For me. I'm more a dark white than anything.) Scott Wedman has done wonders for my shooting. Since I couldn't do much more than lift a basketball over my head early in the summer, I hit upon the idea of using the ample time for good instead of evil. Because I had enjoyed our time together with the Kansas City Knights, I called Coach Wedman to ask if he would be interested in completely revamping my shot. For whatever reason, he was actually enthusiastic about the idea, and so for as long as I wanted on almost any day I chose, I had my very own Mr. Miyagi to help me create the perfect basketball shooting form. We deconstructed my entire routine. I started with hours of form shooting, wherein I would do little more than stand three feet from the basket and concentrate on the simplest parts of a basketball shot.

It should not be lost that my teacher was arguably one of the best shooters in the NBA in the late seventies and early eighties. Consequently, I was willing to listen. I'm glad I did. Not only is my shooting form about 247 percent better, my general attitude toward basketball has improved. Wedman is a calm soul, a far cry from some of the coaches of questionable sanity I have had over the years. His ease with life meshed nicely with my own neurosis. As much as I hate to admit it, his New Age, relax-at-all-costs philosophy has rubbed off on me. I have an entirely new approach to the game of basketball.

We're still working on my approach to life.

Now that we are all caught up, we can examine the situation at hand.

I have known for about two weeks, via my agent's suspicions, that my release from the Bulls was imminent. When I called the secretaries in Chicago to have them reserve a flight for my trip back to the Windy City for my doctors' appointments, I got further confirmation. I could tell by the woman's voice that she was not too sure she was supposed to do such things for a lame-duck basketball player. I was forced to wait a day so that she could confirm with the GM that it was acceptable for them to pay for my flight. (I was, after all, following up with their team doctor on an injury that had occurred while I was playing for the team. I wasn't going back because I missed Chicago's unique combination of gridlocked traffic and horrid weather.) Among the people I called upon my arrival in Chicago was the assistant trainer for the Bulls. In our conversation, I made a remark about my impending joblessness and he replied, "Oh, so you know, then." I knew, yes, but was not aware that everyone else around the organization was privy to the information. There's nothing like existing as a joke.

On the morning of my CT in Chicago, I dutifully got up early and drank the barium cocktail of which I have grown so fond. (I swear the taste gets worse with each successive scan. As these things always go, someone in the manufacturing process was probably charged with improving the flavor, but only succeeded in making it so sickly sweet that it is likely worse than the original.) Whereas in Kansas City it would have taken a week to learn my results, here in Chicago, with the impetus of the Bulls behind me, my results were given to me in minutes. The good news was that my friend the hematoma has shrunk to the size of a Ping-Pong ball. The doctor on hand, one of the original battery of physicians assigned to my case, pronounced me fit for any activity except bungee jumping with the cord tied directly around my kidneys.

After my morning o' fun, I headed back to the Bulls' training facility, where I met with the general manager of the Bulls, John Paxson. He was very cordial, as general managers always are, and informed me politely that the team would be releasing me. He said that "guaranteeing me" would limit their roster space too much and so I had to go. He mentioned that he would love to see me in the Bulls' training camp but that he did not know exactly what the roster situation would be when that time came around. I told him that I was not sure I would be able to come to training camp for free because my previous attempts at such (Los Angeles, Atlanta, et al.) had not worked out particularly well. He said that he would see how the salary situation played out and let me know.

After my formal esteem-bashing, I was invited to the house of one of the Bulls' assistant coaches for dinner. We had become friends while I played for the team in the spring. Over some fine food with his family, we discussed my future plans. He encouraged me to stay in Chicago in order to utilize the facilities available, with the intent of attending training camp and competing for a roster spot. I told him that I could not really imagine making that decision after being, in essence, fired by the team that very day. He said I should not be so prideful, that I am young and it is too early in my life to be bitter.

But let's be honest. John Paxson told me the same thing that every other GM in the process of releasing me said, and at this point there have been a few. He said, without saying it, that I am not good enough for the Bulls to pay me to play basketball. He glossed over it, but that's what GMs do. They're like CEOs—they make vanilla statements. They want to soften the blow. They are humans, and like every other human, they don't want to be perceived as mean. So they say things like, "We really like the way you play—we just don't have any roster spots available." Which, again, is true, but it isn't the whole story. The statement should read, "We really like the way you play— we just don't have any roster spots available because we gave them to other players who we think are better than you." The process is like that of a breakup. It is much easier to say, "This isn't going to work out" instead of "This isn't going to work out because there must be someone out there I like more than you."

September 22

This fall, like every other since my college days came to an end, has been one filled with uncertainty regarding my basketball future. Each week has brought with it a new option or rumor; it has been exhausting. The people closest to me probably think I have been going about a deliberate misinformation campaign because my answer to the dreaded question "Well, Paul, where are you going to play this year?" changes on a nearly daily basis. Over the last two months, I have probably spoken to Keith Glass a hundred times. (And to think that a year and a half ago I believed I could get by without a cellular phone. Maybe by next year I'll have multiple phones like some of my teammates.) Keith started in on my year's basketball plans before I could even really play basketball again; he was throwing out possibilities even before I had been cleared to break into something more strenuous than a jog.

The scrambling my thorax took certainly forced us to rethink my summer. (I use the word *us* instead of *me* a lot when referencing my choice of basketball destiny—I seem to think of my agent and me as an inexorably linked pair, especially if I am discussing decision making, as in "We don't know what we're going to do" or "The team wants us to decide before Tuesday." It is a bit like having a multiple-personality disorder. In fact, maybe I do have one of those. That would explain the calls from the lady with the Jamaican accent looking for the goat heads I supposedly took.) (There I go again, making my parenthetical statements into parenthetical paragraphs. Attempting to read this must be like trying to read something in another language. I'll start over.)

If I hadn't been injured, I would have played in the NBA's summer league for young players and free agents with the Bulls. If that had gone well, the Bulls might have kept me on for the year. At any rate, other teams, both domestic and foreign, would have seen me play and, potentially, would have developed some interest. Since I had just graduated to brisk walking about the time of the summer league, however, our plan for basketball world domination was shot to hell. So Keith was forced to sell me without having a test-drivable floor model at his disposal. Fortunately, while I am by no means a household name in the basketball world, those in the know have a vague idea who I am and what I have done and, since I have not yet assaulted a team-mate or blown up a coach's house (although both would have been justified on an occasion or two), basketball teams do still want me to play for them.

I used to think that Keith did a great job of not telling me about possible job opportunities until they actually turned into formal of-fers. In fact, his relative silence might have been more meaningful than I realized. It could be that those were the only things he had to discuss with me. It seems that he now tells me about all sorts of out-landish possibilities before they are even remotely viable. In a way that is nice; I have some time to wrap my mind around the concept of traveling to some faraway place to live for a year, as opposed to the more harried way, which usually involves the words *decision* and *to-morrow*. Two of this year's early possibilities were a team in Spain and one in St. Petersburg, Russia. I think the Spanish team made an actual offer, but it was not in the price range befitting a basketball player of my ability and pedigree. (What an arrogant ass I can be. Mostly it was in a small town far from anywhere I would want to live.) However, I was intrigued by the idea of living in St. Petersburg. I have always wanted to play in Russia, which makes no sense, I realize. It is cold there and it has only been about fifteen years since they were hoisting flags bearing the letters *CCCP.* But I think it would be interesting. Keith met with the guy representing the team while the rep was observing the summer league in which I was supposed to be playing and said that he thought there was about a 60 percent chance the team would make an offer. They never did.

There are probably several reasons for the discrepancies between what Keith and I believe might happen and what actually does happen. The most important is the telephone effect. Much like the game of Telephone that we all played back in our post-potty-training days, the actual meaning gets distorted along the way (and back then I doubt any of us was translating from Russian to English). My guess is that it goes something like this:

Russian general manager to team official B (via the author attempting a bad Russian accent on the printed page): This Paul Shirley, he play for Chicago Bulls. He is good?

Team official B to Russian agent: You find out if Paul Shirley good enough to play for our team.

Russian agent to American pseudo-intermediary who happens to speak both languages: Team inquires about Paul Shirley for next season.

Psudeo-intermediary to Keith: I think a team in St. Petersburg might be interested in Paul for next year. They probably have about Y number of dollars to spend.

Keith to me: A team in St. Petersburg is interested. I think there is a 60 percent chance they will make you an offer for Y number of dollars in the next few days.

And so I find St. Petersburg on the map and wonder whether it is tolerable in February. Meanwhile, the Russian GM forgot he ever mentioned my name in some vodka-induced haze and has moved on to worrying about where he will take his steam baths next year.

So, let us get down to the sequence of events that has led to my next destination. (Believe it or not, there actually is a destination. Or at least I think so.)

A rather serious offer from Greece came my way about three weeks ago. A team called Aris, which is in Thessaloniki, which doesn't really matter, offered a three-year contract that would be contingent upon the team securing me a European passport—a Polish one. Taken at face value, that sentence would seem to be one that would come out of a crazy person's mouth, but from a basketball standpoint it makes sense. Receiving a European passport would be a very positive development in my basketball career. Each European team is allowed only two Americans, so being "European" increases one's versatility from a personnel standpoint, and thus usually increases one's salary. I was not thrilled with the prospect of a return to Greece, but in the long term a passport would be a very big deal. The financial terms were a bit worrisome, considering the raping I took the first time I was in Greece. The contract was backloaded: I would have made $120,000 the first year, $180,000 the second, and $240,000 the third, which implied that they wanted to see how I did before they actually shelled out any money. (Read: if things didn't go well the first year, a mysterious loophole voiding the contract would be found.) The contract would have allowed for an NBA buyout after each year, so if a team in the States wanted to retain my services, they could, for a steep fee. We kicked the idea around for a while and Keith renegotiated the first two years of the deal to an average of $160,000, but I was put off by the long-term commitment and turned it down. Since the longest relationship of my life to date lasted a whopping five months, it would appear that committing myself to three years of anything goes against my philosophy. I'm not even sure I'll want to play basketball in three years. I could decide that supporting a rampant heroin habit would be easier to do on a regular paycheck and give up this rat race.

At the same time as the Aris deal, another offer came in from Greece. (I must have done something right while I was there. Or they know a sucker when they see one.) This was a no-brainer. Decent team, bad town, money at about $150,000, no passport. No thanks.

After the orgy of Greek interest, the planning of my future, at least for this year, cooled for a week or so—which meant that I spoke to Keith once daily instead of once hourly. Then all hell broke loose. A team from Poland supposedly had interest, enough that Keith thought it would soon be an option. They did not make a formal offer, but wondered whether I would accept a one-year deal worth about $200,000. Often teams will ask whether I will sign for a certain amount without actually making an offer. It is a way to save face. It is comparable to asking a girl, "If I were to ask you out, would you say yes?"—that is, a little childish. I don't know what they have to lose by making an actual offer. Maybe ridicule at the hands of their fellow team officials. "Ooh, Paul Shirley turned you down, huh? You guys must really be in trouble. Maybe you should consider plastic surgery and some breast implants."

Keith was not all that excited about Poland, but I was verily intrigued, mainly because I am odd. The team in question plays in the Euroleague, which is the top international competition in Europe. By comparison, both teams for which I have played in Europe, in addition to their domestic competitions, played in a league just below the Euroleague. A team's Euroleague participation makes a roster spot very attractive to a player—it adds instant credibility to one's resume.

While we were kicking around the idea of going to Poland, a friend of mine from Greece called. He now works for Olympiacos, one of the top two teams in the country. We have stayed in touch since my time in Athens, so I was not surprised to hear from him. But when we spoke, he asked if I had any interest in playing for Olympiacos. The team's management was starting to make decisions for the year, and my name had been thrown around. I told him I would be very interested in playing for the team (another Euroleague team, only in a city I know I can tolerate). He said they would not be making any decisions anytime soon, so he would get back to me in a few days. He called back in five minutes with the authority to offer a contract worth $200,000 for one year. I told him I would have to talk to Keith and think it over for a while. He replied that there was not much time, that they probably needed a decision in a few days. Ah, the Greeks . . .

Keith called his Polish contact and told him that I would sign for $300,000. The contact reported back that the team was going to ask the sponsors for the money and would know the next day by 2 P.M. Coincidentally, the Greeks said that they were going to need to know at almost exactly the same time, which I immediately discounted, since that is the sort of thing Greeks always say.

When our vague 2 P.M. deadline rolled around, Keith had not heard from his Polish contact. By comparison, Olympiacos had called him six times that day. In their final call, the Greeks got impatient. They said they needed to know within thirty minutes or they would have to move on and find another player. Keith in turn asked them to confirm that my contract would have a clause guaranteeing my payment, with language to the effect that if the team was late with payment by thirty days, my obligation to the club would cease, with them owing me the balance of my contract. They would not agree to this clause, causing the following thought to streak through my brain: *That's strange. They know I'm leery of a return to Greece. They say they'll pay me but are afraid to put it in writing.*

I told them no. Keith was on board for the rejection and told the Greeks. He called me back within ten minutes to say that the team had relented and would put the clause guaranteeing my payment in the contract. Sounded reliable to me.

When I turned down the job in Greece, I thought that the Polish deal was still a possibility. Not so. Keith's contact in Poland never heard of any further progress; last he knew they were hoping to drum up $280,000, which would have been plenty to get me on a plane to Gdansk, but that was the last we heard from that outpost.

At the same time that we were dealing with potential European destinations, Keith told me that interest from NBA teams was rising. Of course, it wasn't monetary interest as much as it was volunteer-work interest, but it was interest all the same. He had received calls from Portland, Phoenix, and San Antonio. (I have glossed over our dealings with Chicago at this point. Suffice it to say that my hunch was correct. The team would have allowed me to come to training camp, but the fact that they have eighteen guys under guaranteed contract for fifteen spots and that they are completely apathetic toward my abilities would imply that they have very little interest in paying me to play basketball anytime this year. And I held them in such high regard at one time. So sad.) Keith then told me that I would probably go to Phoenix to work out sometime the next week.

Phoenix quickly lost interest, saying that they already had a player like me in my alma mater's Jackson Vroman. We never really heard back from San Antonio. Portland invited me to training camp while having fifteen players under contract, but I was assured that their master plan called for them to trade two players soon, conceivably opening a spot for a player like me. Cleveland entered the mix—one of the people who had liked me back when I was annually playing summer league with the Cavaliers had ascended to a level of some power—and they invited me to training camp. Their situation looked good, as they had only twelve players on guaranteed deals, but their interest in me seemed lukewarm at best.

So it briefly appeared that I would go to training camp with either the Portland Trail Blazers or the Cleveland Cavaliers. I spoke to both teams myself and got a better reaction from Portland. I told Keith about my conversations. He said, "Okay, let's go to Portland." (See, the multiple-personality thing works both ways.) He told me he would call the GM and get it done. Again—this is becoming a theme—he called back within ten minutes. "I don't like it," he said. "He gave me only 20 percent odds that they would actually make a trade that would help you. You're not going to Portland."

The most recent events, as reported to me by Keith: Cleveland called to disinvite me to training camp, at which point Keith panicked and called Olympiacos in Greece to see if that team remained interested (they had upped their offer to a two-year deal worth about $470,000 total, with a Czech passport thrown in). He considered backsliding to Portland but instead called Chicago to see if I could find a home there, if only as a way station. While he was on the phone, Coach Scott Skiles happened to mention that a different player in whom the Bulls had been interested had mentioned that he was going to receive guaranteed money (a token amount to show commitment to a player) to go to training camp with Phoenix because the afore-mentioned Jackson Vroman had recently broken his hand. In a tizzy, Keith called Phoenix to ask why they hadn't called him. They apologized and said that they were again interested in me but had just not gotten around to calling about my services. They then said they assumed he would want some guaranteed money for me in order to get me to go to training camp there. Keith said, "Of course we do"—even though I actually had zero training camp invites on the board. The Suns offered $15,000. Keith asked for $25,000, but they called back and said their final offer was the same—$15,000, which we were going to accept all along.

And so as of right now, this instant, I will go to training camp with the Phoenix Suns with my first-ever NBA-guaranteed money. It is not much, but it's a start. And it could change by tomorrow.

October 3

By now, the reader may have gleaned that I get illogically uptight when I am about to embark upon another of my basketball adventures. Because I cannot seem to endear myself to one particular team enough that they would want to keep me around for any significant period of time, I am faced with new frontiers entirely too often. After some thought, I have come to the conclusion that my anxiety about each new situation has less to do with the basketball aspect of the thing and more to do with some sort of fear of relocation.

I made my trip to Phoenix several days ago so I could begin to acclimate the team to my basketball stylings. The trip itself was relatively uneventful, except for some luggage issues in Kansas City. It turned out that my enormous bag was eleven pounds over America West regulations. I had only one bag, so the nice homo (I write that not as an insult but as a descriptive noun, as he was quite gay) at the ticket counter suggested that I find a gift shop and pick out one of the bags they had on sale—spending $15 for a crappy satchel would be cheaper than paying the $50 overage for my obese piece of luggage. I have learned to do all I can to avoid raising my own blood pressure at airports, so instead of debating with my new friend the logic of the fact that my bags' combined weight would continue to be sixty-one pounds, and unless America West Airlines is that concerned about the health of its employees' spines that it is actually trying to minimize the weight of each individual bag to save on herniated disks, changing the distribution of my clothes would still result in me contributing the same weight to the payload of the plane, I marched over to the gift shop. He was right—bags were half off, and while it hurt my pride a bit to see "Ladies' Hnbg—$14.99" go across the display on the cash register, my savings of $35 helped salve the wound. And I got a kick-ass African-themed tan-and-brown bag out of the deal.

I spent my first two days in Phoenix working out under the guidance of the assistant coaches and played in a few hours' worth of pickup games with the team. My workouts went well. After the second day, I had an odd encounter with one of my teammates in the shower. (Always a good way to start a story, eh?) He asked about my basketball past, and we made general professional basketball player small talk. I asked about his history, even though I already knew the answers. (He is a bit more well known than I, but there was no reason to give him the satisfaction.) About the time I was gathering up the courage to ask him about his gigantic penis, he noted that when he had first seen me walking into the locker room, he had not thought I was a basketball player. "I just thought you were some dude." (Which makes sense; six-foot-ten guys who are not basketball players wander into NBA locker rooms all the time.) He added, "But you can play, man, so now I know." All a part of my grassroots campaign. Earning respect, one gigantic black guy at a time. And barely avoiding embarrassing genitalia questions along the way.

Other than two strong workout days, I have not done much that has been affiliated with the Phoenix Suns. Most of the players—the ones who know they have a long season ahead—took the end of the week and the weekend off. I pieced together some workouts in their off time. Be prepared, and all that.

Training camp is in Flagstaff, Arizona. I am told that Flagstaff is located at an elevation of 7,000 feet. We played at the University of Colorado in Boulder each of my four years of college. Boulder is located at an elevation of just over 5,200 feet. I thought I was going to die each time we played at Colorado. Seven thousand is greater than 5,200. I hope they have oxygen masks available.

October 10

When I get tired, my demeanor changes greatly. It would be difficult to describe me as happy-go-lucky under the best of circumstances, but I like to think I keep myself in a laid-back state of mind whenever possible. Right now, however, a description of my general emotional and mental status would definitely not involve the term *laid-back*. Exhausted? Yes. Slightly unstable? That too. But *laid-back* is unquestionably a no. Therefore, I must be tired.

Early in the week, we left Phoenix for training camp in Flagstaff after an afternoon of meat-market physicals wherein each player was given a checklist that listed nine different medical departments—including dental, orthopedic, and vision—and was told to visit a new room for each and, in the process, complete his sheet of paper. It felt like we had been dumped off a bus at Ft. Sill in 1967. Evidently, the assembly-line approach does not lead to the most in-depth physical examination—the subject of my kidney/spleen injury, easily the most severe career hiccup anyone in the room could possibly have presented, was mentioned exactly once, and that was by the team dentist. He asked, "Oh, are you the guy who had that crazy injury in Chicago? That sounded like quite a deal. Open your mouth and let me have a look at those teeth." It is reassuring to know that I am in such good hands.

As I lugged my bags into my hotel room in Flagstaff, one of my teammates walked past my open door while searching for his domicile. When I looked up, I noticed that it was Quentin Richardson, with a girl—his fiancée, as it turned out. Quentin Richardson is engaged to the singer Brandy. This turn of events angered me a bit, mainly because nobody told me that I could have brought the bovine-eyed, mediocre pop singer I am dating to training camp.

I think it's clear by now that if I were not an athlete by the nature of my DNA, I would probably despise athletes in general—not because they are necessarily bad people or are particularly unfriendly, but because they are so one-dimensional. That being said, Phoenix has on its roster a couple of guys I can tolerate, and one who I think would be a good friend if I were to, say, actually be on the team more than three weeks. I recently ate two meals in the same day with both the player with friend potential, whom I will call Casey, and one from the former category (those I can, at most, tolerate), Frank. At lunch, after our salad was served, Frank actually said, "Hey, guys, let's say grace." (Begin inner monologue.) *What the hell? Did that really happen? Will I survive this without laughing?* Fortunately, the two of them already had their heads bowed, so neither could see my grimace/smile.

As I reflected on their lunchtime behavior, I ran some possible scenarios through my mind. For example, what if I said, *Hey, guys, my religion requires that I sing the first two minutes of "Woolly Bully" before dining. So could you sit there in silence while I publicly express my beliefs?* That wouldn't be kosher. So neither is asking me to sit there quietly while grace is said. It happened again at dinner, which verified that I had a genuine zealot on my hands. But now on to the real problem. Casey and Frank have played together for two years in Phoenix and, I gather, are good friends. Now, even though I wanted to make some kind of remark about Preacherman to Casey, I had to bottle it because he has known me for approximately six days. His loyalty lies with John the Baptist. But I cannot be expected to maintain radio silence under such circumstances. Eventually I will explode under the pressure of too many unsaid cynical remarks.

In other unintentional-comedy news, I bore witness to a little locker room skirmish after one of our recent practices. Each of the Northern Arizona University basketball lockers is equipped with an accompanying stool for the sitting pleasure of the user, except for three of the lockers, which had low-slung, soft chairs in front of them. The players who had been given lockers with the more comfortable seating situation—coincidentally, the stars of the team—became very attached to their chairs. When the chair of a player I will call John mysteriously disappeared one day, he found reprisal in stealing the nice chair from one of his fellow luxury-accustomed comrades—let's call him Andy. This did not sit well with Andy. When he arrived on the scene to discover that his chair was gone, he took exception with John, who he knew had taken this chair. Heated words were exchanged, the gist of which was that the situation was not acceptable, that just because John's chair had been taken by someone else, it was not okay for John to take Andy's chair. John laughed off the comments as absurd and told Andy, "If you want your chair back, go find mine." The rest of us were chuckling; we saw the absurdity of the situation. But we could tell that a Pakistan-versus-India level of confrontation was brewing. Both players knew that the rest of the locker room was watching and so were unlikely to back down. Andy stalked off, saying that it was better for him to leave before he lost his temper. He returned after a brief absence with what I could see from my close proximity was a glint in his eye that implied that the amount of time he had spent elsewhere had not been sufficient to calm him down. He asked John if he was going to return his chair. When John declined to appease him, Andy began to threaten John with bodily harm. This got a rise, literally, out of John, as he stood from his upholstered paradise to protect his pride. Some of the bystanders recognized the potential for disaster and got between the two potential combatants, which seemed only to exacerbate the situation. (I was not a member of the intervention—I was interested to see how far they would push the envelope.) The verbal war continued, and as the volume with which each insult was delivered increased, its coherency, oddly enough, decreased. Then Andy, feeling that his pride was going to be damaged irrevocably if he did not take immediate action, lashed out and threw a punch at John. His blow did not find its intended mark, glancing harmlessly off John's shoulder. What followed was both predictable and boring. Players rushed to break up the impending fight. Before long, it was merely a funny story at dinner. However, I no longer had any desire for one of the soft chairs and may never again.

As I mentioned, I am pretty damned tired. We have had five days in a row of two-a-days (there's something wrong with that). I am spent. I have actually played quite well, especially early on, but my body seems to be at the end of its proverbial rope. I cannot seem to catch my breath, all references to the altitude aside. The time between practices does not seem to be enough for any real recovery. I think it may have something to do with the late jump I had on getting ready for the year; I really had to condense my training into a shorter period than normal, and that may be haunting me now. However, two-a-days are finally over; I hope a return to a less sadistic schedule (and a friendlier altitude) will be kind to my personage. If not, a precipitous decline in my basketball performance could be around the corner.

October 12

I count on hotel restaurants to provide me with somewhat bland but generally tolerable nourishment for many of my meals—too many, probably. It has been a source of disappointment to learn that the quality of the food at my current place of "residence" is sub-par, to put it entirely too nicely. (I think the final straw was finding that the sausage on the pizza was cut-up pieces of the morning breakfast buffet's links.) Because of this shoddy food, I am willing to go far afield, even without transportation, in search of a decent meal. Recently, I set out on what I knew from a previous experience to be a half-mile walk to eat at a restaurant I had earlier found to be to my liking. After enjoying a nice chicken Bolognese at Valenzi's, I bid adieu to my newly acquired friend, the Suns-loving Greek who runs the place, and hurried to a nearby Walgreen's to pick up some foodstuffs for my hotel room. I was in a rush to get back to my room, so I wasted no time in picking out some Frosted Mini-Wheats, milk, and bottled water (I'm not sure what that weird taste in the hotel's tap water is, but it's not something good). I paid for my goods, attempted to dodge the personal space of the antihistamine- and Kleenex-toting germ carrier behind me in line, and rushed out the door for the half-mile trek back to the Hilton Suites. As I started my walk, I could tell that my decision to buy both a gallon of milk and a similar quantity of water was going to be hard on the trapezius muscles during the hike home. With this in mind, I was in no mood to respond when hailed by a random stranger behind me on the sidewalk. But he persisted, and because he was wearing slacks and a dress shirt and not sweatpants and a ragged-out Garfield tee, I asked him what he wanted. I'll let the dialogue take over:

Stranger: Hey, I'm not a lunatic or anything, I just wanted to ask you a question.
Me: Yeah, what's that?
Stranger: Well, I will avoid the obvious and not ask you if you play basketball because you're so tall. Do you play professionally or something?

At this point I could tell that this person was obviously not a man of his word, as he had contradicted himself completely. His nervous manner was starting to concern me. Also, I was becoming more aware of the fact that I was alone on a dark street speaking to a random man in a city about which I knew very little.

Me: Actually, I do. I play for the Suns right now.
Stranger: The Phoenix Suns?
Me: Yep.

I decided that I was dealing with a well-dressed hustler. I thought he would soon make some sort of outlandish claim—that he was stuck in Phoenix and needed only six additional dollars to get his car fixed so that he could drive back to Tucson. Unfortunately, what followed was nothing so simple.

Stranger: Okay, well, I have a question for you, but I'm not sure how to ask it. I don't know you, so I don't know if you are a religious person . . .

Me: I'm not.

I thought this simple response would be sufficient to prevent the impending Bible talk. Again I was incorrect, not in judging the effectiveness of my preemptive strike but in guessing the next tack of the questioning.

Stranger: See, I'm only about five-four, and you're, what . . . ?

Me: Six-ten.

Stranger: Right, right. Well, what I want to know is . . . because you are so tall, does that mean that, you know, proportionally, you also have a really long penis?

Stop the presses. Reset all clocks. Fade to white.

I managed to sputter out, "Uh, I don't think it works like that," before walking off at an exceedingly brisk clip. I was so completely and utterly taken aback by the hairpin curve our conversation had taken that I was not able to muster anything other than shock. I did not register anger, fear, or outrage. Only confusion and surprise.

Because I had a long, lonely walk to consider the above encounter, I was able to come to some conclusions about the situation. First, I decided that it is completely ridiculous that at no point in my life was I given the tools needed to deal with such a situation. Well, maybe I was, actually. How appropriate that don't-talk-to-strangers rule turned out to be. Second—and this is the only possible explanation I can find—I think I was perhaps being hit on by a homosexual. I don't have a lot of evidence to back up my claim . . . wait, yes I do— the man asked me about the nature of my genitalia on the street. He also had a wicked lisp, and while I realize that "Paul, just because they talk like they're gay doesn't mean they are," my experience tells me to stick with my instincts. Of course, there are exceptions to every stereotype. If an Indian (dots, not feathers) shows up in electrical engineering class, it is possible that he is a stone-cold moron. However, it is more likely that he is going to blow away the curve. If a person talks like he is gay and asks dudes about their private parts, it is possible that he likes girls. It is not, however, likely.

October 21

If I were reading this, I would have a hard time finding much pity for me. But damn, this life in limbo is no fun at all. (Yes, I know. Same song, forty-third verse.) Every time I see a coach or management type headed in my direction, I wonder if that day will be my last with the Phoenix Suns. This level of anxiety goes against everything I have set out to accomplish here, and it is totally counterproductive . . . but it comes too easily.

When I set out on this particular venture, I had a great go-to-hell attitude working. I knew that, whatever the outcome of training camp, I would pocket $15,000 and would be exposed to a new set of decision makers—good for background work down the road. Not to mention that I would have a chance to play myself back into shape after a summer that was, for reasons outside my control, less than productive. I think my basketball ability benefited greatly from my approach. I've played loosely; the results have been great. I have impressed people to the point that a roster spot with the Suns is very much a possibility. But now that I have made it this far, my mental state has tightened—and it shows on the court. I suppose this would be considered normal. Anytime one gets close to a particular objective, it is only natural to become slightly anxious about the possible result.

However, in my case, this makes little sense. I have been through this rigamarole before, so what's the use in panicking? And it remains that the worst-case scenario involves an extra $15K for me. As of now, I am resolving to once again let go a little more. I truly have nothing to lose. As my father always says, in a hundred years no one is going to remember anyway. So tomorrow it's back to playing with a little more joy and a little less control.

Okay, enough of all that self-affirmation BS.

After practice today we had a meeting entitled "The Business of Basketball." Prior to the gathering, the former sole owner of the Suns, Jerry Colangelo, described the purpose of the meeting as a chance for us players to learn more about the intricacies of the business side of the game of basketball. I was intrigued, as I thought I would be exposed to some of the finer points of salary-cap management or the ins and outs of the collective bargaining agreement between the players and owners. The actual topics disappointed. Our engagement began with a video that laid out, in detail, why it was important for us to each be "nice guys" in the community. It was explained to us why the ten public appearances required yearly of each player by the NBA should be viewed not as obligations but as opportunities: "Your life after basketball is much longer than your life during basketball, so you should always be on the lookout for possible contacts. You never know which of the people you meet out in the world today is going to be on the other side of the door you are knocking on tomorrow." Jesus F. Christ. If a basketball player has not figured out that he ought to be nice to some people now so that they might help him later, he is not going to be swayed by some badly done video featuring George Gervin. More important, if my name is Alphonso Basketballplayer and I am making $6 million a year for the next four years, I could give a good goddamn about future business contacts. The only business contacts I need are those of a good accountant and a financial planner with an IQ slightly above 105.

The meeting continued with the new principal owner of the Suns outlining for us his path to wealth. (I have seen a lot of insecurity in my time; his would rank near the top.) He is a banking and real estate investor and his journey to country clubdom began with a modest financial gift he received from his mother at age twenty-two. She gave him $150,000 . . . which would be a decent start. The main topic of his presentation was that he is the smartest man alive because he managed to invest wisely and has accrued some cash based on his wise decisions. He claimed that the money he invested has returned an average of 40 percent annually because of the good management policies of the bank with which he is associated. (It was never really clear in what capacity he exists with said bank.) He next gave a little math lesson, telling us that the average bank makes a 15 percent yearly return. If he had gained at that rate for the last twenty years, he noted, he would have accumulated a measly $3 million at this point. He then quizzed several players as to what they thought $150,000 invested at 40 percent for twenty years would now be. The guesses, by some people who obviously missed compounding interest day in middle school math, were the ridiculously low figures of $11 million, $12 million, and $14 million. As I was furiously calculating in my head, in the hopes that I could destroy the punch line of this impressive-to-fifteen-year-olds speech if called upon to do so, he announced that the figure was actually $125 million. When the applause and calls of, "You're such a badass, Mr. Owner-guy!" died down, he continued . . . with no conclusion at all except that he is a very rich individual who now owns a large part of the Phoenix Suns. The moral of this story is that an hour of my life was wasted, never to return.

I suppose I should mention some basketball-related information. We have played four preseason games to this point. I have played exactly zero meaningful minutes, but we are rather good, so garbage time has come frequently. In our first game, I played about nine minutes and managed to squeeze off seven shots, scoring six points. I actually played quite well, and there was much joy in all the land. My next blowout time got a little hairy, as we allowed Seattle back in the game in the last couple of minutes and had to stave off their furious rally. It was fun, though; I actually felt like I was playing in a real basketball game. I did not make an appearance in a game in San Antonio, information that would have been useful the day before when I was trying to decide between a quiet night in my hotel bed and a evening of eight balls and strippers. In our most recent game against Utah—which we won by a cool forty-one points—I again got to play out the last nine minutes of the game. I was not able to shoot the ball with quite as much frequency, but did score four points. (By the way, it is not lost on me how insignificant all of this is—back to my not-going-to-matter-in-a-hundred-years comment. I scored four points in a damned preseason game. Yippee. But at the time, it seems so important.) We have four preseason games to go. By this time next week, I should know my fate with the Suns.

November 1

After practice today, I was forced to fend off congratulations from reporters, of all people. I will be on the opening-day roster of the Phoenix Suns—certainly an existence worthy of best wishes. A few of the journalists who follow the day-to-day business of the Suns have taken a liking to me and my relatively stereotypical long-shot-does-good story. Because they have seen me dealing with the ups and downs of this life on the brink on almost a daily basis, I think they were genuinely happy to see me make the team. I had to temper their enthusiasm, however, because—as is usually the case in my basketball career—my triumph would be short-lived.

When the Suns' management invited me to training camp, they didn't think I would make the team. Fortunately, I was able to change my odds by playing very well for the last month. About a week ago, I was told that everyone was extremely happy with the way things had gone, that the coaches loved having me on the floor and that the players enjoyed having me around. Along with this news was a caveat, as always. I was informed that the chances of my time in Phoenix being extended past the preseason were highly dependent on them succeeding in making some roster moves in order to save some money. My source told me that I still had a good chance to make the team absent any personnel moves. But a transaction or two would increase my chances.

Last week, our third point guard, Howard Eisley, disappeared in the middle of a mini road swing to California. I knew that his contract was a point of contention with management, and lack of playing time was a point of contention with him. I also knew that his contract situation was one of the main ones about which my informant had spoken, so I was very curious about his whereabouts. After some sleuthing, I learned that both sides had finally agreed to a buyout of the two remaining years of Eisley's contract. He was set to make either $13 million or $14 million for the next two years—ridiculous numbers for a backup to the backup, even by NBA standards. After some arm-twisting, Howard agreed to take an amount reported to be upwards of $10 million to do nothing. He is now a free agent and, in addition to the money being paid him by the Suns, can sign with another team. (Eisley is actually a pretty good guy. I genuinely liked him but am still a little baffled why it took so long for him to agree to a buyout of any kind. I can imagine the conversation: *So you're saying that you'll pay me $10 million and all I have to do in return is* not *play for your team. I'm really going to have to give that some thought. . . .*) At any rate, the transaction freed a roster spot, along with, theoretically, some money that could certainly be used to pay my salary. My future looked brighter.

This weekend I was told that no real decision had been made regarding my fate with the team. However, I learned that I would be kept around at least through the first game, mainly because it would not cost them anything to do so. The team had guaranteed me $15,000 to come to camp. During the preseason a team gives its players an advance of sorts—$1,500 a week of walking-around money. Four weeks times $1,500 equals . . . the Suns have paid me $6,000, leaving $9,000 owed. During the actual season, which starts either today (November 1) or tomorrow, the team pays non-guaranteed players like myself by the day until a date in January, at which point the remainder of the player's salary is guaranteed if the player is still on the team. My minimum salary, based on the number of years I have "played" in the NBA, is something like $720,000. Divided by 180 days, the length of time over which the salary is paid, that comes to $4,000 per day. Which means that the Suns can keep me around for about two and a quarter days without having to commit to paying me anything more. I was told that while the coaching staff would like to keep me, if the management could not make another money-saving move (read: trade a certain player, who will remain nameless, and receive only future draft picks or cash in return), I would be sent home after my two- or three-day regular-season stay.

Note: $4,000 a day in the NBA is far superior to $700 a week in the CBA.

Today after practice I returned to my home away from home, the Hilton Suites here in Phoenix, in a relatively pleasant mood. That changed quickly with a phone call from the Suns. During the call, the assistant director of player personnel joked about the condition of my back. My back is fine, of course, but the Suns need a reason to put me on the injured list. Only twelve players can dress for the game; because we have fourteen, two of us will be on the injured list even though no one on the team is actually hurt. I felt a bit of conspiratorial glee, as if I was actually part of the inner workings of an NBA team for a change. He told me he was next going to connect me with the GM, Bryan Colangelo, because the GM was required to formally tell me that I was being placed on the injured list. Colangelo also joked about my faux injury and then said that he wanted to let me know where we stood.

He began by telling me how great I am—always a bad sign. A conversation that starts with one person ticking off the other's positive traits usually ends up going in the opposite direction. (See also any breakup, ever.) He went on to say that the new owners of the Suns had recently paid $400 million to buy the team and would not allow any "frivolous" spending. He noted that while the coaches would love to have me around, it would be impossible for him to justify keeping me to the owners, especially as I would have to spend much of my time on the injured list. To that end, he informed me that the Suns would release me later in the week. He then went back to friend mode and said that he would try to push my release date back to Thursday because that would result in my not clearing waivers until about Monday morning, allowing me to receive payment for those extra weekend days. If he could not slide that by the owners, he would have to cut me on Wednesday (incidentally, the day the Suns open the season at home against Atlanta). But, he said, he would try to get me the extra $8,000. He closed by saying that he has seen a lot of European basketball; "having watched you play, I would think you would fit in well over there."

I probably did a poor job of expressing exactly the level of condescension that was conveyed over the phone. In our short phone call, Colangelo managed to imply that while paying me the absolute lowest possible salary allowed by the NBA would be frivolous, paying Shawn Marion enough that he can sit around on the team's chartered 737 wearing earrings that cost $25,000 each is a sound financial decision. Without saying it, he said that while the team's owners could afford to shell out a cool $400 million in order to buy a showpiece basketball team, the extra $720,000 it would take to keep me around would not be "lean management."

I especially enjoyed the part where he acted like he was going to do me a huge favor by pushing back my release date by a day. Like I would think, *Wow, Bryan, that is nice of you. That extra money will heal the emotional wounds caused by having committed nearly every waking thought for the last month to how I can be a part of your team and then getting as close to it as a person could, only to have it jerked out from under me at the last second.*

I was quite thankful, too, for the little dig about European basketball. As in, *Paul, maybe you should stop this nonsense. You're a tall white guy who can shoot. Go back to Europe. We don't need your kind here.*

At the conclusion of the call, I was left with the strong feeling that someone who thought he was much smarter than me believed he had truly convinced me of something, namely, that my presence with the Phoenix Suns was a burden he could not bear.

When the madness was over, I fell onto my hotel bed and burst into tears.

So that's that—I will be a member of the Phoenix Suns for anywhere from thirty-six to sixty more hours. Keith tells me that the Bulls have some interest once again. Olympiacos in Athens still calls on a daily basis. The basketball journey will continue. The problem—and what he doesn't understand—is that I don't really want to go on to another place. I was struck this morning, when I arrived at practice and was greeted as an equal, how nice it is to be a part of a team that allowed me to feel like I was welcome. For a change, people seemed happy to see me in the morning. They noticed that I'd shaved for the first time in a month (perhaps a Samson-like mistake) and cared—or at least acted like they did—how I responded when they asked me what I had done on my day off. I suppose that is how people generally behave, but it is new to me.

I don't know how many more times I can do this.

November 15

I would like to relive my actual dismissal from the Suns because, well, apparently I am a masochist and enjoy opening old wounds.

As I mentioned, the powers that be in the Suns organization told me that they hoped they could slide a couple extra days of employment by the owners, thus gaining me a few extra dollars for my trouble. So I did not know when I would be exiting the region, but I knew I was not long for the world of the Suns. While somewhat liberating, it was not a particularly pleasant feeling. During practice the day before the first game, I went through the early drills as usual, but then stayed out of the way during the controlled-scrimmage portion of practice. I assumed that the coaches would appreciate my actions; I would not be taking the time of someone who needed the work. And, truth be told, the fight, at least regarding the Suns, had faded out of me. While I was standing there acting like I gave a damn about what was going on in front of my eyes, one of the assistants came up and asked, in a genuinely inquisitive manner, "Did someone tell you to sit out today?" I replied, "No, but they did tell me that they will be cutting me today or tomorrow." It was not the response he was expecting. Deflated a bit, he said, "Oh, I didn't realize that decision had been made."

On game day, I arrived for the shoot-around expecting a management ambush at any time. I survived a light workout without losing my job and then set off for the weight room. After toning up my massive frame, I sauntered into the nearly deserted locker room, looked around, and decided that the management crew must have thawed its heart and was going to allow me to stay for another day. Not so. The

GM was lurking around the corner. When I finished showering, he sat down with me and laid out the facts. Nothing new was said, except there was mention of the fact that a guy named Bo Outlaw had just been released by the Memphis Grizzlies and that there would probably be speculation about, and perhaps, completion of a contract between Outlaw and the Suns. Outlaw had played in Phoenix prior to being traded to Memphis, and everyone in the desert had liked having him around. Because I was reeling a bit, and because I was worried about getting as many Phoenix Suns T-shirts as I could before I left, I did not raise the one important point that came to mind—which revisited me when the Suns did, in fact, sign Outlaw a few days later.

Namely: in order to get rid of Bo Outlaw, the Memphis Grizzlies had to release him and buy out his contract, to the tune of something like $6 million. By my logic, the Memphis Grizzlies wanted so badly for Bo Outlaw *not* to play for the team that they paid him $6 million to do it. I realize that this is repetitive: *see also* Eisley, Howard. But it is such a bizarre concept, I can't keep stop thinking about it. Apparently the fact that the Grizzlies thought so little of Outlaw's play that they paid him *not* to perpetrate it upon a paying audience was not a cause for concern among the management of the Phoenix Suns.

I was reminded recently of the good that all of this rejection is doing me. I received a call from an old friend a little while ago. He said that he had seen that I had made the Suns' opening-day roster, but could not find my name in the first game's box score. He had gone as far as calling my parents' house to investigate, to no avail. After some more research, a mutual friend had given him the bad news. While we were talking about the situation, he said that I must be getting pretty tough, that all the rejection I was getting could only make the rest of my life seem easier. I think he is right. I can't claim to have seen it all, but I have had my share of disappointments over the last few years. Each one makes the prospect of something as simple as a bad breakup or an inopportune job loss seem less and less disastrous.

November 25

This year's Thanksgiving dinner was not among my best. The food itself was not too bad, but the location left a little to be desired. Instead
of dining in the friendly confines of my grandmother's house, I decided to branch out. I ate my Thanksgiving dinner this year at the
world-renowned restaurant that is found on the lobby level of the Ramada Plaza Hotel at John F. Kennedy International Airport in New
York. I was blessed with such a culinary opportunity because I am en
route to Russia to play basketball.

When my agent called with this particular employment possibility,
I was intrigued. As I have noted before, I've always wanted to play in
Russia at some point in my career. (Why, I do not know.) And the par-
ticulars of the contract matched up nicely with my plans for the year.
One of the players on the team I will soon be joining, called UNICS
Kazan, got hurt a short time ago and the team needs a replacement.
Because it is unknown how soon the player will be able to return, my
stint will be somewhat temporary. If, after a month, the team has had
enough of my brand of basketball, they can send me home without
further obligation. If they do want to keep me around, however, I can
opt to leave if their treatment of me has not been up to my standards
(for example, no harem included with my apartment). If both parties
agree that it would be a good idea for me to stick around, the same set
of options applies after the second month. After two months, if the
lovefest continues, I will stay for the remainder of the year. I've heard
of very few contract offers with such flexibility. If there is NBA interest while I am in Russia, I can leave (after a month) and make a
triumphant return to the United States. If not, I can stay, if they will
have me.

Intellectually, it makes sense. Emotionally, however, it is a disastrous plan. I am not sure what made me think I could deal well with
leaving for a very foreign land on Thanksgiving. I must have gotten
greedy—the financial aspects of this contract are rather tremendous.
(One month's guaranteed salary is about what I would make as an en-

gineer in an entire year.) But my team is in a city called Kazan, which is about five hundred miles to the interior of Moscow (that would be toward Siberia). The words I've heard used to describe the place include *godforsaken* and *hellish;* more often, people just change the subject, as in "What is Kazan like?" "Uh, I hear that league is a pretty good one." And let's be honest, Russia is still scary. Moscow seems doable, but people disappear from other parts of Russia. (Okay, maybe such events were more likely in Stalin's time, but that wasn't all that long ago.) This morning, while I was awaiting clearance to exit the Russian consulate here in New York with my new Russian visa (more on that later), I noticed that one of the old ladies near me was holding a passport issued by the USSR. I am all for rejecting the propaganda that made up a lot of my Cold War–era social studies classes, but I cannot shake the feeling that at least a little of that stuff they taught us about the good old Evil Empire had to have been true.

If I pull it off, the trip from Kansas City to Kazan will be one of my all-time greatest accomplishments. For whatever reason, it is not as easy to get into Russia as it is to enter a run-of-the-mill European country. Upon arrival in, say, Spain, presentation of one's passport is sufficient—they don't need to know of one's travel plans in advance. To enter Russia, in addition to a valid passport, one has to have a letter of invitation from someone in the country, two passport photos for a Russian visa, a properly filled-out visa form, and most important, $350 in the form of a certified check or money order. I am not sure why Russia has such stringent rules about allowing Americans in; one would think its leaders would be more, not less, welcoming than the rest of Europe. Under normal circumstances, a traveler could take care of the bureaucratic mess through the mail, but due to the time crunch under which I was working, I had to appear at the nearest Russian consulate in person. (Consulates are conveniently located in the well-spaced cities of New York, Washington, D.C., San Francisco, and Los Angeles.) This meant that on my way out of town, so to speak, I had to take a day to secure my visa, which I found to be fantastic news. The Russians were able to coordinate my trip from New York to Kazan but said that they couldn't make reservations for travel within the United States. (Evidently they don't know how to use a computer.) So they secured my flight out of New York, sent a letter of invitation for me to the consulate, and left me to deal with the rest. I, of course, learned all of this exactly one day before I was to leave my home country.

I flew out of Kansas City, arrived at La Guardia, retrieved my bags, hailed a cab, rode to the aforementioned Ramada, and settled in for about two hours of real sleep. (Mostly because sleeping at the Ramada JFK is more like actually sleeping in the terminal at JFK—they apparently did not spend much on soundproofing the walls.) I woke up and got another cab for what was supposedly going to be an hour-and-a-half journey into the heart of Manhattan. It took twenty-five minutes, so I had some time to kill at 8:30 on Thanksgiving morning. As it turned out, it was fortuitous that I arrived so early; after a short walk down to Central Park, I returned to find a line forming about half an hour before the consulate's opening at 9:30. I was definitely the only American in the line. It was educational, though, as I met a man from Kazan while standing there. I asked him if he had liked the city. His eyes got wide and he shook his head. Reassuring.

At 9:30, a Russian fellow opened the large door into the consulate. I did not make it in with the first batch in line—a tiny old man and a family who had both clearly been behind me in line somehow slipped past. After a few minutes, more of us were allowed in. At this point, my lack of training in the Russian language proved to be something of a hindrance. Everyone else seemed to know where to go, so I followed along and sat down in front of a matronly woman behind some Plexiglas. When her reply to my, "Do you speak English?" was no, I thought I was sunk. Fortunately, the gatekeeper found me and pointed me in the direction of the visa room, so my panic attack was short-lived. Once inside, things went rather smoothly, actually. After deliberating on the "Have you ever used drugs or been a drug addict?" question for a few minutes, I turned in my application, picture, passport, and money and twenty minutes later was rewarded with my very own dual-entry, three-month Russian visa.

November 29

As I lay awake in a New York hotel room a few days ago, waiting for the next morning's flight to Moscow, I wondered why I was dreading the trip so much. The feeling in the pit of my stomach was like the feelings before summer camp, before the first day of college, and before my first-ever NBA tryout all at once. I didn't really know why. I think it had a little to do with the extreme foreignness of my destination and a lot to do with the fact that my brothers dropped me off at the airport on their way to our grandmother's house for Thanksgiving. (Note to self: no more traveling on holidays.) When I told people about the journey, they said things like, "Ooh, that's so exciting." And I suppose they were right, it is exciting—kind of like a heart attack or a gunshot wound is exciting. They all get the blood pressure going, just not necessarily in a good way.

My dread was not misplaced. Early indications are that Russia and I are not going to get along well. The last four-day stretch has arguably been among the most miserable of my entire life.

That being said, it is funny how a friendly face, even one on a stranger, can improve my mood so drastically.

Getting to Kazan and dealing with all of the trappings of the journey took the fight out of me. So given that I woke up this morning at 5:00 for no reason except that my body thinks it is in some mystery time zone somewhere over the Atlantic and could not go back to sleep, which made me think seriously about retirement from European basketball, I was overjoyed to find some camaraderie at the breakfast buffet. I was roaming the line, attempting to explain that warm milk on my cereal was not going to do the job (cold milk: *moloko khalodnyy,* or maybe *khalodnyy moloko*—I've not yet learned whether the adjective comes first or last), when a pleasant English voice came piping out of the only other breakfast participant, a youngish Russian lady. She helped to translate the reason I was getting a big *nyet* in response to my request. The kitchen had originally had some cold milk—three liters, in fact. But they had used the lot of it to make the porridge. Mollified, I bit the bullet and used the hot milk. My cereal was terrible, but at least I did not have to simmer my way through breakfast, pissed because I could not get my point across.

My roll did not stop there. After breakfast, I headed to the business center for the first time in my stay here. (It had been closed. I don't know why. Maybe the clientele is too busy sitting in their rooms, being miserable.) While I was using the Internet, a man came in to wait. As I was leaving and he was saddling up, he noticed my lack of linguistic skills and asked where I was from. I told him that I lived in Kansas and was now playing basketball for the local team, UNICS. When I returned his line of questioning, he pointed to the Atlanta Hawks shirt I was wearing and told me that he was a writer for the Atlanta paper, in Russia to interview a Thrashers player who had taken a job with the local hockey team while the NHL is consumed by a lockout. After we were finished with our little medium-world moment, the other fellow in the room piped up with, "Kansas? I studied at Shawnee Mission East for a month, but a long time ago." In a hotel somewhere near one of the four corners of the earth, I ran into a guy who has spent significant time at the high school that is approximately twelve blocks from my home in Kansas City.

Those encounters may keep this particular entry from being the absolute most negative one I have ever written. If I had hammered something out twenty-four hours ago, the results would have made the Smiths seem jovial.

When I arrived at the Aeroflot desk in New York after an hour of waiting in a dot-filled line that smelled like a boiled combination of sweat and feces, I was greeted with, "Passport and ticket, please." (Is the fact that Indian people smell so terrible off-limits? It need not be; I believe our only hope of solving this global problem is by attacking it head-on.) "Well, here's my passport, but I think my ticket is an electronic one." The Russian lady behind the counter destroyed my rebuttal by informing me that Aeroflot does not give out electronic tickets. I should not have been surprised—the airline still uses a hammer and sickle in its emblem. I said that I had no paper ticket and didn't know what to do. She softened a bit and asked for input from her fellow in-

checkers. In the time it took for her to return with an envelope with my name on it—the one containing my actual ticket—I had decided that I was split exactly fifty-fifty on whether I wanted the problem solved. If she had come back with no ticket, I would have been provided a convenient escape from my trip to Russia, one akin to the chicken exit near the roller coaster called the Orient Express at Worlds of Fun. (Kansas City reference.) Fortunately for my pocketbook, and unfortunately for my mental well-being, there would be no easy out.

My flight to Moscow was uneventful. I actually got a little sleep, and while Aeroflot's business class is not on par with that of British Airways, it still beat the hell out of sitting in coach.

When I arrived in Russia, a frumpy, unilingual Russian man met me at the exit of the baggage claim as planned. After a two-hour drive through snow-covered Moscow without a whit of conversation, he guided me into the other airport in the city. (Really—no English. None.) He did not manage to provide me with much information, but he was able to get across that I was going to have to pay something to the next airline for the overstuffed bags of winter clothes I was portering around. With that nugget dispensed, he abandoned me to the clutches of Domodedovo Airport. For seven hours—my flight to Kazan wasn't until late that night. I spent most of my time attempting to dry the contents of my backpack, which had become soaked as my bag rested on the floor of my driver's shitty car. (I don't know why.) I'm sure I looked like I had an advanced case of obsessive-compulsive disorder as I sat there fanning through the most-affected items for several hours. But it gave me something to do. Because I knew no one, and because the few people I cautiously approached quickly shot down my hopes of an English-only conversation, I was left with a dilemma or two: leave my bags to the mercy of any airport hoodlums in the area, or allow my bladder to explode. After several hours dominated by the latter option, I broke down and got my baggage cart as close as possible to the lavatory door before making a run for it. (I realize that all of this seems a little paranoid, but what the hell do I know about what goes on in Russian airports? Especially Russian airports filled with extraordinarily creepy-looking men who look like they might eat me if given the opportunity.)

Eight-thirty finally came and I was able to check in for my flight (on Siberian Airlines, no less). I picked my way through the security check and was on my way. In Europe, many airports employ buses for the transport of passengers from the terminal to the plane. Once they are out on the tarmac, the citizenry are hustled up Nixon stairs and into the plane. In a lot of places, this procedure makes sense; it probably cuts down on gate congestion. However, Moscow is not a lot of places. Instead of spending my boarding time in a nice, heated rectangular tunnel, I spent it outside in the snow, choking in the pleasant −10°C night air. While waiting to board the plane and contemplating whether my testicles would ever re-descend, I decided to commemorate the moment. (I did not write my name in the snow. Although that would have been awesome.) I got out my newfangled camera and snapped off a shot that I hoped would contain some snowflakes and the Siberian Airlines insignia. After I did my best Ansel Adams, I felt a tap on my shoulder and turned to find an unsmiling member of the Polizia in close proximity. I thought I was a goner. He said something in brusque Russian. I took it to mean, "No more pictures." I hope it was not, "You've been marked. Next mistake results in a ten-year stay in the gulag." I put away my camera, got on a plane that closely resembled one of the transports they show in Vietnam War movies, and passed out.

I was met in Kazan by Elvira, the woman with whom I had communicated before starting my journey. We walked from the airport into the tundra, and I was stowed in the back of a panel van with two Russians whose identities remained a mystery. Elvira spoke passable English but wasn't particularly forthcoming with information as we drove the thirty minutes through pitch-black countryside into the city of Kazan. By the time I got to the Hotel Safar, it had been almost exactly forty-eight hours since I had left the comforts of my house in Kansas City. I was thoroughly disoriented and in no mood to find that my hotel room was the worst in which I had ever set foot. My bed was a mattress on the floor, and the only possible explanation for the carpeting choice was a fire sale on indoor/outdoor at the local emporium. I dodged some mildew for a quick shower and then collapsed for what I hoped would be a nice long rest before I was expected to be anywhere in the morning.

It was not to be. As I said, I woke up at about 5:00 A.M. I was not in good shape. In retrospect, I realize that I was totally warped from the trip, exhausted but not able to sleep, and extremely hungry. At any rate, dealing with the entire situation became a monumental task, and I lost my mind. I had not been so distraught in a long time. I thought I'd left behind my homesick days about ten years ago (not an easy task, I might add—I'm kind of a pussy), but I was incorrect. I called home after contemplating a trip out of my thirteenth-story window. I'm thankful that my mother was available for calming, she did a bang-up job of getting me to focus on the short-term goals of leaving my room and finding something to eat. (If these writings seem filled with complaints, imagine twenty-six years of them. That's what my mother has had to put up with so far. Amazingly, she seems to have maintained her sanity. Most of it, anyway.) After finding some nourishment, I was able to calm down and then actually went back to sleep for an hour or so.

My first practice as a member of UNICS Kazan was uneventful. I felt like hell, but I managed to muster a few smiles and act like I was happy to be in the gym. The entire team was not around for the morning workout; it was more of a supplemental practice, which was nice, as I was able to meet the coach under somewhat less formal circumstances. Fortunately, his English is passable—exactly the second person in Russia I've met with that skill set. He took the opportunity to pass on some tidbits of information that I found quite . . . odd. I had been under the impression that I was in Kazan to replace an injured player. The coach informed me that he hoped my stay would be a long one, so the team wanted to evaluate me first before adding me to the roster. He told me that I would not play for the first seven to ten days, saying that he wanted to let me have a chance to fit in. I said that I would do whatever he needed me to do. I'm such the coach's dream.

That night, I was introduced to the team as Paul Shirley, in Kazan on a tryout. As I gave a little wave, my ego took a swan dive. My brain said, *Tryout? What do you think you have here, the 1986 Boston Celtics? Give me a little credit.* But that quickly subsided as I realized that (1) I get paid the same either way and (2) as far as I can tell, Russia causes me to have suicidal thoughts, so the faster I can get out, the better. After my own little pick-me-up moment, I sat through some film and tried not to fall asleep.

Let me revisit the statement immediately preceding in which I implied that the country formerly known as the Soviet Union makes me want to kill myself. Well, it does. At least, this city does. First of all, it is cold. Really cold. The type of cold that we Kansans experience from time to time but know instinctively should only be viewed safely from the inside of one's home. I learned that the high today was something like −10°C. And that was on a sunny day. (This is November, by the way.) I can't imagine what possessed a group of people to come upon this spot and decide, "Damn, but isn't this one hell of a place. We ought to build a city here." They could have been fooled in May, but come October, a couple of abandoned huts should have seemed like an acceptable loss.

Next problem: lack of even the most basic friendliness. Perhaps glasnost never made it to Kazan, or maybe it is the aftereffects of all those USSR years, but the average Russian carries a look on his face that says, *Lenin didn't smile; neither do I.* I don't need vapid grins and bouquets on my doorstep, but the occasional glint of joy in the eyes would not be frowned upon. The lack of general friendliness spills into my next problem: the language barrier. Sure, Russian is hard to learn. (Today's letter of the day is Ж. I don't know what it means, but it sure is cool-looking.) That's not the real problem, though. Greek was difficult, too. But in Greece, when I tried a phrase, I was usually greeted with a slightly condescending smile or laugh, like the one given a child who tried to use the word *obsequious* in his everyday conversations. Here, the look I get says, *What, are you retarded? Say it right, idiot.* Which makes me want to say, *Hey, assbag, I've been here for forty-eight hours. I'm doing my best,* which quickly devolves into, *Wait, didn't we win the Cold War?* But that redneck line of thinking really flies in the face of what I stand for, so I try to cut myself off before I get to that point.

Last, this place is a little scary. At about 3 A.M. last night, a group of Russians were loudly attempting to get into the room next to mine. But that wasn't my first thought. When my slumber was interrupted by the sound of their fists on a door, it sounded a lot like they were trying to get into my room. My anxiety might have been a consequence of the spy movies and the anti-USSR propaganda we Americans were fed from age six. Whatever the cause, it was alarming to hear gruff Russian voices separated from my head by four feet and a very flimsy wooden door in the middle of the night. I like to avoid the melodramatic. But I think it is safe to say that my chances of disappearance are significantly higher in Kazan, Russia, than in Mission, Kansas.

The good news is that the worst is probably over. There will be some odd situations ahead, but I don't think I could possibly feel as bad as I did that first morning here. The important thing is that I remember, when this all over, to *never do this again.*

(I'll probably forget.)

December 4

They gave me a Volvo to drive, which is great because the chances that I will need the protection provided by the famously safe Swedish carmaker on the streets of Kazan are quite high. Every day that I make it to the gym without a fender bender is a small miracle. The city's drivers are probably not inherently bad—the driving conditions simply provide them with no opportunity for success. First of all, the streets have no markings. No lane lines, no turning lanes. The roads are one big racetrack, with the added obstacle of cars choosing entirely new directions of travel at a moment's notice. It is not so bad when the streets are confined by some boundary, such as buildings, a canal, or a bridge abutment. However, when a widening occurs—near an intersection, for example—all hell breaks loose. Drivers jockey for position as if the checkered flag at Talladega is awaiting the first car to the opposite side of the bulge in the road's geography.

My drive to the gym is about three miles. Two nights ago, it took me thirty-seven minutes to get there. If I had jogged it, I would have beaten my car there. Of course, I would have died from hypothermia, but since we're discussing a fantasy world anyway, I can pretend that I could have done it.

The journey began innocuously enough. The area around my hotel was, as usual, devoid of any activity. (Good for driving, bad for, say, finding a nearby restaurant.) Once I arrived at the intersection with the main road into town, the fun began. I made a right onto the bridge across the Kazanka River and merged into traffic. So far, so good. At this point, I took notice of what sorts of vehicles were in my general vicinity so as to predict the strange maneuvers their drivers might make. From largest to smallest, my fellow combatants were as follows:

1. Track-bound trolleys
2. Buses powered by overhead wires
3. Large self-propelled buses
4. Self-propelled minibuses
5. Cars

The trolleys and electric-powered buses are fairly easy to avoid. But they're relentless. Their drivers seem unconcerned by the prospect of a charge of vehicular homicide; their style would best be described as aggressive. However, both are confined by their tracks or wires, so avoidance is possible.

The minibuses are another beast altogether. They move with no predictability, and their drivers apparently think that a 180-degree turn in the flow of traffic is often a good idea. Some days, these buses are the bane of my existence.

Cars are always a nuisance. Generally, they are of the Russian-made Lada type. (Of which the Sputnik model seems to be most popular.) Their degree of unpredictability varies inversely with their worth. For example, the rare, newish Mercedes is less likely to jack-knife itself in the quest for a parking space than is the ubiquitous, decades-old Sputnik.

With the identities of my competition in mind, I crossed the bridge over the Kazanka River. While doing so, I noticed the ice fishermen on the river and wondered why they don't build themselves shacks like Minnesotans. Then I realized that they live in Kazan. That anyone chooses to live in such a place would imply that good judgment is obviously in short supply here. Traffic on the bridge was slow, so I wandered into the middle of the road like a local and used the area covered in trolley tracks as a fast lane, keeping an eye out for the Bolshevik-era trolley cars at all times. At the far side, I was faced with my first stoplight and its five possible light conditions:

1. Green
2. Red
3. Orange

And then it gets more complicated.

4. Blinking green, signifying impending orange—a pre-caution caution light, as it were
5. Red and orange at the same time, meaning, about to switch to green—a head start, perhaps

I suppose that these extra light combinations were created in an effort to give motorists more information. Unfortunately, the plan has backfired. No Russian driver wants to be left behind, so each car is already well in motion by the time the green light comes on. Of course, the cross traffic has not yet cleared the intersection, resulting in a snarl of cars headed in all directions as each driver attempts to extrapolate from past experience with crazy people what his comrade might attempt, while trying to avoid the trolleys and buses, which are bound by no traffic laws. At the same time, every man behind the wheel is furiously wrenching on his window crank so that he can vent his frustration with the nearby driver who had the gall to actually wait for a green light, all while trying to decide which should govern his mitten usage—the cold outside air, or his need for a cigarette. Nicotine wins, but the time it takes him to search for a light causes him to miss his chance for forward progress, angering the man now jammed perpendicular to him, beginning the cycle again.

And that's just the first intersection.

After the first traffic light o' hell, I was given a brief respite by an area of road that is probably eight lanes wide—if lane lines were to magically appear. It was a moment of calm before the storm. After the brief traffic angioplasty, the artery is quickly constricted to a two-lane road on the right side of a canal. Since it is the only road into the center of the city, the road was full, as usual. (It has been reported that I once reached 20 miles per hour on this road, but those reports are unconfirmed at this time.) Blessed with good conditions, I found the going to be only slow. Under normal conditions—which include (1) a stalled car ahead, (2) the driver of a large truck deciding that the entire right lane is a good place to park, (3) a small accident that won't be cleared until the two participants quit yelling at each other, and (4) inexplicable circumstances involving stray dogs, pedestrians, and so on—movement is impossible.

After inching along for a mile or so, I found my landmark, a strip club on the left side of the road, and crossed over the canal. I took my next right and found my nemesis awaiting me—the most disastrous intersection I have seen in all of the world. (And I mean that.)

Traffic at this intersection is never fast-moving; the situation is further complicated by the pedestrians present because of its proximity to the center of the city. Said pedestrians are not rational human beings. They will jump in front of a car without fear. They are often old and appear to be holding on to their sense of balance tenuously. The intersection proper marks the confluence of two trolley tracks, meaning that trolleys are never far and are often turning, which is not a speedy process. For whatever reason, the lights are badly timed: green lasts about six nanoseconds.

For me, the path through the intersection followed its usual preset pattern. A trolley was stopped by a group of pedestrians crossing out of turn. A driver traveling perpendicular to the trolley thought he could beat a red light and got stopped in the intersection. Traffic flowing parallel to the trolley received its red-orange combo light and headed out into the havoc. One lane's flow was blocked by the car. Someone in another lane began an attempt at a twelve-point turn into a side alley, leaving the rest of the participants a winding path that was soon blocked by an old lady stumbling through a pothole. Chaos and much honking of horns ensued. Each new driver to arrive on the scene decided that he was the one getting a raw deal and tried to bull his way through.

Eventually, enough people realized that driving out into the intersection never actually solves the problem, the lights began to have meaning again, and I finally got across. From this intersection, I had only a few trolley tracks to dodge before I arrived at the arena, calm and collected and ready to practice.

Oh, did I mention that the streets are always covered in snow?

So far, I have not made my trip from the hotel to the arena en route to a game in which I would actually play. I haven't even donned a uniform. In fact, the team recently departed for a game in the city of Novosibirsk, leaving me in Kazan to practice with the junior team. (The coach originally told me that I would travel to the game even though I would not play. When I found out it was a seven-hour flight and three time zones away, I begged my way out.) The player I thought I was here to replace, Chris Anstey, has arrived back on the scene after an appendectomy and should be ready to play in two weeks. It appears that the team is awaiting word on whether another American, Ira Clark, will receive a French passport, as he has been promised. If that happens, I think I will then be added to the roster. Like most European leagues, the Russian basketball federation allows only two Americans per team. If Clark does not receive dual citizenship, the team will be forced to choose whether it wants to keep him or me. (Anstey counts as one American, even though he is Australian— not worth the explanation. Clark is the other.) By the time he would receive the mythical passport, I will have only about two weeks left on my contract. (I am now thinking of this only as a one-month tour of duty; something amazing would have to happen for me to stay past December 25—like all the snow melting and a beach appearing.) I could conceivably play in about four games before taking my leave of this hellhole. On the other hand, they could decide not to pay the fee (it costs a certain amount to change players on the roster) and stay with the current roster, leaving me out in the cold, so to speak. While I think that actually playing might make the time go a little faster, I don't know that I care that much. If there is no real future in it, it is difficult to put forth any effort. And if the coaches are going to continue to treat me as if I am nothing more than a nuisance, I have very little motivation to care one way or the other. There is the money thing, I suppose. I need to become a little more American and embrace the materialistic.

December 9

My team plays in an international competition in addition to its participation in the Russian league. Shockingly, it is not easy to get in and out of Kazan for the trips to the international games. In fact, I might file our return trip from a recent game in Macedonia under "Most Ludicrous Travel Itinerary Ever." We left a hotel in Skopje, Macedonia, at 5:15 A.M., on a bus to the Skopje airport. Departed from Macedonia at 7 A.M. Arrived in Frankfurt, Germany, at 9:45. Left Germany at 10:45 with a 3:30 P.M. (Russian time) arrival in Moscow. Rode a bus two hours across town to the "bonus" airport in Moscow. Waited. Departed Moscow at 10:30 P.M. Arrived in Kazan at 11:45 P.M. In all, it was an eighteen-hour journey. I could travel from New York to almost any city in the world in that amount of time.

Our stay in Skopje started off well. The ride into the city took us through modern-looking, semi-civilized streets, and my opinion of Macedonia was at an all-time high. It would only drop from there.

We practiced the night of our arrival in Skopje and then headed off to bed in what is easily the nicest hotel in which I have stayed in all of my European basketball adventures. So far, so good. Because we had traveled to Macedonia a day earlier than usual, we had another day to wait before the game. (I don't know why. See above difficulty regarding travel in and out of Kazan. It didn't really matter to me—a hotel room in Skopje beat my mattress on the floor back on Hoth.) Our day-before-the-game ritual included a double shot of practice, a concept of which I am none too fond. I managed to wrench some odd muscle in my back during the first practice, which was not encouraging. I can deal with only one negative stimulus at a time, so I was dismayed when my stomach began to roil just prior to the second practice. I managed to hold things together through the workout; in fact, I had one of my best practices since joining the team. When we got back to the hotel, the team gathered for the evening meal. I played my part, except for the eating-of-food aspect, with my mind on my room and a hope of some back-pain and upset-stomach management. I asked the team's trainer (who speaks less English than I do Russian; how does a team expect to deal with American players in this capacity?) for some help with my back; he came to my room and gave it a good rubdown. (Insert gay-sex joke here.) I did not mention the clash of microbes that was going on in my digestive tract. As I have mentioned, I generally like to keep my complaints to trainers down to one at a time. After some run-of-the-mill diarrhetic trips to the bathroom, I fell into a restless sleep.

My trusty little Timex travel clock informed me when I awoke that it was 2:30 in the morning. I knew something was amiss. I wasn't sure what was going on, but I did know that (1) I needed to be in the bathroom and (2) my body needed to be oriented in a direction opposite the one usually used in the vicinity of the toilet.

When I was finished, I spent some time lamenting the end of a nine-year vomit-free streak—and then I cleaned myself up and went back to bed. Sleep did not come easily; I think my mind knew that something big had happened—or maybe I was just sick. The next morning, after a few more bathroom bouts of a slightly more conventional manner, I managed to summon the team doctor to my room. He gave me some voodoo pills and sent me back to bed. (Actually, I should not make fun. I have found European medicines to be quite effective. I don't know if that implies a lack of government oversight or that I have not yet developed a tolerance for their drugs, but their stuff seems to work.) No shoot-around for me that day. I was not displeased, as I certainly had enough things on my plate, not the least of which was starting a new vomitless streak.

Our esteemed coach informed me before we left on our road trip that I would probably not play in Macedonia. I didn't protest my inclusion on the travel list because, as I may or may not have made clear, I hate the city of Kazan and thought the adventure would do me some good. My position vis-à-vis playing did leave me in something of an awkward spot with my teammates. Because of the language barrier with most of them, it was difficult to explain that while they may have perceived that I would be playing in this particular game because I was on the trip, that had never been in the cards and my bout of food poisoning had not been the cause of my absence from the lineup. That being said, had the coach wanted me to make my UNICS Kazan debut in Skopje, I might have had to decline. Come game time, I was still in pretty bad shape. I had only subtracted calories over the previous twenty-four hours, and my back had definitely not benefited from my night of trips to the bathroom. Needless to say, I was pleased to watch the game from the sidelines.

It was quite a game. Reminiscent of my time in Athens, the temperature in the gym was being maintained at about 55° F. The court had more dead spots than a barn floor and appeared not to have been swept for years. My team came out the victor, to the dismay of the crowd that hovered over us the entire game, showing its displeasure by occasionally spitting at us. (I managed to contain my Artest-like reactions, but only because I was in street clothes.) The best part of not playing was still to come—in the fact that I was not forced to use the despicable showers in an attempt at a body cleaning. I guess a little out-of-place microorganism and a crazy coach are worth something after all.

December 15

Soon after our return from Macedonia, we left Kazan for Turkey. While I remain a streetclothes-wearing spectator, at least I'm getting my money's worth on the exotic-travel front.

A second trip to Istanbul confirmed what I thought after my first visit there—that Istanbul is a fantastic city. It is dirty and the people generally smell like gym socks, but I like its personality. My first journey to the city was with the Greek team for which I was playing at the time. Because of the eons-long dispute between the Greeks and Turks, I was kept insulated from most of the Muslim historical sites. Instead, my tour guides confined me to ancient Greek churches and the like, so I did not see what is probably the most famous site in historic Constantinople (as my still-bitter compatriots called it for the duration of our visit), the Blue Mosque. Now, one would think that a learned person like me would remedy that gap in his touristic adventures when he had the chance. Instead, though, I chose to while away my hours in Turkey with the most American of pastimes—shopping. I cannot say that my adventures in consumerism were without their share of culture, however, as they occurred at the Grand Bazaar.

The Grand Bazaar was not what I expected. I had envisioned some sort of dusty, Indiana Jones–like city square, with giant pots, monkeys, and men wearing turbans, brandishing scimitars, and yelling things in Arabic (or Turkish, I suppose). From an economic standpoint, my vision of the bazaar has a couple of flaws. First, the open-air arrangement I had dreamed up would allow inclement weather to wreak havoc on the proceedings, and second, the burly Turks with swords wandering around in my fantasy would most definitely scare away gullible tourists and their bulging wallets. In fact, the bazaar is not all that different from the standard mall in Suburbia, USA. The décor is different, and the food court is not as easy to find, but the theory behind both is similar.

When our cabdriver dropped several of my teammates and me at the entrance, it did not take long for us to be initiated into the customs of the bazaar. Leading to the entryway was a short, brick-lined street like something out of a Harry Potter book. Before we cleared that street in order to enter the bazaar proper, we were whisked away by a man selling leather jackets who had ingratiated himself to Ivo, my Croatian teammate, by calling to him in his native language. Ivo was in fact shopping for leather coats, so it did not take much to convince him to follow. We followed and were led into a dead-end alleyway, where we found ourselves in a miniature mecca of leather shops. I was fairly confident that we were about to be mugged but was comforted by my earlier decision to carry a sword of my own—kind of like the one Morgan Freeman's character in *Robin Hood* used. Unfortunately, it was tucked down the right side of my pants, so I knew I was going to have a devil of a time getting it out if . . . (Okay, that was retarded and I made it up. It seemed to fit into the story though, so I went with it.) Anyway, when we got into the shop, our newfound friends began assaulting us with entreaties to buy leather jackets. They actually had two coats with long enough sleeves for Ivo. Unfortunately, they were more offensive-lineman big and not basketball-player big. No matter, though—the shop owner simply sent his runner off to who knows where to secure another option. While he was gone, there was a commotion outside in the shopping cul-de-sac. Our shopkeeper quickly shut the door to his store at the first sign of trouble, so we were insulated from the situation. As near as I could tell from all the yelling—more from the harsh tones and the rather high volume than any knowledge of the language being used—a man felt he had been cheated by another store owner and was going to retrieve his dignity using the footstool he was waving about. We watched through the glass as some fellow Turks (they had darkish skin and black hair, so I assumed) calmed their companion. Crisis averted. As the situation was being resolved, our courier returned with two new options and sauntered in as if nothing had happened outside. My teammate declined to make a purchase, and we moved on.

The bazaar itself is almost entirely underground, or at least seems to be. (There were no pamphlets and everyone there was peddling something, so I was not able to get any facts.) It contains something like three thousand different shops, each the size of an average bedroom. The shops' level of formality ranges from, at the top end, places that accept credit cards to, at the bottom end, a man standing at the crossroads of two paths, offering, "You wanna buy a carpet? Come with me." Everyone I saw spoke some level of English, along with several other languages—it makes good business sense to have such ability. The walkways are clean, and the ceilings are very high and well lit, so the place is relatively welcoming. But because the complex is constructed like a maze (for obvious reasons) one can become disoriented quickly. I have no doubt that I could have wandered for hours without understanding which way I was going.

Having acquainted myself with the setup, I dove in and started looking around to see if there was anything that interested me. I found some potential Christmas gifts and made a few purchases. I then followed my teammates around for a while and watched Ivo participate in some disastrous negotiations. He was again looking at two leather jackets—one for him, one for his wife. After some back-and-forth, the shop owner told him that the best he could do was $700 for the two. Ivo then made his first mistake and started acting wishy-washy, saying he did not know what he wanted to do, that he wanted to think about it, instead of furrowing his brow incredulously and threatening to leave—the method I found to be most effective. The seller then proposed $680. The small discount threw off my teammate and he said, "How about $500?" To which the owner's eyes lit up. He raced over and said, "You got it!" His enthusiasm betrayed him, though, as my friend knew he had been had. We beat a hasty retreat, and Ivo lived to bargain another day.

I write as if I am some sort of master at bargaining. The truth is that, by purchasing something, I was probably raped on the price. For example, I returned to the bazaar the day after our first there because, miraculously, I had located some shoes for myself and wanted to drink that well dry. I inquired at several shoe shops to no real success before finding a store that had a pair I liked. I tried them on and considered what I might pay for them. I looked up at the salesman from the cushions on which I was sitting and asked what he wanted for the shoes. (For background, I am talking about some semi-athletic shoes that I would wear casually. They would probably cost $65–75 in a store—if that store carried shoes for gigantic humans.) He said $120, which was ridiculously high. But I think his strategy worked. If he had said $80, then I could have countered with $25. As it was, I came back with a $40 offer. He said $100. I said, "No, thanks," and got up to leave. He quickly came down to $75, and I thought I had him where I wanted him. I again told him no and began unlacing. He asked what the most I would pay was. I said $45. He said, "$60, and that's as low as I can go." But it wasn't. Eventually, he came down to $45 and I had a new pair of shoes. The beauty of this exchange is that we both came away happy. I felt like I had gotten a pretty good deal on some shoes I liked. On the other hand, he knew that he had paid $8 for the shoes because they were either knock-offs of the real thing or had been pushed off the back of a delivery truck. Whichever it was, he had made a gigantic profit by getting $45 out of me. So in the end, I'm a sucker, no matter what the price.

December 19

That I am in Kazan, sitting awake in this shithole of a hotel room, with the light above the door blinking on and off as if it cannot decide its role in our arrangement and my window open to the cold air in order to compensate for the overly hot radiators that I cannot control, makes what I am about to write all the more absurd.

(Did I mention that when I checked in after our recent road trip, my refrigerator contained a half-empty bottle of water? Someone probably tested it for poison. Nice of him.)

When we left for our last road trip, we were bid farewell at the Kazan airport by the president of the team. In his remarks, he mentioned that he was glad to see me with the team but was disappointed that he had not gotten a chance to see me play. He mentioned that I should remain ready, as my time might come at any moment. That statement, or translation thereof, turned out to be quite prophetic.

I watched my team's game in Istanbul in civilian clothes. We (they) lost against a team called Fenerbahçe. (I write the name only

for the fun provided to the reader in attempting to decipher its pro-
nunciation.) The next day, we departed Istanbul for Moscow and a
game there. While in Moscow, we were actually given an afternoon to
ourselves. I took advantage of the opportunity and set off for downtown to see the headquarters of what my textbooks always told me
was the most evil place on earth. It proved to be quite an accomplishment, if only because I was able to successfully navigate Moscow's
subway. When I headed into the bowels of the city, it was with the
knowledge that I had deciphered the metro systems of Barcelona,
Athens, and Paris, all without an entirely firm grasp of any of those
cities' native languages. However, those mass transit experiences
were aided by at least a little English posted somewhere. Not so in
Moscow. All Russian. Not a letter in English. Russian is not an easy
language to read. It's like Greek, only harder. With Greek, most of the
letters, while foreign, are at least unique to the Greek alphabet. In
fact, I can think of only one exception—*P*, which is rho or *R*. In Russian, *H* means *N*. A backward *N* means *I*. *B* means *V*. (Actually, Greek
has that one, too. I stand corrected, by myself.) There is a *3* that
means *Z*. And my personal favorite, the *W* that means *SH*. Awesome.
At any rate, trying to read the names of stations on the fly in this code
is not easy. And as I had set off on my journey into the center of the
city at almost exactly 5:00 P.M., the rush hour crowd of dark-clad, unsmiling faces was amused neither by my confusion nor by the fact that
I was using 0.67 square feet of prime potential hustling and bustling
real estate while I stood staring in total bewilderment at the metro
maps. Thankfully, I had asked at the front desk of the hotel exactly
what trains and switches I needed to make. After nearly throwing in
the towel, I finally made the mental leap needed and got on a very
rickety subway train and found my way to my destination—Red
Square.

My map was a poor one, so when I emerged from the subter-
ranean maze, I was surprised to find myself in front of the Bolshoi
Theatre. I looked around outside and moved on. (I admit that I was
name-dropping. I'm a little disappointed in myself. I don't care much
what the outside of the Bolshoi Theatre looks like—I thought it would

make me sound more cultured. I'm sorry.) I wandered around as I tried mightily to get my bearings using the free "cultural map" I had been given at the hotel.

Eventually, I found the Kremlin, and was not disappointed. The Kremlin itself is simply a castle set on a small hill. It is quite big and impressive and would certainly inspire me to fall in line with the party way. I snapped a few pictures and then set off across Red Square itself. Lenin's tomb was closed—it was nighttime. The building housing it is somewhat out of place in its location—austere and modern in an area filled with grand and showy monoliths. (It dawns on me as I write this that maybe that is the point. I guess the Bolshevik revolution was a bit of a reaction to the decadence of the czars and an attempt to simplify life. It only took me three days to put that together.) From Lenin's tomb, I could begin to see St. Basil's Cathedral, which is one of those monuments that, like the Eiffel Tower or the Parthenon, is actually more impressive than one could imagine based on photographs alone. The onion-topped spires really are as colorful as advertised; the place is put together well.

After hitting the high points, I wandered through some shopping districts to get a feel for the locals and then made my way back to the hotel without much event, which I found to be very surprising.

At breakfast the next day, Ira Clark, the American player whom I am in line to quasi-replace, walked into the room without greeting and said, "I need to go home." He had just learned of a serious illness in his family. As I was sitting in the lobby before we left for practice, one of the assistant coaches found me. He said, in very broken English, that the head coach had decided that he wanted to activate me before the next game (in two days) but needed to confirm that I was intending to stay around for the next month, as activating me would cost the team a $50,000 payment to the Russian basketball federation. I would then be registered to play and the team would have officially changed Americans. I told him, flatly, no. He was surprised and asked me why. I related what I have been feeling all along: that I had been marginalized and treated as if I were trying out for the team. Not to mention the fact that the city of Kazan is not exactly a tourist destination and my living arrangements had not been ideal. I also noted I had come to Russia thinking I was going to play, not just practice. He led me to a phone so that we could call the head coach and I could tell him of my decision. The head coach attempted to convince me to change my mind. When he could not, he told me to postpone a final decision until he could speak with me in person at the evening practice. I accepted that plan and waited with anticipation for the inevitable awkwardness of the encounter.

That night after practice, the head coach sat me down and attempted to talk me into staying for another month. At one point, he was nearly begging. I found all of the kowtowing to be very strange. I had not played in a single game, nor had I been setting the world on fire in practice. In fact, I have shown less aptitude for shooting the ball during my time here than during any other span in my life. But, judging by the newfound affection, I've done something right. (Or more likely, the coach realized how difficult it would be to bring in and train another American at this point in the season.) I told him again that if I had to give him a final answer right then, it would be no. I also noted that if I were to consider staying, I should not do the considering while in Moscow, a place of relative civilization. I needed to return to Kazan and its awfulness before making a decision. He agreed to my plan, although I don't think he agreed that Kazan is awful.

He asked me again the next day—game day. We were to play CSKA Moscow (pronounced chess-kuh) (oh, and moss-cow, in case of retardation), the biggest and best team in Russia, so he was anxious for any advantage he could get. Ira Clark was still in the city, as he would not leave for the United States until the next day, so I found it curious that the coach continued to press me. I told him that nothing had changed. He said that he would ask me again before the game, and that I should be ready to play. Even though it seemed absurd—as I mentioned, the team would have to pay $50,000 to put me on the roster—I had a hunch that I might make my first uniformed appearance.

We arrived at the arena behind schedule due to the murderous Moscow traffic. After helping the team get settled in the locker room,

I wandered into the lobby of the arena to await the start of the game. The coach found me and asked me yet again if I would stay around for the next month. I told him that my mind had not changed. He said, rather brusquely, "Okay," and walked off. Ten minutes later I saw him huddled with the assistant coaches, and my something-weird-is-about-to-happen meter fell all the way to the right. He called me over and asked me if I was ready to play that night. I said, "Sure." He told me that the president had shelled out the $50,000 and that I should find a uniform. I would be playing instead of Chris Anstey. The coach had told me earlier that he did not think Anstey was quite ready to play, as he was still recovering from his appendectomy. I had an hour to prepare for my first game in a month and a half. (Or, if I don't count preseason games—and I probably shouldn't—my first real game in about nine months.) And against the best team in Russia, one of the best in Europe. Awesome.

I played terribly. Everything was out of sync. I was passive, could not catch the ball, could not finish around the basket, and was generally a disaster. We lost by five or seven. I scored two points.

I hoped that my poor play would simplify the situation. Maybe due to the constant nagging, maybe out of greed, I was starting to consider the idea of staying in Russia for a little while longer. While I still did not like much about Kazan, I was starting to tolerate the entire situation, mainly because I had found someone—Chris Anstey—whom I could stand for more than fifteen minutes at a time. He and his wife have tolerated my frequent presence at their apartment and have even cooked the occasional meal for me. They may be saving me some money that otherwise would have been earmarked for a therapist later in life.

December 30

I'm a liar. I went to the team and proposed a deal. The team went for my swindle. Consequently, I am still in Russia.

The terms were a little ridiculous. I told them that I would stay for twenty days if they would pay me a month's salary for that time period. I did some math; that wage scale is the same that I would receive if I were in the NBA—hence the proposition. I thought I could survive twenty days if I could justify in my mind that I could do no better— financially, at least—in the United States. And the team virtually fell over themselves to agree. I don't know what is wrong with them; it's not like I'm giving out free postgame hand jobs.

My first real game with the team was a roaring success. (I'm not going to count the game for which I was told to dress only one hour beforehand.) We played a team from Israel that had beaten my team handily in their first encounter. I started the game, which came as a surprise, and we roared out of the gate—pardon the sportswriter- speak. I scored the first four points of the game, which was nice since it was my first appearance and the crowd didn't know quite what to make of the longhaired American. We piled up a lead of more than twenty points by halftime but weren't finished. I gathered that the Jews (it was mostly Jewish guys—that was not a slur) had embar- rassed my team the first time around, and our coach was not going to let them forget it. We ended up winning by fifty, scoring 109 in the process—not an easy task in a forty-minute game. I really played well, finishing with fourteen points and nine rebounds, which in itself is not all that impressive. But I had a good game—it was the most fun I've had on a basketball court in a long, long time.

After the game, I was invited/required to attend a Christmas- themed dinner party thrown by the owner of the team. It was quite a spectacle. Fortunately, I spent most of the night with Chris Anstey and his wife, so I had an outlet for the remarks that were brewing in my head as the night wore on. We arrived in time for the first of the evening's many toasts, given by the owner, who heads a large chain of banks and is the vision of the stereotypical rich old Russian man. Con- tributing to his general ugliness was the strong impression that he'd downed at least a fifth of vodka the previous night. He speaks no En- glish, is probably sixty but looks eighty, and constantly has a woman half his age on his arm. While I listened to his speech—or, rather, his speech washed over my ears, as it was in Russian—I wondered if a person like him takes note of the halfhearted nature of the laughs and handshakes or if he just ignores it.

When he was finished with what was, I'm sure, a truly inspirational piece of public speaking, it was time to get down to the business of picking at some appetizer platters. While we waited for further nourishment, we were entertained by/subjected to a very bad saxophonist accompanying piped-in Kenny G. After he left to sporadic applause, I began looking around for some real food. Instead, I was treated to another toast in Russian, this time by our head coach. Fortunately, his was not as lengthy, so we were not made to wait long for a repeat of the musical stylings of our saxophone-playing friend. This cycle repeated itself—boring toast, odd entertainment, me looking around for foodstuffs—and I fell into a daze, until the girl wearing the nurse's uniform came out. Prior to the dinner, one of my teammates, Kaspars Kambala, had translated for us a brief synopsis of the evening's entertainment agenda. He had mentioned that there was supposed to be some "erotic dancing," but I'd assumed he had said that only to get his wife's blood boiling. When the girl came out, I realized that he had not been kidding.

I should back up and do a better job of setting the stage, as it were. Those invited—players, coaches, the team doctor and trainer, a few team officials—had been encouraged to bring along their families. Most players brought only their wives, leaving their children at home. One player brought his one-year-old daughter, but his wife had taken her home after she managed to crawl under the length of the forty-foot table in just under two minutes. The fact that there were no children in attendance upon the arrival of the "nurse" was unfortunate only because their absence allowed the comedic value of the very awkward situation to wallow about three percentage points lower than its potential.

Before the girl could even be off with her outer layer, Kambala's wife ushered him out of the room in protest. I am not a proponent of wife beating, but come on, loosen up. After that, the girl got down to business. She only managed to bare the upper half of her body, which seemed half-assed (excuse the choice of words). She took a lap around the table and then, without fanfare, retired to the next room.

After another toast, I was called to the front of the room to lead the singing of a Christmas carol of my choosing. I was not thrilled. But I've learned over the years that protests only make matters worse. It is best to seize the request before it becomes any more demeaning. Since I didn't want to take off my shirt, I rushed to the front of the room before the situation became even more bizarre. I wish I could write that I came up with an interesting carol, but that would be untrue. I went with "Jingle Bells." I don't mind speaking in front of a group; singing, however, is not listed under the "Skills and Unique Abilities" section of my resume. I even failed to begin the song correctly, in two ways. First, I left out the "Dashing through the snow" beginning. To make matters worse, I started off singing "Jingle Bell Rock" and had to change gears quickly when I realized my mistake. Fortunately, there were only about four people in the audience who realized I had made a grievous melodic error. Even if the Russians knew the song, most of them were too drunk to care.

I returned to my seat with hope that my caroling would be rewarded with some actual food. Not so. We had only been served the aforementioned appetizer platters and some broth that took more calories to consume than it provided, so I was beginning to get a little cranky.

After another toast, the ante was upped, and more strippers came out. Male strippers. Plural. The Kambalas made another swift exit, as did two of my more insecure teammates. (Leaving the scene under such a circumstance does not actually make a person appear more heterosexual. It only seems to raise the question "What is he really afraid of here?" On to another tangent: it seems that a popular question these days is "What if you found out you had a gay teammate? Would it bother you that he was showering with you and seeing you naked?" This baffles me. It is not like being around a gay dude is going to turn me into a homosexual. Plus, he might be able to give me hair-care tips.) The male burlesque show was truly hilarious, as the poor guys were dancing around like, well, a couple of fairies (and I mean that in the most Tinkerbell, ballet-like way I can) while most of the audience either laughed or made remarks under their breath. They took off their shirts and then finally slunk off stage right. I'm not sure what the organizers of the event could have been thinking. Having the female stripper was pushing it, undoubtedly. But two male strippers? Seriously, who could have decided, "Yeah, that will go well with the semi-formal dinner and the Santa Claus entrance"? (I neglected to mention that Santa Claus, or the Russian equivalent thereof, had made a white-beard-stained-with-red-wine appearance earlier in the evening. It was an uninspired performance.) Which reminds me, none of the strippers used a Santa Claus theme. It seems like that would have been a no-brainer.

Next we took a twenty-minute break for dancing. Still no food, of course. Most of the party moved to the next room and its dance floor, which gave me the opportunity to witness the team president and the entire coaching staff attempting to dance to current pop songs. The dancing—or, more appropriately, unnecessary arrhythmic stress on some aged hips—was not a pretty sight. The most awkward aspect was that no one was really dancing with anyone. In fact, the group had a three-to-one male-to-female ratio and the dancing was taking place in one big circle, as if everyone was waiting for someone to take the lead and begin a break-dancing contest in the middle. I was glad to be able to watch from the other room—the awkwardness on the dance floor was straining the gauge. My viewing was interrupted by a lady who appeared to be the wife of one of the coaches. She told Chris and me that the president wanted everyone to dance. Wrong thing to say to me. If I had been considering going out there to break it on down, the dancing orders relieved me of that sentiment. My dancing policy is pretty simple: I try to avoid it, for the most part. There are exceptions, weddings being an obvious example. But even in that case, my dancing is generally limited to the type that involves a partner and some sort of preset routine (such as slow dancing) unless one of two conditions holds: (1) I am in a really, really good mood or (2) I am under the impression that dancing with a particular person could somehow later lead to sex with that person. At any rate, neither of my stated requirements was fulfilled in this situation, so I stayed in the dining area.

When everyone was finished expressing his inner Fred Astaire, we were eventually given some food. The entertainment fizzled out from there: our final troubadour recited poetry. In Russian, of course. After three hours of very little food and a whole bunch of strangeness, I was finally able to leave, and one of the strangest evenings of my life came to an end.

January 13

It's official. I'm leaving Russia soon. Following my deal/swindle for an additional twenty days, the coaches asked me to remain until the end of the season. While their desperation was flattering, it did not overcome my need to leave. But before I could go, I had to deal with one final road trip.

We traveled to the Czech Republic to play a team in Nymburk, which is about an hour outside of Prague. The trip itself was a doozy. We left Monday night from Kazan to fly to Moscow, where we stayed in easily one of the grimiest hotels in which I have ever slept. It looked like it was built in the 1950s and seems to have been maintained in the style of the era—for a communist country. While there, I had my first exposure to a faucet shared by both the sink and the bathtub. The principle is a little militaristic, I suppose, but a long tap that swivels between the two is rather efficient. After a night's sleep, we departed for Prague. Our arrival there was hailed by something I had not seen in ages—the sun. It was as if someone had taken the gray 3D glasses away from my eyes. So much color. Green grass. Red roofs. I don't know how the Czechs stand it. I kept looking for the sludge-colored cars . . . houses . . . streets . . . dogs . . . people. . . .

My team had lost to the Czechs the first time the two had played, so a win in Nymburk was a necessity. (Maybe a little too much gravitas there. Sometimes I get caught up in cliché fever.)

I did not have high expectations for much playing time in Nymburk. In the previous game, a home win against a team called

Khimki, I had gotten the distinct impression that the process of phasing me out had begun. I didn't start—the first time that had happened since I began playing for the Russians (with the exception, again, of the game when I was notified of my impending participation sixty minutes beforehand)—and had played only seven minutes, scoring a whopping two points.

I again did not start against the Czech team, but was one of the first off the bench when our coach was once more reminded that one of our two marquee players still has learned neither how to play defense nor how to pass the basketball to his teammates. I did not come out much after that, and had a really good time. The team we were playing was certainly not the '87 Lakers, but they were a tenacious bunch and the win was a satisfying one. In my little niche in the world, there are few better feelings than grinding out a victory away from home. There is something about stealing the glory from the home team that gets me going.

The postgame mood was pretty somber, mainly because my team is filled with assholes like me who cannot enjoy a win if they feel they were in some way slighted by the coach regarding playing time, being yelled at, et cetera. The locker room activities were the same as usual: our coach never showed to make any postgame remarks, three players retired early to the showers to rush through a pre-cleansing cigarette—all the things that any functional basketball team does after a game. After I made my way out of the zone of positivity that was our locker room, I found myself waiting in the lobby of the complex with one of the other team's Americans and the mother of another one. While we were engaged in conversation, she asked where I was from. When I said Kansas, she said, "Isn't that in Nebraska?"— and was not kidding. There should be tests that a person has to pass to be allowed to continue living. The American player with whom I was waiting turned out to be a good guy, so we ("we" being my usual partner in crime, Chris Anstey, and me) got his number and promised to call him when we got back to the hotel.

We were greeted at the hotel by a meal that featured a large amount of moldy bread. I cannot say that I have ever been served moldy bread at a restaurant, so it is a good thing I went to the Czech Republic; I might otherwise have missed out on that experience. (That sentence came out a bit wrong. I in no way want to imply that all restaurants in the Czech Republic serve moldy bread. Just the hotel restaurant at the Bellevue in Nymburk.) After plowing our way through the chef's demonstration of his apathy toward his job, we called our new friend and set out for the center of the city.

We met the American, Adam, and one of his teammates and began the age-old ritual of finding somewhere to go. As usual, this entailed our host asking dumb questions like "Where do you guys want to go?" To which the obvious response is "Well, since we don't live here and couldn't give a good goddamn anyway, why don't you just pick a place?" In our case, that place was a pizzeria near downtown Nymburk.

The four of us sat around a table in the pizzeria until it closed, sharing stories about idiot coaches and brain-dead teammates. Chris and I supplemented the poor excuse for a meal provided by the hotel with some pizza, and the group consumed several beers until it was time to leave. (The total bill was about $10—cheap living in the Czech Rep.) Adam's Czech teammate had developed some rapport with two of the waitresses, so we told him to convince them to meet us later at another bar. We also somehow picked up a Czech girl with whom the teammate had a passing acquaintance; she would prove to be nothing but a nuisance, mostly because she smelled awful.

We hiked a few blocks to a dive bar in the center of town. After a while, the two girls joined us. (Europeans, unlike many Americans, often actually do what they say they will do—if they say they will come to a bar in half an hour, that is probably what they intend to do, as opposed to the average American, who will say that with no intention of ever showing up.) For the next few hours, there was a lot of talking with minimal understanding, some dancing involving a stripper pole placed conveniently near the stage, the consumption of alcohol, the taking of several pictures, a lot of making fun of the stinky girl without her knowing it, and all in all, a memorable evening for all involved, or at least for me. Maybe the rest of the group does that on a regular basis, but I can without a doubt say that I will never have another night quite like it, not because of anything monumental that went on but because I will never be in Nymburk at my age under those circumstances ever again.

We all left the bar at 3:30 A.M. Our wake-up call for the bus to the airport was at 5:30 A.M. I was disappointed that we had to leave the Czech Republic—I had taken a liking to one of the pizzeria girls. However, I couldn't figure out how that was going to help anyone, since I had two in-country hours remaining. My new friends came to the rescue, sort of. As I moaned about the problem, Adam called his teammate, who was in the midst of taking the two girls home. (Chivalrous of him.) I was put on the phone with the girl with whom there had been some spark. She said that she would meet me in front of our hotel at 4:15. Chris went to bed and told me to make him proud.

As I stood on a darkened plaza in Nymburk waiting for a girl to appear and for us to do God-knows-what before my team left in an hour and a quarter, I considered the absurdity of the situation. I rated it somewhere between high and very high. I was officially out of my element. It was great. There is something freeing about being so far from home. In such situations, life becomes surreal. I've had a fair number of such occurrences, and each time I think, *This is not the sort of thing you do, Paul.* But they keep happening, so apparently they are the sort of thing I do.

Marketa appeared from the dark just as I was ready to pack it in and try for forty-five minutes of sleep. I asked her if she wanted to go inside. She said no, that we should go to a bar nearby. It was probably for the best. We chatted for a while and then I walked her to her home, which was around the corner from the hotel. I kissed her and walked back to my room in time to pack up my bag and get on the bus.

I'm sure I'll never see her again.

January 17

The hits just keep on coming here in Russia. I can't get out of this country fast enough.

I am currently embroiled in a long process that I hope will eventu-

ally result in the return of some of my clothes. I generally make an absolute mess out of the hotel rooms in which I stay, and find that the
floor is a great place to store dirty clothes until it is time to check out.
One of the maids here disagreed with my methodology and took it
upon herself to take some of my soiled whites to the laundry. Unfortunately, they have not reappeared. Today I made a trip down to the
front desk to see if I could learn something about my clothes' whereabouts; the woman there told me to go back to my room and wait
while she called the chambermaid to straighten things out. (At least
that was what I thought she was doing.) After twenty minutes, a
knock came at my door. I found a maid outside speaking rapidly in
Russian. Luckily, one of the front desk workers was down the hall; she
translated that the maid was asking if I wanted my room cleaned. I
sent her on her way and explained the situation to the woman who
had accompanied the maid. She said, "Wait two minutes." About half
an hour later, a different maid, this one bearing a striking resemblance
to Olive Oyl, only without the quality dental work I would expect from
a run-of-the-mill cartoon character, made an appearance. She was decidedly not holding my clean clothes and began making hand motions
that were intended to simulate washing clothes, implying that she had
come for the clothes that I needed washing. I shook my head and tried
to smile, closed my door, found the Uzi that I keep in my bag for just
such an occasion, and went on a killing rampage in the hotel. Actually,
I chickened out and once again called the woman at the front desk.
She assured me that everything would be taken care of. Doubtful.

The coach once again tried to persuade me to stay before the
team left for Kazan, but it was to no avail. He told me that I still had
time to change my mind, but he did not say anything to make that
likely. So my exodus from Russia has begun, albeit slowly. I did offer
the team a final proposal, one that would have nearly doubled my
monthly salary, but they didn't go for it. I think they gave it some serious consideration, but the numbers were so outlandish, it would have
been difficult for them. In the interest of full disclosure, I will say that
they did up their offer to a cool $55,000 a month, net of taxes, for the
rest of the season (four months), but that was not quite enough to

make me want to continue to deal with Russia. Of course, the above number is a ridiculous amount of money, and I have been going over and over in my head why I cannot seem to bring myself to simply endure another 120 days for the sake of my bankbook. I think I realize that I acted young and dumb to turn down such money; I just don't care. The beauty of my current lot in life is that I can afford to be so wanton. It is possible that I will regret these poverty-making decisions at some point, but I don't think it is likely. My current life-theme is less about planning for the future and more about enjoying what I am doing while I can. (It's true, I do have emotions.)

With regard to basketball, I think the decision to leave was undoubtedly a good one. I'm quite sure that I am a worse player than I was when I left the United States. Since my goal (alert: potential soul-searching ahead) with regard to my basketball career is really only to see how good I can get at it before I quit, a few more months on the downslide was not going to help.

My contract came to an end a few days ago. At the request (begging) of the coaching staff, I stayed to play in one last game since I was going to be in Moscow awaiting a flight home anyway. We lost the game, thereby destroying my hope for a triumphant exit from Russia. I did not play particularly well or particularly badly. In fact, I had little impact on the game, other than some comic relief provided when I blew a wide-open layup in the first half. Our opponent was just behind us in the standings, so our loss was devastating.

As punishment, our coach banned us from leaving the hotel after the game. I was, of course, no longer under contract to the team, nor under any obligation to follow any rules set forth, so I felt no remorse when four of us set off for Moscow proper. (The hotel was not close to the city.) I'm not sure what the enforcement plan was; Chris Anstey actually walked past the coach on his way out of the hotel. When asked where he was going, Chris said, "We're meeting people in Moscow," which I guess was not deemed direct disobeyance of the order to "not leave the hotel."

We rode into the city in two cabs, Chris and I in one, Shammond Williams and Ira Clark in the other. Those who had told us we were far from Moscow had not lied; it took about fifty minutes to get there. Once in the city, we ate at a terrible American restaurant that under normal circumstances would have offended my sense of taste, but because the others in the group did not have a trip to the United States in their immediate future, I could not fault their need for a bit of Americana. After the meal we meandered down to a club that the rest of the group knew. Since it was Sunday night, the place was nearly deserted. Two of the few patrons were retrieving their coats as we entered; had they left, the place would have been completely empty. But when they saw us slide up to the bar, the two girls from the coatroom decided their exit could wait, and sidled over to us. Their English was limited, and their look was a little on the whorish side, so we were somewhat suspicious of their intentions. One, whose name was something Russian that I have forgotten, claimed to be a tailor, of all things. Her friend, who was better-looking if one could overlook the zombie-like stare and pallor of her skin, did not speak English, but we learned that her cover story was that she was a student.

As the halting conversation progressed between the two of them and Shammond and me (we happened to be nearest them), my internal whore-o-meter went from 65 percent sure they were hookers to 90 percent in a matter of minutes. The Russian girls should have realized that we were going to be poor marks when they saw that we were drinking tea; had they fully understood most of the things we were saying, they definitely would have realized that we were not actually interested in their wares. We were more interested in making each other laugh. At one point, when the conversation had died down again, Shammond blurted out, "Do you have sex for money?" The ringleader of the group of two acted embarrassed, and then whispered in my ear, "Maybe two girls at same time?" which I relayed to Shammond. He asked, "How much?" They replied that it would cost $600. Having pushed the envelope as far as it needed to go, we turned away from them and went back to talking among ourselves. When we got up to leave for the night, the girls followed us as we made a final circuit of the building to see what we had been missing while we had been talking to hookers. The English-speaker made a last-ditch effort with me, saying (this is a direct quote), "Maybe now we go back to your hotel, relax, little sex, what you call—ménage à trois?" I gave her a smile and a no, and they finally left, which actually surprised me. Aren't whores supposed to negotiate?

The story does not end there. (Well, as far as the prostitutes go, it does. My moral code is not all that stringent, I suppose, but paying for sex is unacceptable. Unless she's a Maori. Then it has to be done in the interest of a good story.) When we left the club at about 1:30, we needed a ride home. The sister of one of our Russian teammates worked at the bar; she offered to find us a ride. We had originally planned on calling the same taxi we had taken into the city—we knew the driver knew the way home—but realized that it would probably take twenty minutes for him to find us. Our friend the worker bee assured us that the club's doorman could find a ride for us immediately.

The two cars that arrived at the club were definitely not taxis. But that makes sense—there are very few actual taxis in Russia. Most of the taxiing that goes on is done by private citizens in their own cars. I don't know why; it probably has something to do with an impotent government and its lack of regulations regarding such things. I do know that it takes a good deal of trust, at least for me, to get into a total stranger's car. I realize that I do not know most taxi drivers personally, but it is reassuring to see the cabdriver's registration hanging from his rearview mirror.

The two drivers seemed amiable enough and recognized the name of our hotel straightaway, so I thought we were in relatively good hands. In retrospect, however, we should have waited. About forty minutes later, when our driver was hunched over the steering wheel with a baffled look on his face, Chris and I realized that our trust had been misplaced. Shammond and Ira's car was following us; eventually their driver flashed his lights and our driver willingly pulled over for a powwow. We had a card with the hotel's phone number and suggested that either driver call the hotel for some directions. One did; he spoke to someone for ten minutes. During these ten minutes, Chris and I came to the sobering realization that we were in a total stranger's car in a very rural area somewhere outside of Moscow, and that this was about all the information we had about the situation. Not a great feeling, really.

After the talk, our driver came back with a purposeful look in his eye. We drove on . . . for about a mile. When we stopped again, both drivers got out and lit cigarettes, and Chris and I wondered what the hell was going on. We finally ascertained that they had told the hotel to send someone out for us and were waiting at the predetermined intersection for the hotel shuttle. In the meantime, I tried to call the hotel. I explained the situation as best as I could to the receptionist. After claiming that she did speak English, she listened for about twenty-five seconds and then hung up. Fantastic. We waited for a few more minutes before the other driver decided he would figure out our route home. He set out so confidently that I regained some hope.

Finally, we stopped at the building he thought to be our hotel; it looked more like the entrance to a junkyard, complete with guard dog, and was definitely not the Atlas-Park Hotel. At this point, I coerced our driver into talking to the hotel on the phone. Five minutes later, we were at our destination. When we gave our driver the pre-arranged 1,000 rubles, he seemed miffed, as if we should have rewarded him for finding his way back from being totally lost. What a country.

January 19

Because the Russians apparently have absolutely no talent for logistics, my trip home was interrupted by a stay in the Ramada Plaza Hotel at JFK in New York—the same place I'd stayed before my departure in November. They could not put together a trip that got me home in one day, even though they had a nine-hour time change working in their favor. Oh well, it gives the entire trip a bit of symmetry; it's like going through the levels of depressurization after a deep dive. Or, perhaps more accurately, like being brought back from a hypnotic state—complete, I hope, with some amnesia regarding the last two months.

Apparently I am a memorable fellow. The man at the hotel restaurant in New York recognized me right away. He said, "Weren't you here on Thanksgiving?" I'd like to think that his memory of me was aided by my winning personality, but I would guess that it had more to do with my height. I can pretend, though.

Aside from some long lines in the Moscow airport and the unnecessary stay in NYC, the trip across the Atlantic was relatively easy. The same driver who had shuttled me between airports when I arrived in Russia picked me up at the hotel outside Moscow and drove me to Sheremetyevo Airport for my flight to New York. On the way, the team's general manager, Elvira, called to make yet another last-second offer and plea for me to stay. (It must seem that I am making this up to boost my own ego. In fact, I was as surprised by it as anyone.) I gave her another polite no. Once at the airport, the driver—who until now had shown no sign of speaking English—managed to put together, "Team not pay for this. You pay me $100." I do not know if mustering the courage for his attempt at extortion caused him to sweat more than usual or if it was merely the turning in my direction that did the trick, but at that moment I was overpowered by the most repellant, nausea-inducing case of body odor I have ever encountered. It was like a mixture of mildewed socks and rotten teeth. The stench did nothing to convince me. Instead, I opened the door slightly in order to let in some cold air to kill the smell and then called Elvira. She answered expectantly, most likely assuming I had changed my mind and wanted her to get me a flight back to Kazan. Instead I disappointed her and told her to get Stinky off my case. She succeeded, and I beat a hasty retreat from the car.

The flight home consisted of the following:

T minus 10 minutes   I get on and realize that, for all the worldliness I like to pretend I have, I still feel a bit out of place in the business-class section of an airplane. That being said, I feel a little less out of place in Aeroflot's business class, as it is easily the worst I have seen. Which is the case only because neither Siberian Airlines nor Tatarstan Airlines, which tied for the honor of worst planes I've ever seen in operation, had anything above coach.

0:02   The guy next to me stinks. Great. Why do they think they need to wear so many clothes? The smell is not quite as bad as that surrounding my driver, but it is reminiscent.

0:15   Speaking of clothes, I notice that my outfit of track pants and a T-shirt is decidedly out of place here. Then I think, *Did these people really believe it was a good idea to wear a suit for a ten-and-a-half-hour flight?*

0:21   I receive a menu. I am momentarily confused by the entrée list. I understand "Salmon Steak" and "Vegetable Tortellini." "Bee Fillet," however, throws me for a loop. Let me think now . . . I have heard of most cuts of meat but know nothing of the bee fillet. Is this an insect delicacy? Hmm . . . It says it is wrapped in ham. That rules out bugs, I suppose, as it would be hard to wrap a bee in ham. I look over at the side written in Russian, hoping for some help. I see БЕЙФСТАК, which, because I am a damn genius, I can read as "Beefsteak." Problem solved. I guess my time in Russia was not wasted after all.

0:37   I pull out the little TV at the side of my seat and discover that the current movie being shown is *The Princess Diaries 2*. Son of a bitch.

0:41   I stow my TV. I gave it a chance, but that is one terrible movie.

0:42   I evaluate my entertainment options. I have about a hundred pages left in my book. I bought a magazine in the Moscow airport, but that won't last long. In addition to smelling bad, the man next to me is Russian and I cannot even begin to explain how tired I am of broken-English conversations, so he is out. Thank Jobs for my iPod.

1:10   Dinner is served. I leave my caviar untouched, to incredulous stares from my cabinmates. I want to say, *You realize this shit tastes like fish eggs, right? Who decided that was a good thing?*

1:26   My bee(f) fillet arrives. It is not good per se, but it gives me something to do, and for that I am thankful.

1:45   Aeroflot rallies and brings me an amazing dessert concoction. The whole meal is something of a microcosm of Russia itself: nothing of substance is worth a damn, but the girls look pretty good.

2:00   I notice that the outside air temperature is −70° F. I wonder how it can be so hot inside

the plane. I push my pant legs up and become a true sight to see—a six-ten guy
with a plain white T-shirt and some track
pants pushed up above his calves wearing
white socks that match his skin after two
months under the clouds of Kazan. I consider inquiring as to whether the flight attendant can find a Busch Light so I can
complete the stereotype.

2:08   By my calculations, *The Princess Diaries 2* has to be over soon. Surely they
wouldn't . . .

2:15   "Walt Disney Pictures Presents" . . . *The
Princess Diaries 2.* Shit.

2:20   I begin a rotation that goes something like
this: iPod alone, iPod while reading maga-
zine, iPod alone, reading book with no
iPod, back to the iPod alone. I pass out for
about an hour.

4:30   Christ. Six hours left. Back to the rotation.

6:15   I drink my second bottle of water and mar-
vel at the fact that I have not yet visited the
lavatory. When I am seventy, I will yearn for
these days.

6:37   It hits me that I will be home soon. I think,
Four more hours, that's nothing. I am jubilant.

6:41 Four more hours? What am I going to do for four hours?

7:12 A snack is served. On its way to my mouth, my salmon and mustard-seed pâté falls off the cracker-like piece of bread on which it is sitting. I calmly pick it off my paper place mat, replace it on the bread, and send it on its way. Cultured, I am.

8:01 I begin work on my masterwork, a list of my top fifty albums. Again, the iPod comes through.

8:45 I order a brandy. Brandy? Who the hell am I?

9:40 I finally make a trip to the toilet. Always a source of entertainment, both for me and for anyone lucky enough to see someone of my stature attempt to fold himself into an airplane lavatory.

10:12 They hand out the customs declaration sheets. We're almost there. I am given pause by the fact that they are only in English. Seems it would be difficult to fill these out if one did not speak the language, like if one were, say, Russian. We Americans are lucky that someone decided that English would be the intergalactic language of choice.

10:16 My seatmate moves and a wave of funk is blasted my way. My concern for the Russian people is obliterated.

10:35   We touch down, five thousand miles later. I
                             am happy but exhausted. It is 6:45 P.M., but
                             my body thinks it is 2:45 A.M.

Arrival plus 20 minutes I hand over my passport to a black lady be-
                             hind the immigration counter. She smiles
                             and says, "How was it?" I reply, "Terrible, I
                             don't think I'll go back to Russia." She
                             smiles again and says, "Well then, welcome
                             home." When I complained in Russia about
                             the fact that no one there ever smiles, I was
                             told that the opposite was true in America;
                             that people smiled too much, without any
                             meaning behind the expression. There is
                             something to that—we are probably too po-
                             lite at times and often do not say what we
                             mean, but that lady's smile seemed awfully
                             nice to me.

January 24

I left Russia with no real plan for the rest of the year. I thought I would
come home, play out the year with the minor-league Kansas City
Knights, and hope for a ten-day contract in the NBA, but most of all
enjoy the fact that I was not in Russia. I thought I had a good chance
for a call-up but was not going to be all that disappointed if one did
not come my way. It probably was not the most ambitious plan, but
then again, it seemed open-ended enough to be to my liking. Strangely,
my lack of any real direction may have resulted in one of the most
amazing turn of events in my life.

I arrived in Kansas City on a Wednesday night, still disoriented
but delighted to see two of my younger brothers awaiting me at the
airport. We had a quick dinner at Outback Steakhouse (because nothing is as American as a poor attempt at co-opting another country's
culture) and I fell into bed. Thursday held a trip to my parents' house

to see the rest of the family. That night, sometime before or after one of my mother's typically fantastic culinary creations, I got a call from my agent. Keith told me that the Phoenix Suns were considering making a trade that would send three of their players away in exchange for only one player. He did not know many details but said that the Suns had called him to inquire about my availability should the deal go through. He thought that if it happened, it would be the next day, so I should stay close to my phone. I informed my family and, for the most part, forgot about it for the night. Such things—the type that seem too good to be true, that is—have not figured prominently in my basketball career to this point, so that I dismissed the scenario as extremely unlikely should not be particularly surprising. My reaction was that there was very little chance the team I already knew—the one that had some players I actually liked, in addition to being one of the best teams in the NBA this year—would sign me. It would be too easy.

I woke up Friday and, after my whopping one day off (travel days do not count as days off; I would submit that they are harder on the mind and body than a full day of practice), made a trip to the gym with the hopes only of breaking a sweat and checking to see if I had forgotten how to shoot a basketball in the four days since my last game in the former USSR. I accomplished that goal and on the way home checked in with Keith. He reported no real developments except to say that the Suns' GM, Bryan Colangelo, had called him early that morning to say that the trade had not yet been made, but if it was, I would definitely get the call as a replacement for the departed players. He noted, however, that he had been told that if it happened, the trade would go down at noon Eastern time. That it was then 2 P.M. Eastern time and he had not heard anything was a little alarming. I decided that even though there was a good chance doing so would jinx the entire setup, I probably should get home and start unpacking some of my bags.

While I was waiting to transfer loads of wash, I made a few calls to catch up with people with whom I hadn't spoken in two months. One of my calls was to a friend who works for the New Orleans Hornets, having survived the purges that removed Coach Floyd from his post there. He happened to mention that he had overheard a rumor that his employer was about to pull the trigger on a trade that would send Jimmy Jackson (for whom the Hornets had traded one month earlier, only to have him refuse to report for duty) to the Suns for Casey Jacobsen, Jackson Vroman, and Maciej Lampe. He thought the deal was all but done—their equipment guy was readying uniforms for the new acquisitions. My jaw dropped at least three inches. When I recovered, I told him how his news was particularly interesting to me, and promised to keep him informed about further developments. When I hung up, it was all I could do to keep my newfound information to myself. I told my brothers but kept careful watch on their Internet usage over the next hour. A little while later, just as I was putting my third load in the washer, Keith called to tell me that the trade was done and that I should be ready to go to Phoenix, possibly as soon as that night. When he told me that the deal had gone through, I put him back on his heels a little by naming the players involved. He was duly impressed with my insider information. As I ratcheted up the pace of my laundering, I waited for more news. It did not take long. When he called the next time he said coyly, "I have bad news and good news. The bad news: I wasn't able to get you the ten-day with the Suns. The good news: I was able to get them to sign you for the rest of the year."

I spent Friday night in a daze. I had invited people over for a poker game at my house; it played on, but my concentration level was at an all-time low. (Such is the excuse for my poor performance.) I flew to Phoenix on Saturday at noon, and upon my arrival I underwent a physical that consisted of a doctor asking if anything had changed since the last time he had seen me in Phoenix: it took approximately three minutes. After my clearance, I returned to the same hotel where I'd spent a month in the fall, and wandered around in confusion. My brain was completely overloaded.

Keith called the next day, just prior to my first regular-season game with the Suns (not counting the one at the beginning of the season before which I'd cleaned out my locker). He said, "Well, Paul, there are some issues with your contract." I thought, *Okay, here we*

go. The real nameplate they put over my locker and all the rejoic-
ing by team personnel—it was all part of the plot to help make the
ten-day they are going to offer more palatable. I knew this was too
good to be true. He continued, "Yeah, they want to have an option on
next year."

"What? Who gives a damn? They can have an option on each of
the next ten years, for all I care. Is this contract guaranteed for the
rest of this year? Yes? Well then, sign it before they change their
minds." (This is the reason that from the outside, such as in the news-
paper, it appeared that I signed a two-year contract.) I signed my
copy of the contract exactly twenty-six minutes before our game with
the New Jersey Nets. I suited up but did not play—probably fortunately for everyone, as my body continues to show some confusion as
to what time zone it is in. We won, and my second stint as a Phoenix
Sun is off to a glorious start.

February 3

It is quite possible that I have the best job in the world. The following
are my vocational requirements:

1. Travel around the country on a chartered jet.
2. Stay in the finest hotels our land has to offer.
3. Practice basketball occasionally.
4. Sit on the bench during games and cheer for my teammates.
5. Once in a while, play a few meaningless minutes when the
   aforementioned teammates have stretched a lead into the
   thirty-to-forty-point range.

It's a tough gig.

I can vividly remember being about twelve years old and watching
some NBA game or other with my father and hearing him say about
some white guy at the end of the bench, "You see that guy, Paul? He's
got the best job a person could want—backup center in the NBA." I
am neither a center nor even a backup. I am a backup to the backup.

I have even less responsibility than the guy we were talking about. Add in the fact that my contract is guaranteed for the rest of the season, meaning it would take a meteor crashing into the earth, or at least an unprecendented fiscal crisis in Phoenix, for me to worry whether I will have a job in two weeks, and my dad was right—I do have the best job a guy could want.

I was in Phoenix for exactly forty-eight hours before leaving again. The Fates decided that I had not had quite enough traveling in the last month, so they decided my return to the Suns would coincide with the beginning of a six-city, ten-day road trip. Our journey would take us to all the way east to New York, back across the country to Milwaukee, again to the coast and Boston, north into Canada for a game with Toronto, down south(ish) to Memphis, and then back to the Kazan-like climate of Minneapolis (actually, it felt a lot like spring there; it must be global warming). I spent the first few days of the trip in a kind of afterglow, hardly believing I was where I was. I watched us score 133 in a win against the Knicks, pull out an ugly victory against the Bucks, and squander a big lead over the Celtics but hold on to come out on top, all from the end of the bench, fully clothed in my warm-ups. My days were spent confirming the rumors regarding my whereabouts and walking around about six inches above the ground. Heady times.

In Toronto, the Suns scored forty-six points in the third quarter, which has to be some sort of record. This scoring orgy left us ahead by thirty going into the fourth. The seemingly insurmountable gave our coach, Mike D'Antoni, enough confidence to throw into the action me and a couple of other guys who had not played. We played great defense, allowing the Raptors to score only ten straight points in two minutes. Seeing his hard-fought lead being whittled away, Coach D'Antoni escorted us out of the game. The starters managed to right the ship, and we were allowed back in with about three minutes to go. My totals were five minutes played and 0 for 1 from the field (it took me about forty-five seconds to get up my first shot), with one random assist.

Our five-game win streak came to an end in Memphis. They found the secret to success against the Suns, which is to score more often than we do. (We play a rather fast-paced game, mainly due to point guard Steve Nash's ability to get the ball up the court in a hurry on offense. When I say that the secret to success is to score more often than we do, I mean it somewhat seriously. Because of our blitzkrieg mentality, most teams are taken aback and get down early, which results in their taking bad shots, allowing us to rebound the ball and get it out for easy baskets. The problem only gets worse as a team gets further behind, leading to the ludicrous point totals we sometimes accumulate.) The Grizzlies were actually able to make enough shots early to slow our advances into their defense, thereby creating a half-court game that was more in their favor. I will now stick a knife in my own ear because I sound like a basketball analyst.

We got back on the winning track against the Minnesota Timberwolves. In fact, at one point we were up by forty in Minneapolis. (The Suns truly have to be seen to be believed. Our every game should be on television just to get people excited about the NBA again.) I was the last player off the bench, logging the final three minutes of the game. I did not get a single shot off, which is inexcusable.

As I've mentioned before, I might have the best job in the world. So I shouldn't complain. Ever. But playing so rarely is hard on my psyche.

There certainly is no shame in being the eleventh man on the best or second-best basketball team in the world right now, but I am still struggling a bit to come to grips with the idea. (Eleventh because we have only eleven players. Apparently, the league will soon make the team sign another player.) I really have never been in this situation, at least not for any length of time. Now that I am faced with half a season of it (and beyond), I am disappointed with my reaction. I have always maintained that I would be perfectly happy to cheer on an NBA team from the bench, contributing in practice and in a minimal role on the court. But I am presently in exactly such a role, and I fear that my hold on happiness might be a tenuous one. It isn't that I think I should have any other role. The Suns don't need me or anyone else right now. They're doing just fine. I guess I feel like I need to contribute something more. I have an overwhelming need to prove that the Suns' trust in signing me for the rest of the year was not misplaced and that I am worthy of the honor, as it were, of being with the Suns and not with the Kansas City Knights. Since I doubt that the situation is going to change, I need to learn how to enjoy my time in some capacity. Otherwise, I'm going to be the uptight guy in a situation where there is no call for such behavior.

I'm not sure most basketball players would have these thoughts. However, it appears that my self-esteem, especially as tied as it is currently to my basketball abilities, needs constant booster shots. It is difficult to get a representative sample of how I am doing on the court in three or five minutes of end-of-the-game blowout time. In fact, in our last game, against Minnesota, I had the ball in my hands in a position where I could do something aggressive toward the basket exactly one time. Because it was an isolated event, I spent the rest of the night replaying that one move time and time again. Should I have shot it first? What happened when the defense collapsed? Was there someone else to whom I could have passed the ball? How close was that rather large man who was impeding my progress, and was there something I could have done that would have allowed me to score? This analysis is of a play that literally took less than a second to unfold. I'm breeding my own case of obsessive-compulsive disorder. It should be noted, too, that I am the only one who gives a damn about this; the coaches are not analyzing my 180 seconds of play while trying to decide whether to play me more. And for once my future with the team (for this year, anyway) is not dependent on management's opinion of my play.

Logic tells me that my problem will work itself out. I will get a few real practices under my belt and will start to feel like a productive member of the team. (Our practices on the road trip, because they always fell between two game days, consisted of light shooting and some walking around.) I'll learn to relax at the far end of the bench and will see my limited time on the court as a reward for the hard work I put in with the Suns this fall and not as punishment for some imagined basketball ineptitude. Then maybe that cushion of air will come back.

February 12

While I do love my new job, I cannot submit that the situations in which I find myself have gotten any less maddening.

While waiting after practice for the start of a short road trip to San Francisco, I sat down at one of the computers in the palatial players' lounge that adjoins our locker room. No one was using the pool table, the DVD player, or any of the multiple video game systems available to us and our stunted maturity levels. One of my teammates was sitting in one of the leather recliners, watching the Discovery Channel and a show about Milton's *Paradise Lost* on the huge flat-screen television on the wall, mainly because he thought the program was about religion, not about the author's take on it. Another teammate was absently talking on his phone while eating something that had come out of the gigantic refrigerator near the couches. When he looked up from his food, he noted the program and said, "Man, I wish I could come up with an idea for an invention. I could make some real money then."

Of course, the show was not even remotely about inventions, unless we accept that writing a book could be called inventing a book, which is a bit of a stretch. It was on the Discovery Channel, which does spend a goodly amount of time focusing on inventors and their wares, so the mental leap is somewhat understandable. More important, the player to whom I refer uses his Las Vegas–based education to pull down upward of $14 million a year. I doubt many inventors can instruct their accountants to fill in such a number on their 1040.

Such moments remind me that I am in desperate need of a benchmate. NBA games are long. Really long. There are all kinds of breaks in the action, mainly of the media time-out variety, so there is plenty of standing around. Granted, I should probably be, oh, paying attention to what the coach is drawing up during these time-outs, but they are so long and frequent that even the coaches run out of things to say. It is at these times especially that I need a partner in crime—someone who will see the humor in the fact that the poor girl in the dance contest shown on the scoreboard screen is merely a prop for the obvious eventual winner, the middle-aged fat guy who lifts his shirt over his head to expose the world to his man-pregnancy. I need someone who will not be afraid to rate the members of the dance team in descending order of most realistic breast implants. I need someone who will help me keep track of my NBA All-Ugly Team. Most of the people who play think they actually need to concentrate on the games, so they cannot be bothered with my attempts at self-entertainment. The trainers and other support staff—my usual outlet for such sophomoric comments—are isolated behind the bench, out of range. Which leaves my two fellow non-playing players, each of whom presents problems of his own. First, both are basketball players, so the chances of them having the same sense of humor as me are slim. One of them is married and a religious wing nut, which removes him as a potential recipient of any comments involving the objectification of women, curse words, or anything that degrades another's self-worth—basically, my entire in-game repertoire. The other candidate is a little better but is generally too scattered to be able to focus on something as intricate as a detailed analysis of the strategy needed to make the choice among a free throw for $777, a three-pointer for $7,777, or a half-court shot for $77,777. By the end of the game, my eyes must be crying out for help, there are so many pent-up snide remarks stored away. Obviously, I need to start playing, even if it is only as a distraction from the rest of the circus around me.

February 24

My line from our most recent game, a home engagement with the Los Angeles Clippers:

Min: 1 FGA: 0 FGM: 0 REB: 0 A: 0 F: 0 TO: 0

Ostensibly, I did very little that day. A recounting of the day's schedule would lead one to believe otherwise.

Game-day practice, the shoot-around, started at 9:45 A.M. On a normal day, practice begins at 11:00. I have not yet figured out why our shoot-arounds are so much earlier; it seems counterintuitive. One would think a coach would want his team to get more rather than less rest the night before a game. Needless to say, this earlier start time throws off my policy of sleeping until 9:00 whenever possible. It really is a rough life I lead. At some point during the season, the players decided that it was too cold on the main floor of the arena so early in the day, so shoot-arounds were moved to the more temperature-friendly confines of the downstairs practice court, thereby negating what was, I thought, one of the only reasons for a shoot-around—acclimating oneself to the baskets to be played upon that evening. So, after arriving around 9:15, I made my way down to the practice court. We watched film of the Clippers, warmed up, and then broke into two groups for some light shooting. As is always the case, we inside players reported to one end of the court, with the guards heading to the other. When we are told which direction to head, the coaches say, "Bigs—this end. Wings—down there." They do not use *littles* as the opposite of *bigs* because the guards decided that such a term was too demeaning. When we got to our respective ends, we did drills that resulted in shots specific to our positions. After five minutes, we switched ends of the court, which seems somewhat pointless since, again, we were not in any way getting used to the rims on which we would be playing that night.

When we finished with another five minutes of tremendously useful shooting that was not repetitive in the least, the team got back together and we ran through some of our plays. Next, we moved on to something a little more constructive—the scouting of the opponent, in this case the aforementioned Clippers. The coaches identified some of us as stand-ins for Clippers players and took the team through a walking rendition of some of their plays. I was selected neither as a Sun nor as a Clipper, so I stood on the sideline and tried to keep my mind from wandering, with little success. (It should be noted that if I am having trouble staying focused in such a situation, there is no telling what most of my teammates are processing. I think some of them began planning next year's Christmas list.) For fifteen minutes or so, the coaches positioned the stand-in Clippers in one spot or another and talked about what our opponent might do in certain situations. In actuality, most of what they said was forgotten before it was even learned—but at least the coaches could say they had done their jobs. We gathered at center court, listened to one final pep talk, put our hands in the center of a team huddle, and broke with a "1, 2, 3 . . . Suns!" for the first of many times that day, and I went off to shoot some free throws. Others followed suit. When 11:00 rolled around, most of the team scattered. Those of us who would not be playing much later in the day stuck around; after my free throws, I worked with one of the coaches for about twenty minutes before calling it a morning. As I passed the training room, I popped open the compartment marked *17* (my number with the Suns) on the old-lady pill reminder contraption and washed down my two daily multivitamins, one of which leaves an earthy aftertaste, the other of which has a 5 percent chance of being some kind of steroid. After drugging up, I found my way to the showers and my daily contemplation of why, by comparison, we white guys are blessed with so little. As usual, I was sent no answer, and so was resigned to finish my shower in ignorance. Afterward, I made my way to the lounge area so that I could be an asshole and not answer the e-mails I had received, before leaving the arena at about noon.

The game was at 7:00, so I reported back to the gym at around 4:45. I was actually not the first one to arrive. Quentin Richardson, who may sleep in the building, was already on the scene. Interestingly, he never really does anything with the extra time he spends there—in fact, he rarely even goes out to the court to shoot prior to the game. I think he just really, really likes being in the locker room. Or maybe he doesn't have a TV at home and likes to catch his BET at the arena. Most people call Quentin "Q." As I've mentioned before, I feel strange using a person's nickname if I don't know him all that well. But "Quentin" seems a little formal. So when I saw Richardson sitting at his locker, my greeting consisted of me stammering my way through "What's up, Queue . . ." just as I turned my head, hoping he wouldn't notice my awkward hello as I walked to my locker.

I donned my uniform, which never fails to produce a small rush of pride, and moseyed into the weight room, where I had promised earlier in the day to meet the strength coach, Erik Phillips. We went through a slightly more organized workout than we had the previous game day. On that occasion, I had jokingly suggested that we make that day's regimen a cycle through one of everything in the weight room. He waited a beat and said, "Okay." So we did. Because Erik's great . . . and because he's happy to have someone who occasionally does what he says to do. Because I was the only one in the place, I got to listen to something other than the latest offerings of Trick Daddy, which made my time there significantly more tolerable. After forty minutes in the weight room, I had made so much progress that Erik stopped me with, "That's it, Paul. You are officially too strong. There is nothing more I can do for you." (I can dream.) Finished, I took a quick stroll back through the locker room. Most of my teammates were either getting treatment or furiously wasting time—not that I would have been doing anything different if I had been about to play thirty or forty minutes that night. Bored, I meandered out to the court.

An NBA arena has a certain buzz prior to game time. The media people are checking the lights, the trampoline dunkers are discussing their routine, ushers and other various peripherals are wandering around with nothing to do until the fans arrive. It is my favorite part of the evening.

My reverie was interrupted by one of the assistant coaches who— almost more than I—needed something to do. He put me through the beginnings of a workout until he was distracted by one of the starters, who had come out earlier than usual to shoot. I was kicked to the curb and so drafted one of the ball boys to rebound for me until another assistant coach appeared. As is always the case, he had not seen me do anything to that point, so he started me into yet another workout. (In this way, my day can be a bit *Office Space*–like.) A few more players drifted out of the locker room; we coaxed one of them into playing one-on-one with me until it was time to return to the locker room.

With forty-five minutes left until game time, we bigs met with the assistant coach in charge of us, Marc Iavaroni. Our meetings are quite a sight. Iavaroni usually spends most of his time attempting to keep the attention of his class as he goes through the keys for the night and the tendencies of the players we are likely to guard. It's like a board meeting, if the members of the board had ninety-second attention spans. Iavaroni is a relatively enlightened fellow and usually fits in a jab or two at those whose minds have wandered, so I am kept entertained. (Again, I feel that this should be everyone's overriding goal.)

After a brief film session with Iavaroni, we rejoined the group in the main locker room for a pregame briefing. We watched, as a team, some clips of the, uh, Clippers on video, and Coach D'Antoni went through some of the main keys to the game. It turned out that Steve Nash would not be playing; D'Antoni left out the fact that we were 0–3 this year without Steve. (Feel free to change that *we* to *they* since I was not yet around for those games—I'm trying to feel more a part of the team by co-opting their success as my own.)

After another, "1, 2, 3 . . . Suns!" we commenced wasting time in the locker room. In my experience, NBA teams do not generally get too excited about warming up and so don't take the court until about eighteen minutes remain before the game. We are no different. Our reluctance to take the court left an awkward period where we all wandered aimlessly for five minutes. I moved out of the locker room and for the fourth time that night greeted the guy who guards the locker room door. (Each time I am forced to give him a fist bump, I want to say, *Stick out your goddamn hand and I'll slap it. Putting your fist out does not make you any cooler, nor does it make your lazy eye appear any less strange.*) With seventeen minutes to go, we followed the flag-carrying male cheerleader types onto the court to the cheers of the five thousand people who actually show up fifteen minutes before the game. We jogged through some layups and then broke up into chaos, which involved some players shooting, some stretching, and some wandering around in between. After a few minutes of this, we gathered back up for some slightly more intense layups. With two minutes to go to game time, we dissolved back into random shooting. Shawn Marion went to the free-throw line and Jake Voskuhl stood just in front of the basket waiting for Shawn to shoot his first free throw, whereupon Jake goal-tended it and both he and Shawn broke into laugher. I cannot even begin to imagine the many levels on which their inside joke must work. Evidently it has staying power; they re-peat their routine before every game, and their reactions to it haven't dulled in the slightest.

We then all reported to the free-throw line and stood respectfully as a man named Lou Rawls massacred the national anthem. Appar-ently, he is a local favorite; the crowd did not seem to share my opin-ion of his singing abilities. I have heard the name Lou Rawls before, but after the butcher job he did on the anthem, I cannot imagine that it was because of his rampant musical talent. As with every game, after the anthem my teammates and I did our cute little high-five-in-a-row thing that, while a bit seventh-grade-girlish, is kind of cool. As we finished, the Clippers were introduced to a lukewarm reception. They are neither a particularly good team nor a particularly interest-ing one, so our fans could muster little enthusiasm. Then, like always, the lights went out, and the screens positioned around the top of the stands lit up with the introductory video, which is actually among the best I have seen. Afterward, our starters were introduced. Usually, the list begins with Amare Stoudemire and ends with Steve Nash, which is a good setup for maximum crowd pleasure. Without Steve in the lineup, the anchor spot fell to Joe Johnson, who, while good, does not carry the same cachet as Nash, so the introductions did not have their usual punch. After Johnson was introduced, the capacity crowd was in a mild frenzy, and those of us left out of the starting lineup skipped out to the free-throw area, where we performed our next pregame ritual of forming a circle linking arms over shoulders, bend-ing down, and swaying back and forth around the figure of Bo Outlaw, who bounces back and forth while making guttural grunts with each change in direction of the circle. I am not a huge fan of the tribal dance routine but, as always, did my best to endure it without com-ment. As our little hullabaloo ended we gathered again, performed yet another "1, 2, 3 . . . Suns!" and wandered back to the bench. Coach D'Antoni pulled the starters together for some last-second words of encouragement, we did one more "1, 2, 3 . . . Suns!" and I found my place three seats from the end of the bench and prepared to be enter-tained.

Because the routine we go through prior to a game is relatively dull and repetitive, the opening tip of the Clippers game provided a refreshing change of pace. As I took my seat, I realized that for the next couple of hours I had nothing to do but watch a basketball game. Even though at this point I have seen enough live sports to last a lifetime or two and am rather jaded, I can still appreciate the beauty of the chance to watch an NBA basketball game from the front row.

The game started as NBA games often do—sluggishly. My eyes started to glaze over after about three minutes. I'm concerned about my burgeoning case of ADD. I did well for my first few games with the Suns, with my focus on the events at hand lasting well into the fourth quarter. Now, the concentration ship sails away sometime before the first media time-out, which comes at the first dead ball after the six-minute mark in the first quarter. Before the game had even reached that point, I had begun scanning the crowd, looking for interesting people and/or attractive girls to watch throughout the game.

At the whistle that signaled the first time-out of the game, I hustled out of my chair to meet my team on the court, giving the obligatory high fives and words of encouragement that certainly do not come that easily to me. I am not particularly enthusiastic in general, so cheerleader is not a role that I fit all that well. But I did a good job of providing some enthusiasm, and wandered back to the huddle as the coaches made their way out to their usual meeting point near the free-throw line in front of our bench. We cleared a path for the coaches to get back in front of the starters, who were now perched on the bench, with the rest of us surrounding them in a half circle. Because it was early in the game, and because we had not exactly blown the doors off the Clippers, Coach D'Antoni had plenty to say. As usual, his message was delivered in an impressively calm voice that rarely rises above a conversational tone. The players in the game made a valiant effort to appear as if they cared about what he was saying, some other modifications were made, and the group was sent back into the fray.

While D'Antoni was exhorting my teammates to greater heights of physical performance, I hovered near the back of the huddle, trying halfheartedly to see what was being written on the dry-erase board with basketball court markings. After about twelve seconds of this, I was distracted by the dance team—I think it had something to do with the outfits they were wearing, along with the fact that they are much better-looking than my teammates—and lost all focus on the events of the huddle. It is a good thing I was not sent into the game; I don't think I would have had much of a chance of being on the same page as everyone else. As my teammates marched back into battle, I hustled back to my end of the bench in order to stake out my seat. The three of us who sit at the end (Bo Outlaw on the end and Jake Voskuhl to his left, with me next) have settled into a routine regarding our seating arrangement. The rest of the group cannot seem to figure out where they fit in and are constantly jostling for position. Thus, I have taken it upon myself to make sure my end-of-the-bench comrades and I have adequate space. Jake and Bo applauded my work. Content, I settled back into my seat, only then realizing that I had not paid the slightest attention to what had gone on in the time-out. I chastised myself for my behavior and I resolved to do better. I would have plenty of chances. In NBA games, mandatory media time-outs seem to come around every nine seconds.

I was proud of my work in the subsequent time-outs. I lost concentration only when something truly entertaining, such as the trampoline dunkers or the Kiss Cam, was on the docket. For time-out entertainment, it is hard to beat the Kiss Cam. Whoever came up with the idea is a crowd-pleasing genius. Kiss Cam came sometime in the second quarter in this game against the Clippers. I watched out of the corner out of my eye while Coach D'Antoni scribbled on the board. He had his head down, so he did not notice until it was too late that all five players sitting in front of him were staring unabashedly at one of the screens in the arena. And who could blame them? The story line is predictable, yet infinitely entertaining. Things got started with some twenty- or thirty-somethings who were obviously married, or at least dating. A hearty but restrained kiss was shared. So far, so good. At some point, the mad genius operating the Kiss Cam switched gears and managed to catch an awkward teenage couple in which the male involved thought he had found an automatic free pass to first base while the girl covered her face and giggled. The encounter ended with a chaste kiss on the cheek. Back to a few average couples, one of which went for the assault kiss, wherein the man leaned over his girl-friend or wife and tried to suck off her entire face. Comedy gold. Pan to the two co-workers who came to the game on company tickets. One was significantly more attractive than the other, and much like the awkward teenage couple, the encounter ended badly. The woman—the better-looking of the two—was especially insecure, and acted mortified. She even went as far as to shake her head as if to say, *Seriously, like I would sink that low?* which, in my mind, should at the very least be worth a VD rumor around the office. As the Kiss Cam neared the end of its run of glory, the crowd found itself staring at an older couple. Par for the course, the two were completely oblivious to the goings-on. It took a nudge from their neighbors to get them into action. The moment of truth had arrived. The director of the spot had to be shaking with fright; the success of the entire segment depended on the retirees. Occasionally, the old folks glare at the camera and refuse to budge, even with much encouragement from the rest of the crowd. But this couple stared blankly into the camera for a few seconds, then realized what was wanted and made good on a dry kiss born of decades together. The crowd went wild and, as usual, every-one thought that love had a chance.

Which made the rejection all the more awkward when I immedi-ately tried to make out with Bo Outlaw.

Back to the action. We muddled through the second quarter and took a ten-point lead into halftime. I found myself in the middle of the pack as we walked back into the locker room, which meant that I faced a dilemma as hands came out of the stands hoping for a quick five. *Do I slap them on the palm and act like it was really my hand they were seeking, or skip them safe in the knowledge that they don't even know who I am and couldn't care less if I give them five?* As is most often the case, I opted for the former—it is not my job to know the whims of every individual fan. We passed by the guy who guards the locker room door, whose fist was held out yet again. I bumped it, for about the fifth time that evening. I found my way to my chair and waited for some heavy-duty basketball knowledge to be distilled. The coaches met briefly in their office area and then came out to talk about some adjustments. After Coach D'Antoni said a few things, he turned the floor over to the assistants. The first had something new to say, the second had a little less, and the third, looking like the first two had stolen his ideas, resigned himself to silence. We gathered in the middle of the locker room, broke huddle again, and then slowly wandered out to the court, where we repeated a very abbreviated version of the pregame warm-up.

I found my seat again, the game resumed, and I started wondering if I was going to get to play. The Clippers were displaying their ineptitude at every opportunity, and it was obvious that our lead might balloon rapidly. Against good teams, a big margin can mean very little, but against a team like the Clippers, a smallish lead is as insurmountable as a forty-point advantage over a good team.

Before I knew it, the fourth quarter had rolled around, and it looked for all the world like the Clippers were done. Down by fourteen with nine minutes to go, they made a late push, but it was for naught. We made it through the first and second media time-outs of the fourth without any major changes, but as the three-minutes-remaining time-out whistle blew, I knew there was a good chance I would need to get rid of my warm-ups. We were ahead by twenty, and LA was spent. Coach D'Antoni called Bo's name; I thought I was next. I did not go in, though, and was a little hurt. As I have said many, many times, I truly hate playing in garbage time. However, it never feels good to get passed over. But a few seconds after the action started back up, Coach D'Antoni called out my name and sent me to the scorer's table. I got there with two and a half minutes to go but had to sit for a minute and a half of game time before I was able to go in. Even then, I only got to take off my warm-ups because Bo saw me stretched out in front of the table and, wanting to do me a favor, fouled on purpose so that I could enter the game. I went in with fifty-eight seconds left. I touched the ball once, but I was about forty feet from the basket, so I didn't have a chance to get off the requisite shot. Time expired and I felt for a second like I had contributed—if only because I finished the game with my shoulders bared.

We walked to the locker room, where the general manager was waiting with congratulations for everyone. As usual, it was an awkward moment for me. I followed Shawn Marion in. The GM said, "Way to go, Shawn. Good win out there." For me it was, "Uh, good win." Coming up with things to say to the scrubs like me can't be the easiest task.

Coach D'Antoni was pleased with our win—the forty-second of the year. He was smiling upon his entry to the locker room. He said very little, and we finished the night off with one last, "1, 2, 3 . . . Suns!" I retreated to my locker, took off my uniform, and put on some practice clothes because my night was not quite over. I walked slowly down to the practice court, where my day had started about twelve hours before, and ran a few sprints under the watchful eye of the strength coach. In the unlikely event that three guys go down with injuries at the same time, my body will be ready, even if my mind is not.

March 10

I rail against religion a lot. I am forced to think about it so much because of its undue presence around athletics. I have seen enough basketball players with one tattoo declaring that "Only God Can Judge Me" accompanying another that states that the wearer is "Brooklyn's Finest" or was "Born a Star" to know that most of these so-called Christians have about as much acquaintance with the teachings of Christ as would a scouting expedition from another galaxy. It is the hypocrisy that bothers me. The religious have done some great things over the years. Without religion, many a native people would have gone wanting for subjugation and oppression. Without religion, hundreds if not thousands of young boys would have been forced to endure a tragic life free from molestation by a trusted priest. Without religion, millions of AIDS viruses would go homeless, left to die on the inside of a third-world condom. Wait a second. I got my good things mixed up with my bad things. What I meant to say was, I can understand the benefits of a religious mind-set. I love a good crusade or jihad that kills innocent byst . . . Dammit, I give up. Anyway, I'm sure that religion has done some good. I just grow tired of seeing people say one thing when it seems convenient but do another when it isn't.

Recently, one of my teammates approached me in a conspiratorial way as our morning walk-through was ending. He said:

(Break in the action. I will now present two stories. One is true; the other is more like what I thought life in the NBA would be like.)

Story 1: "Paul, we're having a little prayer meeting in S____'s room after walk-through. We'll meet up there about five minutes after we are done here. It is something we do on the road all the time. About half of the guys come. I don't know if you are interested, but if you are, it would be great to have you."

Story 2: "Paul, we're going to get together after walk-through and do some blow in S____'s room. I think some strippers are going to stop by and, let me tell you, the crew we found last year here in Seattle was A-OK. They were letting us snort coke off their . . . well, you know. Anyway, this is something we do on the road all the time; about half the guys come. I don't know if you are interested, but if you are, we could probably spare a gram or two."

I'm not sure which of the above options offends me more. I wouldn't participate in either, but if I put the two at the ends of a spectrum, I do believe my potential acceptance would fall closer to Story 2 than to Story 1. Of course, Story 1 is the true one; it is doubtful that my team would be tied for the best record in the NBA if half its membership were doing cocaine on the road. At least on game days. My response to the prayer circle invitation was a quick lift of the eyebrow and a "Huh, that's interesting," which was a far cry from what I wanted to say, which was, *You've got to be fucking kidding me.*

You're going to gather a group of grown men in a hotel room and pray together? Seriously, did no one laugh when you first suggested this?

If I were not such a sissy, I would have gone to the little Bible study session and reported back. But I really didn't think I would have been able to maintain a straight face.

The same person told me a story today.

"Hey, Paul, I think you'll appreciate this. It is a genuine miracle." At the time, I searched my brain for why he thought I would appreciate something involving the suspension of logic, but it became clear shortly. "My brother just finished his master's degree." *Ah, because I'm the "smart guy," I'll appreciate the academic nature of the story.* "He wants to teach at the college level, but he has been pretty nervous about whether he would be able to get into a Ph.D. program. He has prayed and prayed about it, and finally decided to apply to Northwestern, which has the best program in the country for what he wants to do, and Cal Berkeley. Now, he doesn't really know about Berkeley because, you know, there are some weird people out there." *Yeah? You mean free-thinking, overly intelligent people? You're right, I have heard about them—to be avoided at all costs.* "But anyway, he just heard back from Northwestern. Get this, I mean, it is truly a miracle—they're going to give him a five-year scholarship and pay him $18,000 a year. Isn't that amazing?"

I said, "Uh, yeah. Pretty cool. Must be a smart guy." But I am sure the fact that his brother is apparently a highly driven, intelligent human being has nothing to do with the fact that he was the number one selection by his school of choice. No, it was definitely the prayer that did it.

Later in the day, this same guy asked one of the public relations people about some basketballs the team was securing for him. The PR guy told him that they would be in shortly. When the player asked how much he would owe, he was told, "Oh, don't worry about it, we'll get it." Shortly thereafter, the PR guy asked the player, "Hey, I was talking to someone over at St. Mary's Hospital the other day. He was wondering if you had some time next week to get up to the burn unit over there. It wouldn't take long—maybe an hour." The reply was, "Hmmm, I don't know. I don't think I can do it. I know we have those two days off, but I have stuff going every day. Sorry."

The hyperreligious types that seem to crop up more and more, especially in athletics, fall back on their religion only when it is convenient. It is not applicable in all situations. It is only to be used for personal gain and not for the good of others. On the rare occasion when it is used for the good of others, media personnel will be on hand to document it so that personal gain can later be had.

It is important to note that I am not condemning my teammate for refusing to visit the burn center. In fact, as soon as the question was asked, I thought, *Yikes, I hope he doesn't ask me. Disfigured burn victims freak me the hell out.* But that is okay, because I am a selfish bastard—and that cuts across all situations. I do not claim to be a benevolent, even-handed creature.

At the end of the day, I suppose I am not railing against religion per se. I am railing against duplicity and dishonesty. It seems to me, though, that religion is a concept behind which many people find plenty of space to hide their true selves. This, in the end, turns people like me away from anything smacking even lightly of religious behavior because we have seen so many times the behavior of the "enlightened" when the doors are closed.

March 16

When I signed with the Suns for the rest of the season, I was faced with two immediate concerns: lodging and transportation. I solved the first after a few minor hiccups but was at a loss regarding the second. I kicked around the idea of buying a car here, but that seemed extravagant, so I tried to talk my brother Matt into driving my car from Kansas City down to Phoenix, if only for one last hurrah. I thought it would be hilarious to pull my 1996 Monte Carlo into a parking space at the arena next to the BMW 745s and Cadillac Escalades. Alas, he did not want to make the two-day trip, so I fell back to buy mode. After giving it some thought, I decided that I could afford a purchase.

I also realized that buying a car would bring me one step closer to the stereotypical athlete triumvirate (house, car, jewelry) that has eluded me for so long, and if that is not motivation enough, I don't know what is.

After much careful shopping, I bought a BMW M3. (Pause for gagging. I am a cliché.) I decided to pull out all the stops in my transformation into the stereotype. Plus, I thought a German car would hold its value relatively well and would be reliable. Imagine my surprise, then, when it recently began making a very strange noise under the hood. At the time I tried to ignore it, thinking that since I had put only a hundred miles on the car and had purchased it "certified pre-owned," there was no way something could be going wrong already. (Now that I think about it, their claim wasn't much. It could be inferred that the only thing the dealership was certifying was that the car had been owned before.) My optimism was, of course, a blatant suspension of logic. My middle name is Murphy, after all. I drove to our game that night, thinking I could get through that trip and the return to the arena for the next day's practice before dealing with any potential problems—it's all of a mile from my apartment to the arena. On the way to the game, an oddly shaped light came on in the dash. I didn't have the owner's manual with me, so after a rather awkward loss to the Houston Rockets, I drove back to my apartment hoping to learn what was wrong with my new car. (Well, 14,700-miles-past-new car.) When I cracked open the guide, I learned that I was supposed to interpret the lit-up icon to mean that my car's engine needed coolant. I thought, *I grew up on a near-farm in Kansas, of all places. I can solve this problem.* I hopped back in my car with the idea of killing two birds with one stone: I would drive to a gas station I knew well to secure some antifreeze, and let the engine cool while I ran across the street to the IHOP for a late supper. (We were leaving the next morning and I didn't really feel like throwing a meal together.) Then, hunger sated, I would go back to my car and add the necessary fluid to its vital parts and be home in time to pack for our trip.

On the way to my mecca of late-night commerce, the engine began to overheat. The temperature gauge hovered smack in the middle of the red at the far right of the half circle. I became concerned. I envisioned my pride and joy seizing up in the middle of a Phoenix street as I frantically wondered what to do while my engine melted into one giant pool of molten metal. (It was late. My imagination tends to run away from me at night.) I slowed my pace on the way to the gas station and survived the trip without any of my Dali-esque visions coming to fruition. I breathed a sigh of relief and started into my itinerary.

The first kink arrived when I was informed by Habib the attendant that his gas station did not stock antifreeze. Which made sense. It was silly of me to expect a gas station, of all places, to have antifreeze. While I was pondering my next move, a customer slightly younger than I stepped up to the counter to buy two Red Bulls and a tallboy. As he was finishing his transaction, I asked him if he wanted to make a quick forty bucks. (My mind had scrambled for the right number— *Will he go for twenty? Should I say a hundred?*) He thought he did, so I told him that I would give him that sum of money if he could track down some antifreeze for me. I jumped in the backseat of his car and he explained the situation to his girlfriend in the front. We drove about four blocks and found a nice, brightly lit Texaco station that looked for all the world like the kind of place that would carry antifreeze. Sure enough, I came out with a gallon of the finest antifreeze money can buy—if money was given only one option. We drove back to the original station, I paid my driver, and he and his girlfriend abandoned me.

I opened the hood to find a bone-dry radiator. (Warning: I do have a degree in mechanical engineering, but I know very little about cars. My father must be so proud.) I poured almost the entire contents of my jug down the hatch, hoping that the bobber that was supposed to indicate some degree of fullness would soon make an appearance. It did not, but I assumed I had added enough of the liquid and closed the hood. I looked under the car and, finding no greenish puddle that would indicate a leak, started the engine. The temperature needle hovered somewhere between blue and red for a few seconds, and I thought I was saved. But then it raced its way right back to red, this time even causing the red side to blink. Without a cohesive plan, and with all thoughts of a stop at the International House of Pancakes banished from my mind, I made a break for it, hoping I could get back to my apartment. About two blocks from home, the Service Engine Soon light came on and I started seeing a vision of me pushing my pricey imported car through the near-ghetto surrounding my apartment. But I made it home, or nearly. I didn't think my car would survive the trip to the parking garage, so I left it in front of the apartment complex, thinking it would be an easier logistical arrangement for the tow truck driver in the morning.

When I woke up, I called the folks at my dealership and, in an unprecedented show of restraint, used not a single curse word while voicing my displeasure at the turn of events. The customer service department took over and, with remarkable efficiency, had a tow truck at my apartment within thirty minutes of my call. In fact, the entire repair process was quite smooth, which made me wonder: do they manage that part of the process so well because of their attention to detail, or is it merely lots and lots of experience with broken-down BMWs?

After presiding over the loading of my car onto a flatbed tow truck, I hiked to practice. It is a good thing I play for the Suns and not the Timberwolves. (That was a weather joke. I realize that it wasn't great.)

The final analysis was that my car's serpentine belt had shredded, cutting the radiator hose. Apparently, the M3 has a plate underneath the engine that protects it from debris coming up from under the car. This was where all the antifreeze I poured into the radiator ended up.

Here's what it all boils down to for me:

Car	Days Driven	Times Towed
One-year-old BMW M3	10	1
Nine-year-old Chevy Monte Carlo	1,825 (approx.)	0

Hmmm . . .

My walk to practice was accompanied by a large bag. I'm sure that those who observed my passage through downtown Phoenix had no second thoughts about a slightly overdressed giant pulling a massive duffel bag behind him. It was an altogether normal sight. That bag contained clothes for a ten-day road trip that started in Memphis.

Long road trips in the NBA are both great fun and extremely taxing. It becomes completely disorienting to fly from one city to the next immediately following a game. Night becomes day, and day . . . (Sound of vomit introducing itself to the back of my throat.)

I'm afraid the Memphis Grizzlies may get kicked out of the NBA. I could be mistaken, but I think they started three white guys—three American white guys at that. I'm pretty sure there is a rule against that. I guess I'll find out soon, when the league brings back the Cincinnati Royals to fill the void the Grizzlies leave behind.

As I watched our game against Memphis, I realized that I was observing a good-versus-evil match-up of sorts. I grew up watching the Boston Celtics and Larry Bird. When I could watch an NBA game, I would watch the Celtics. Without knowing why, I loved the way Bird and his teammates played the game. At the time, I only knew that they were fun to watch. Now I understand why I was drawn to them. The Celtics, along with other teams of the era, played basketball the right way. They played with reckless abandon, not caring whether they looked cool doing it. Unfortunately, that style quickly faded.

My team is something of a test case for a return to the 1980s Celtics and Lakers style of basketball. No one knows if that kind of game can still be played or, more important, succeed. At some point after the Bird-Johnson era, something changed in NBA basketball. Whatever it was alienated most of the people I know. No one in Kansas watches professional basketball. They first grew disillusioned with the me-first, style-before-substance attitude, but that was not really the reason they stopped watching. They stopped watching because the game was no fun. Coaches had tightened their respective grips, and basketball became a slugfest. The emphasis switched to defense as the powers that be realized that any team, no matter how limited in ability, could win if it stopped the other team from scoring. Consequently, players were taught that it was more important to learn how to play defense than to learn how to shoot a basketball. By the late 1990s I, and most everyone I know, could hardly sit through an entire NBA game.

Which brings us back to our game with Memphis. The Grizzlies are a fine basketball team, to be sure. But they are limited. We are what the game is supposed to look like—players moving, sharing the ball, shooting when they are open, and, most important, playing together. It has taken some time for this brand to reemerge (call it the Nowitzki-Stojakovic effect), but when the game takes this form, it is fun to watch.

Because I had a three-month break from the Suns, I have a unique perspective from which to analyze. I was very excited about this team after training camp. I was less excited when I was told to clean out my locker, but even after I was kicked to the curb, I was hoping for my former teammates to succeed, because I had enjoyed being a part of such an explosive, high-powered team that seemed to be moderately excited about playing the game together.

And now, with our record among the league's best, a return to entertaining basketball seems inevitable. Good triumphed over evil, 97–91.

After we traveled from Memphis to Atlanta, I met a friend of mine named Tara for dinner the night before our game with the Hawks. When we arrived at our restaurant of choice, we decided that neither of us was particularly hungry, so we ordered some iced tea and an appetizer with intentions of a lazy discussion of nothing in particular. After an hour or so, our waitress noticed that I was wearing an Interpol T-shirt (the band, not the international crime-fighting organization). She remarked, with a point in the direction of my shirt, "Hey, do y'all know that they are playing here in Atlanta tonight?"

Interpol could be my second-favorite band in the world, so my interest was piqued.

In a part of my life I would rather forget, I would most likely have passed on the Interpol concert. I would have overanalyzed the situation and thought, *Well, the Hawks are pretty bad, so there's a good chance you'll get to play some tomorrow. Is a concert that may keep you out late worth jeopardizing that opportunity?* The answer probably would have been no. Fortunately, I dragged that guy behind the garage and beat him to death with a snow shovel. I now take a more Zorba the Greek–like approach and am willing to attend the concerts of my favorite bands.

I called my brother for logistical help. He confirmed that Interpol was in Atlanta and would be playing at a place called the Tabernacle. The show was, of course, sold out. Unfazed, Tara and I paid our bill, thanked our waitress for the timely information, and hustled back to my hotel. (I had to change my shirt. No need to be that guy.) The show started at 8:00 P.M. It was 7:30 when we left the hotel. We realized that our lack of guaranteed entry did present something of a problem; when we left I put our chances of finding a ticket at 40 percent.

We were lucky, since the hotel was close to the venue. We were there by 7:45 and were assailed with "You all need tickets?" by 7:48. I hustled over and, given an opening bid of $120 for two, quickly countered with an offer of $100. Face value was $23 each, but the show was sold out, and I was in no mood for haggling with events nearing commencement. The man quickly accepted my offer, mocking me in his mind for being such a sucker, I'm sure. We snatched our tickets and headed for the door.

Interpol was great. The opener, Blonde Redhead, was only fair. But I am not complaining. As the night wound down, I realized what a great life I lead.

I have been known to do my fair share of complaining. Sometimes, like when I am stuck in a frozen outpost such as Kazan, Russia, for two months, it is warranted. Most of the time, though, my complaints are about as necessary as mammary glands on male swine, as the expression (sort of) goes. This part of my life is one of those times.

Now all I have to do is hope the ringing in my ears subsides before someone expects me to catch my balance and make a jump shot tomorrow. But even if that does not happen and I am a complete disaster on the court, it was worth it.

March 23

It's a good thing I have the trainers and other support staff around to keep me sane. I don't know what it says about me, but I call very few former teammates my good friends. On the other hand, my e-mail address list is riddled with the names of athletic trainers, strength coaches, and managers from my various stops along the way. I'm not sure why; it could be because most basketball players have an inherent inability to laugh at themselves and are most of the time worried more about their appearance than anything else.

After a game-day shoot-around midway through our long road trip, I found the weight room in our hotel and met Erik Phillips, our strength coach, so that he could make a futile attempt at sculpting my body to Olympian standards. As we walked into the room, Erik pointed out that one Earvin "Magic" Johnson was sharing our space. He was riding a stationary bike, listening to headphones, and watching a television mounted on the wall in front of him. We didn't really know what to do with this information, so we ignored Magic and lifted weights. Toward the end of the workout, we were joined by assistant trainer Mike Elliott, who was in self-improvement mode as well. Soon after Mike burst onto the scene, we changed the channel of the television nearest us to the same one being viewed by Big Earv. (And I mean *big:* regarding the progression of HIV, someone must have been misleading us back in high school health class.) He was watching a program that was counting down the NBA's greatest finishes. Just as we found the new station, the host began recounting Game 4 of the 1987 NBA Finals. While I finished some lat pull-downs, Magic hit the famous running hook that helped win the series for the Lakers. The three of us were struck by the strange situation in which we found ourselves. Mike, fortunately, came up with a suggestion: "Someone should go over there and say, 'Hey, Magic. Nice shot.' " Because the gauntlet had been thrown down, Erik was almost without recourse. It took him a couple of minutes, but he did it, and it was hilarious, as we expected. These are my kind of people—not afraid to make asses of themselves in the interest of lowbrow comedy. (By the way, after

Erik took one for the comedic team, we all walked over and chatted with the former Lakers star. He was gracious, kind, and charming, like everyone says. I did notice that when I introduced myself, he did not tell me his name. I, of course, know his name—the above paragraph would have been difficult to write without that knowledge. I do not know, however, what I am supposed to call him. Magic? Seems a bit odd. Earvin? Seems forced. It will be a dilemma that haunts me. Anyway, we talked for five minutes and then went our separate ways.)

That night, we beat the Atlanta Hawks and, in so doing, chalked up our fiftieth win. Not bad. I would like to say the mark was set on a game filled with poetic basketball and a high level of play. But if I did, I would be lying, betraying the very little credibility I do have. Writing that the Hawks looked like a very bad basketball team is like writing that living in Beirut would be exciting—true, but not really the whole story. The Hawks were really, really bad. It is almost as if someone picked the players on the floor completely at random. Balls were bounced off teammates' faces, passes were thrown to no one in particular, and, in general, very little coherent basketball was played. At one point, the Hawks actually entered an air ball as their shot of choice on three straight possessions.

A couple of things stood out in Philips Arena, not the least of which was the usual raucous crowd in Atlanta. And, by raucous I mean almost nonexistent. I don't understand how a team in the fifth- or sixth- or seventh-largest city in the United States (I need a fact checker) can consistently play in front of a nearly empty arena. Jimmy Jackson said it best before the game. "Watch out," he warned, "there are a bunch of fans dressed up like seats out there tonight."

I had several Gun-In-Mouth Moments during our game with the Hawks—most of them caused by bad nicknames. I define Gun-In-Mouth Moments (GIMMs) as points in my life when, if I were carrying a gun at the time, I would have to consider putting it in my mouth and ending it all in order to avoid dealing with the further downward spiral of our culture. The first GIMM arrived with the announcement of the starting lineups. Here's the deal: when, after sixty games, the team being announced has a winning percentage hovering around the same area as most pitchers' batting averages, it loses the right to a grand entrance. No more dance team, no more theme song, no more dimming the lights. The players walk onto the court and play the game. That's it. The Hawks did not agree to my deal. They had an overproduced introduction on the big screen, an actual hawk that flew down from the rafters, and even a catchphrase—something like "The Spirit Lies Within."

The Hawks employ two rookies with the first name of Josh. My other GIMMs occurred each time either of those rookies was announced for scoring a basket. Apparently, someone decided that saying "Josh Smith" or "Josh Childress" was not going to be sufficient. So instead, each time Josh Smith scores, the crowd is treated to "J-Smooth for two." When it is Childress, out comes "J-Chill with the assist." An analysis of the situation that does not result in an aneurysm for me seems impossible, so I will stop.

March 25

We had an off day in Miami, which was good news for my legs. Exhaustion was about to set in, what with all the forty-minute nights I had been putting in. Wait—I somehow got confused and thought I was writing Shawn Marion's journal entry. Sorry about that. Regardless, I think a day off is always a good idea. If I were a slightly more conscientious basketball player, I would have used the extra time to do some weightlifting or conditioning. Since I am not, I went to the beach with my trainer and support staff friends.

Steve Nash and Leandro Barbosa joined us by the water after a while. They and the rest of the group spent some time in the ocean (gulf? My geography is not what it once was), while I looked on like the kid who didn't get picked for the kickball game. I had made a grievous error with my wardrobe choice, donning khaki shorts with no auxiliary option when I left the hotel. Poor planning. I did manage to remember to buy some sunscreen at the hotel. I took care to apply it liberally. I may be, with the exception of Kirk Hinrich, the whitest player in the NBA, and was not keen on ruining the rest of the road trip with a blistering sunburn. (Upon further review, it would appear that my sunscreen application skills have grown rusty. A significant trapezoidal area of my back was angry with me for allowing so many of the Miami sun's UV rays access to it.) When my compatriots returned from the water, we listened to the most anal lifeguard ever to grace Miami Beach yell at people for having the nerve to play paddleball on the beach, decided we had had enough, and retired to the pavement for the rest of the afternoon.

The trip to Miami was my first. Neither of my prior partial-season stints took me to the city, so my opinion of the place was a blank canvas. After the trip to the beach, the frame was looking rather bright and colorful; by the end of the day, it was filled with grays and browns. Miami has the same problem as many cities famous for their nightlife—it is chock-full of people trying way too hard to have a good time. Like New Orleans and Las Vegas, it is place that is worth visiting once in a while, but I can't imagine living there. I'm sure that some would disagree, but the place, at least near the beach, has a very false feel. Almost everyone I saw—be they muscle-bound douche bags with bad tattoos or bleached-out, implanted girls—looked as if his or her entire goal in life was to impress those watching. (As an aside, I will now declare the tattoo trend dead. Not just over—that happened a couple of years ago. Dead. Is there anything more passé than the arm or shoulder tattoo on the male of our species or the symmetrical lower-back tattoo on the female? On a further tangent, because this is how my brain works, Tom Gugliotta has the worst tattoo in the NBA. The barbed wire on the biceps is bad enough to put him in the running; the fact that he thought he could get away with not having it complete the circumference of his arm puts him over the top. It is like wearing a tie that is not only ugly but a clip-on to boot. Ugly is at least forgivable; the clip-on aspect makes it reprehensible.)

We gave the beachside area a solid walk-through. My personal highlight was finding out that I was at one point walking a part of Route A1A, which for some reason brought some closure to my life. When I was eleven, as my younger brothers and I would jam to Vanilla Ice on my brother Dan's tape player, I always wondered what "A1A" meant. Now I know that it is a highway that flows through Miami, slowing to become a choked street in South Beach. Hooray. Steve spent a good portion of his time being quite the ambassador for the NBA, stopping for pictures and handshakes with well-wishers. The rest of us watched the bizarre assortment of passersby, and I wondered what percentage of them were planning to snort cocaine at some point in the day. (That's what they do in Miami, right?) Just before we all split up, Steve was assailed by a group of guys looking for photo opportunities. As we stood waiting for him, a youngish girl did a double take as she passed the scene and asked me, "Is that a famous person?" There it is: Miami, where one's worth is measured not by one's own recognition but by the recognition of others.

Before we left Little Havana, I had some time to revisit one of my favorite subjects—my own stupidity.

I can be an absentminded soul. Remembering facts such as where I parked my car, whether I picked my credit card out of the little plastic sleeve attached to the restaurant bill, and a girl's last name is often a challenge. As I spend more and more time around basketball players, my brain power continues to diminish, which is not assisting my functionality within society. I've been on a slow burn since college. Back then, I was at least encouraged to spend half the day around semi-studious types, and my cognitive ability probably benefited. (In my case, über-studious types—the whole engineering thing.) After four years of professional basketball, my brain is a veritable mush. The only bits left are a few quotes from Tommy Boy and a dozen ways to cover a pick and roll.

Case in point: I cannot remember my room number as we change from city to city. Granted, anyone would be challenged (autistics with a gift for numbers excepted) to recall one's room number if he changed hotels night after night. However, the average person would learn from his mistakes and come up with a solution. Not me.

One morning in Miami, I wandered down to breakfast bleary-eyed at 10:30. (That I rarely have to get up before 9:00 is still the most underrated thing about my "job.") We were new to the city, so I hadn't had much time to get my bearings. I have many times sauntered onto an elevator without knowing exactly which room was my target destination. Apparently, those encounters have taught me nothing. After an overpriced breakfast, I was faced with the bill. As I signed my name, I realized that the "Room Number" line was going to stump me. I managed to put together that my number ended in 22; a few moments later, I had a lightbulb-over-my-head moment and felt pretty confident, probably 70 percent or so, that I was on the twenty-fifth floor. I wrote down 2522 and went on my way. When I got to 2522, I noticed that its door handle was very bare of the Do Not Disturb sign I use to keep away groupies. (Ha. Actually, I leave it on at all times so the maids do not come in and mess up the finely crafted rumple I give my bed. With the slept-in look, I can at least pretend that I am at home.) I tried the key, to no avail. I wandered dejectedly back to the elevator, wondering if I was going to have to make the walk of shame to the front desk so that I could find out my room number. Luckily, I had a backup number in my mind, and 2322 turned out to, in fact, be my temporary home.

Unfortunately, I don't think my fifteen-minute detour is going to prove to be sufficient negative reinforcement. When we checked out of the hotel, I examined my bill and found that only one of the two breakfasts I had eaten had actually been charged to my room. Since I was not that thrilled that I had paid $13 for a bare stack of truly awful pancakes anyway—not to mention the $6 orange juice—I didn't call the mistake to anyone's attention and chalked up the experience as research for my post-basketball days. When my brain has completely failed me and I need to eat, they won't be at all suspicious of the bearded, six-foot-ten forty-year-old wearing a faded Suns jersey at the Four Seasons. Especially when he's able to so quickly come up with random room numbers to write on his bill.

Before our game against the Heat, I had a wave of something melodramatic and hokey wash over me. It happened during our warm-up, immediately prior to the game. We had finished our half-assed layup line and I was sitting at half-court, stretching while the players who would actually be participating in the game took jump shots. I looked around at all of the beautiful people streaming toward their seats. I saw the ESPN guys preparing for their broadcast of the game. I looked down and saw my own warm-ups. Then I panicked a little. I wondered if everyone around me was going to realize the fraud that I was. It does not seem all that long ago that my father was teaching me how to play the game on our gravel driveway or that I was playing high school basketball in a town of seven hundred in Kansas. I wondered to myself, *What am I doing? Who am I kidding? I could be about to play in this game between arguably the two best basketball teams in the world. I don't belong here.* And then it passed. I got up, marched over to the basket, grabbed a bouncing ball, took a shot, and melted right back in with my team. Identity crisis over.

March 27

In the four years since my college career ended, I have played for no fewer than eleven professional basketball teams. Of those, I left on my terms in four cases, was either released or not asked back in six, and will know more this summer regarding the last. There are prostitutes who have had fewer jobs over the same span. On one hand, the fact that I have been so nomadic has been priceless. I have traveled to amazing places and met some very cool people. On the other, the transient lifestyle I lead has been less fun than some would imagine.

Our very long road trip ended with a win in Orlando. After the game, everyone was relatively happy in the locker room. We had put together a solid road trip and were excited to go home. (I feel like I had a stellar set of games. Min: 0, TP: 0, FG%: Undefined. Bravo.) I shared in the jubilation. Because of my job description, I do a fair amount of traveling. Consequently, I hate it. I like the idea of seeing new places; it's the execution of the theory that is the hassle. So I, like everyone in the locker room, was anxious to get back to Phoenix. The hotels in which we stay are absurdly nice, but that does not change the fact that the beds have been used by countless other humans.

The flight home was lengthy, which gave us time for a battle royal over the poker table. I did relatively well, making $89 on the night, but felt like I had squandered some opportunities when it was over. When

I finally made it back to my apartment at about 2:15 A.M., I was more than happy to pass out in my bed. I went to sleep content in the knowledge that I had an off day awaiting me in the morning.

I awoke to find my rental apartment, with its rented furnishings, entirely bereft of the raw materials I needed to fix breakfast. (Read: the milk in the refrigerator was spoiled, making cereal a difficult proposition.) I considered my options quickly, not wanting to go from hungry and disoriented to hungry and mad at the world. I settled on a trip to IHOP; since it was already nearing noon, I thought I could eat one big meal that would take the place of both lunch and dinner. (Not a new concept for me. Most of my collegiate Sunday mornings were spent weighing the benefits of either getting out of bed relatively early so I could eat both breakfast and lunch or simply sleeping until noon and combining the two. Needless to say, I usually ate only two meals on Sunday.) I had a relatively pleasant breakfast while watching several post-church families stroll into the restaurant wearing their Sunday best. And then I went on my way, looking forward to a day consisting of very little that could be considered constructive.

I have been asked many times over the years if my life is a lonely one. It is most often a question asked by girls; males tend to think, "Dude, you have the coolest life ever." Which, for the most part, is true. I usually answer the loneliness question with a no because I can rarely say that I feel alone in my travels. It is not that difficult to form friendships in these places I go; most of the time there are souls in the same situation as I, and they too need someone to talk to. However, most of the time my relationships lack depth.

I now have friends scattered all over the world. I will probably never see some of them again. That is not to say I don't want to see them; any of these people, had we grown up together or gone to college together, might be my absolute best friend in the world. But it's hard to reunite with them when they live in places like Melbourne, Singapore, or Izmir. The same holds true for girls I have dated. Had the circumstances of our time together been slightly different, there is no telling what the future could have held. (Most likely their growing quite tired of my cynical, judgmental, and sarcastic view of things and telling me to go to hell.) It should be noted that I have met three girls I later dated on airplanes, and a fourth on a Greyhound bus. Probably not the best plan with regard to the future.

So where is the problem? I am twenty-seven, I have no children, no wife, and no serious girlfriend, and while I'm no male model, I'm not going to make anyone's All-Ugly Team anytime soon. (Incidentally, my version of this year's team has two members from Minnesota, one from the Milwaukee Bucks, one from the Warriors, and one from the Portland Trail Blazers. In the interest of not getting lynched, should I actually play in a game against one of these teams, I will keep the exact identities to myself.) While I am somewhat hard to be around at times, I can be moderately interesting, and have been known to relate an amusing tale once in a great while, so it is not that I doubt my ability to meet people if need be. The only problem is that I do miss these people I already know. It is hard to return "home" and then realize that my real home is scattered all over the world. It would be difficult, even, to call the place where I own a house—Kansas City— a home in the true sense of the word. I have lived there for two years but usually am only in residence for a few months before leaving again. Even there, I feel like a stranger.

People often ask me how long I will play basketball professionally. (It's a very curious crowd, the one I hang around.) I never know what to say because there are so many variables. I could blow out a knee, fall in love with some girl who refuses to leave her native South Africa, or simply lose interest. Really, though, I think I will quit when I have too many days like today, where I feel like a rootless Bedouin. That time is certainly not now—I would not trade my life for anyone's—and it is probably not a year or even two years from now. But it will happen someday.

April 25

The playoffs have begun. I'm generally unfazed by most anything concerning a particular sporting event—I've seen way too many basketball games in my life. But I was a little more excited than usual by the prospect of my trip to the arena for Game 2 of our first-round series with the Memphis Grizzlies.

I am constantly amazed by the ability of others to care about sporting events. I understand being a fan—I grew up living and dying by the nightly fate of the Kansas City Royals. I do not, however, grasp the existence of the über-fan. This is a touchy subject, though, as fans pay my salary. I would reiterate that I understand the idea of rooting for a team. We all need something we can get behind. But enthusiasm seems to be easily overdone; I can't help wondering what makes the crazies tick.

During warm-ups before the game, I noticed a couple of fans directly behind our bench. (This time, neither was female.) One had painted a basketball on his nearly shaven pate; the other had dyed his longish hair orange. They were in their seats approximately four hours before the game, so I had plenty of time to analyze their behavior while assistant coach Phil Weber and I played our traditional pregame match of Horse. (At some point in the year, Phil and I grew tired of drills and began playing Horse at the conclusion of my pregame workout. Strangely enough, our little game is quite an effective indicator for my team's fate. When he wins, the Suns win. When I win, we lose. Our regular-season record was 62–20, which should indicate that I am a fantastic Horse competitor.) The two gentlemen with the creative head coloring kept calm throughout our match—perhaps they were that enthralled by the thrashing Phil gave me. Little did they know how important our game was. (Nor how accurate a prediction it would provide.) When the actual game began the two diehards stood up and unfurled their trump card, a handwritten sign that said something along the lines of:

Hair dye: $8

Tickets: $500

Missing my first day of work to watch the Suns in the playoffs: priceless

Their placard inspired a few thoughts. First, who is the bigger jackass, the guy who is three years behind the times and said, "Hey, this joke will be funny," or the guy who, back at the apartment, said, "You're right, dude, that *is* funny. You totally have to take that to the game"?

Next, if one of our heroes was starting a job that would have theoretically had him working on a Sunday night at 7:30, was $500 for tickets to a basketball game a wise fiscal maneuver? I understand that it is the playoffs and all, but was the abandoning of any potential cash flow worth the sacrifice? Maybe for the Finals, but even then I would be willing to bet that the Texaco has a TV behind the counter.

Last, is missing said crappy job really worth the "priceless" tag? I'm thinking that should be reserved for "bailing on the birth of my firstborn to watch the Suns in the playoffs," or perhaps for "breaking out of the county jail to watch the Suns in the playoffs." Let's keep things in perspective.

Fortunately for my own self-respect, I am missing whatever gene is required to do things like paint my head orange for a basketball game. I think the same set of DNA is responsible for those people who at Pearl Jam concerts scream out totally inappropriate nonsense like "Eddie, you kick ass!" (In other news, I hate exclamation points, and only used the preceding one because it was absolutely necessary. I would like to see others adopt my rule concerning this form of punctuation.)

I recently attended a concert by a band called Local H. The band played one of their crowd favorites at some point—a song called "High-Fiving Motherfucker." The tune is basically a fast-paced romp aimed at skewering the jockish types who think nothing of raising their respective hands and expecting a slap on the palm in return in reaction to some meaningless event. There is nothing wrong with a five—high or low—if it is given in response to a well-performed athletic feat on the part of one of the participants in the five. It is not, however, appropriate if neither party was remotely involved in the sporting contest. The enjoyable part of the song, for me, is that because it is a jaunty number, some of the audience invariably begin moshing. (For those out of the loop, moshing is the random running into fellow concertgoers that often occurs directly in front of the stage.) These idiots, of course, are exactly the personality types the band is making fun of. The irony there is very decent.

I feel like Local H at times. I want the crowd to thrill to the action and enjoy our games, but I don't want them to make fools of themselves. I like to see some dignity, and I don't think I'm alone. I ask not for a moratorium on signs or enthusiasm; I ask only for the signs to be humorous (because, again, my personal enjoyment is the main goal here) and for the high-fiving on the part of crowd members to be reserved only for circumstances of the utmost basketball intensity, with notable exceptions given in cases of extreme drunkenness. I really don't think it is much to ask.

May 2

I have not played a meaningful minute since I rejoined the Suns in January. My role on this team during games is to cheer at the end of the bench, give encouragement to my teammates as they leave the floor during one of the seventy-four time-outs in an NBA game, and stay prepared enough to play should catastrophe or blowout befall my team. I do not, however, play when it counts. I am still trying to wrap my brain around the concept.

A reporter recently asked me if wins were as sweet and losses as sorrowful because of my stunted participation (his question, actually, was nowhere near so poetic—it's easier to make things sound good when a backspace key is available). I was impressed by the direct nature of his question. I don't think he was trying to stir up controversy; he seemed truly curious. Of course, that is his job. I might have dodged a bullet when I chose a more thoughtful answer over *Man, this is some [bovine excrement]. I can't believe I ain't playin'. I mean, what is Coach thinkin', man? All's I need is a chance.*

With my limited role comes a somewhat detached relationship to my teammates. I don't want to exaggerate too much—I am a part of the team and do behave as such—but I don't have the same claim to the results as does Steve Nash. It would be folly for me to intimate that he and I are experiencing the same emotions now that we have closed out the Memphis Grizzlies and moved on to the second round of the playoffs. Such is simply not the case. To me, it goes something like this: if x is the magnitude of the emotional result of one game (either negative or positive), the following are some of the multipliers that would result in an aggregate emotional impact for people with different investments in a particular game:

Starter: 2.0x
Bench player who sees significant time: 1.8x
Head coach: 1.7x
Assistant coach: 1.6x
Me: 1.5x
Trainer: 1.3x
Security guy at arena: 1.2x
Steve Nash stalker: 1.1x
Standard fan: 1.0x
Drunken homeless guy outside arena: 0.5x

To explain for those who were not fans of the word problems at the end of the math chapters, it is pretty simple. We shall use Shawn Marion as an example. After our latest win at Memphis, which did close out the series, but was also relatively ugly, the emotional result (x) was, say, a 7. So Shawn felt an emotional impact of around 14 (2.0×7). I felt an emotional impact of around 10.5 (1.5×7), and the homeless guy sustained one of about 3.5 (0.5×7). This is all slightly changeable based on how seriously the particular player took the game and how attractive the girls he gave his tickets to were, but I think it gives a rough guide.

In words, since this isn't high school algebra class, any feelings I have about a win or loss are going to be slightly dampened compared to Shawn Marion's. If we win the NBA Finals, it is not going to be because of something I did; to take such credit would be extraordinarily self-serving. I may have had some influence; perhaps a play I made back in training camp or an esteem-boosting poker loss I absorbed on the plane helped in some small way. But let's be honest—any impact I have is much smaller than the impact Jimmy Jackson or assistant coach Alvin Gentry will have. The potential range of emotions because of a win or loss is bounded, as I showed in the masterpiece that is the above table, and I think that is the way it should be.

May 7

Most of my colleagues are quite tall. I am no exception at six feet ten inches. When in captivity, on the basketball court, I am able to easily forget the fact that my bones are stretched to an extraordinary length because I am surrounded by other members of the freak show. Not so when I am released into the wild. Then I am forced to remember . . . by stupid people.

After a recent session of the basketball camp that serves as practice while we await an opponent for our next playoff series, I headed to my neighborhood Safeway. I picked up my staples (cereal and yogurt figuring prominently among my selections) and headed out the door. As I was leaving, a man searching for a nearby accountant's office accosted me when he observed my heightful frame and said, "Hey, man, you should have played basketball. You're really tall." *What, basketball? You're kidding. Why didn't I think of this sooner? It's a good thing you came along, man.*

He continued, "Just how tall are you?" I replied with my correct height, which was quite the Herculean effort, considering the retorts that occurred to me. Returning to his original line of questioning, he asked, "So, did you ever play ball?" He was obviously baiting me into giving something away. The smart move was to keep walking and admit nothing. Instead, I said, "Actually, I play for the Suns." As soon as it came out of my mouth, I wished I had a DeLorean. Option 1: no conversation with strange middle-aged man. Option 2: lengthy encounter with strange middle-aged man. Option 1 was the logical choice; I must have sucked in too many air-conditioning fumes while inside the grocery store.

My newfound friend immediately interjected that he was a veteran of the Korean War; it was great that he told me, since that was exactly the question I was going to ask. He then proceeded to tell me about his children, which again was fun because I had been wondering. He apologized for not being enough of a Suns fan to know who I was; I assured him that there were only about two hundred people in Phoenix who did, so it was okay. Then he helped load my goods into the trunk of my car despite my protests to the contrary. (Aren't young people supposed to assist their elders, not the other way around?) Finally, I signed a piece of paper for his wife. ("Harold, what the hell is this? I send you out to deliver some tax papers and you bring me some guy's autograph.") The whole encounter got me thinking about the problem that is the height question.

Telling me I am really tall is not a great conversation starter. It's like walking up to a well-endowed girl in a bar and telling her she has nice breasts—it's (1) creepy and (2) obvious. She's heard it before. It is not a new tactic and is not going to lead to a conversation that ends well. The same (sort of) is true for me. The only possible response available to me is, "And you're really smart." The encounter basically marks the asker as an idiot and me as an asshole.

Next comes the obligatory "Hey, how tall are you?" I have had some time to consider the question and have decided that it is necessary in only two situations: either the inquisitor is in some way unable to judge my height, because the conversation is taking place via telephone or because of the interrogator's blindness, or I am seated. It does not make any sense for someone to walk up to me on the street and ask me my height. He can see how tall I am. Feet and inches are merely arbitrary measurements set up by some English king—they are meaningless without some kind of standard. Basically, to judge a person's height, one of two things is needed, a number value or a visual representation, not both. Unless, of course, there is some sort of underground tall-person collecting going on. Maybe, much like bird-watching, finding someone of every available height is a goal people have.

I really enjoy when people say things like, "Did you know that you are really tall?" Again, asking this question is not a way to convey intelligence. I haven't pulled them out yet, but someday soon I will respond with questions regarding the physical appearance of my foil, choosing from "Did you know that you are morbidly obese?" and "Has anyone ever told you how unbelievably ugly you are?" It's going to happen. After all, much like height, they are only observations regarding a person's appearance.

One by-product of the height conversation is often a comparison to someone the questioner knows and thinks is tall. Invariably, the person to whom I am compared is not really tall at all and the conversation usually ends, unless I am about to be told how big his feet are and how tall the doctors think he will eventually be because, again, I apparently look like I need to know. "Six-ten, huh? Wow. My cousin is six-two and I thought he was tall."

My all-time favorite encounter is the guessing game. In it, a person approaches and says, unprompted, "I'd say you are about X feet, Y inches." Even better is the guess without any preceding statement; the guesser starts throwing out heights from a distance, apropos of nothing. The fun aspect of this pastime is that the person is almost never close. "You're about six-two right?" (I'm serious; it has been said multiple times. I think six-one is the record low.) No. Not even in the ballpark. And let me guess, the neighbor kid is really tall.

These are all more tolerable, though, than the nearly-out-of-earshot comment. Oftentimes when I walk by, I will hear whispers: "Wow, look how tall he is" or "That guy is really tall." It's as if, by being tall, I was not blessed with fully functional ears. Were these people not taught how to use their inner monologues? Yes, I am quite tall, but I know that. Any observation to that effect by others should be kept on the inside, unless the participants are willing to bear the consequences. I don't go around saying everything that is on my mind, but I could. If I did, the airways would be full of "Well, now, that guy is an example of why they made abortion legal" and "Why, exactly, were those two people allowed to procreate?" I think we are all better off with my silence, so no more height questions.

May 16

Tim Floyd, who is one of the people I respect most in all the world, once told me that the reason he likes basketball the most as a spectator sport is because an observer can tell a lot about a person's character by watching him play. In baseball and football, the fans are too removed from the action, and the players' faces are physically covered by either a helmet or the brim of a hat. A player, he noted, can hide a lot behind those impedances. In a game of basketball, the player's emotions are on display for all to see. That's what made Steve Nash's effort in Game 4 of our second-round playoff series with Dallas so breathtaking.

I went to the game in something of a malaise. Our games have begun to run together for me because I have not played in so long that I have considered neglecting to wear a uniform beneath my warm-up gear. Consequently, I was not all that excited to watch yet another basketball game, especially after the emotional high that was our Game 3 win in Dallas. I spent the first few minutes of the game putting forth a lackluster effort in my job as associate cheerleader, but my interest picked up as we struggled through the second quarter. The Mavericks' fans were beginning to get boisterous, which roused me from my stupor enough that I began to take a real interest in the proceedings. Dallas was playing inspired basketball and we . . . well, *inspired* would not be the word to describe the way we were playing—I think *disinterested* does the job nicely. We* made it into the locker room down only by sixteen, which seemed much more surmountable than the twenty-one-point deficit we had faced moments earlier.

At the half, Coach D'Antoni did his best to stoke the fires; it seemed to work, as we began the second half with a higher level of focus on the task at hand. (I was trying to put as many clichés in one sentence as I could. How did I do?) Unfortunately, our efforts failed to dent the deficit; in fact, the Mavericks staved off the charge with shots

*Note: I use the term *we* loosely and to mean "my team," and only because it is the direct opposite of *they,* which I use as a stand-in for "the other team."

that found their mark from all over the court. It was frustrating to watch.

There comes a point in every semi-blowout basketball game when the team sucking the proverbial rear mammary begins to fold. After Dallas managed to effortlessly keep the lead between twelve and fifteen points for much of the third quarter, my team unconsciously said to itself, *Damn. What the hell are we going to do? They just won't miss.* Inner shoulders began to sag, and theoretical faces started to fall.

Then a magical thing happened. Steve Nash absolutely took over the game.

We did not win Game 4 against the Mavericks. In fact, we lost by about ten points. I doubt that many people will remember what happened in the second half of the game. I know, though, that I will never forget it. Steve put on what was unquestionably the single most impressive display of basketball skill that I have ever seen in person. He was absolutely unstoppable. There were times throughout the last fifth of the game that I literally had goose bumps as I stood by the baseline watching him carry the Suns. He made big shot after big shot, at times when a miss would have been absolutely disastrous because Dallas was certainly not acquiescing to Steve's plan of a stirring comeback and was making nearly everything they threw in the direction of the backboard. I think that is what made the experience so astounding—each shot was under such pressure. It is never easy to find such a rhythm, but it is certainly a simpler task when the chips are falling into place—when the game is flowing and when one's team is actually making progress. Steve could have hung his head and resigned himself and his team to a losing fate at any time during his zoning-in, but he never did. As I mentioned, though, we never could close the gap. Our fearless point guard kept us within striking distance for almost the entire second half, but his floormates and he could not come up with the defensive stands needed to surmount the Mavericks' lead.

The greatest part of Steve's forty-eight-point performance came late in the game. He had not really forced a shot all night and had taken what Dallas had given him throughout the game. (In fact, some will say that this was the Mavericks' game plan. I doubt, though, that allowing anyone to score forty-eight was mentioned in the pregame briefing.) On two consecutive possessions near the end of the game, he had what looked for an instant like an open shot, only to have the window of opportunity closed by a fast-charging member of the opposition. In both cases, he found an open teammate who scored. Those two passes drove home what Coach Floyd once said, because anyone watching the game could tell exactly what sort of person Steve Nash is. They could tell that after the game he would deflect any talk of his own performance and instead concentrate on the fact that his effort, as Herculean as it was, was not enough to win the game. They could see that he never gave up on his team as he huddled with them after bad breaks. They watched him shrug off, as best he could, some questionable calls by the referees. In all, anyone who watched Game 4 of the Phoenix-Dallas series now knows exactly what kind of person Steve Nash is. And I don't think that's a bad thing.

May 26

I overheat easily. I think my core temperature must be slightly higher than that found in most everyone else. It doesn't take much to push me over the edge to a slight film on the forehead. Considering my present "home" city, this is all great news—I think it was 170 degrees in Phoenix yesterday. Fortunately, my poor cooling system does not manifest itself in some sort of rancid body odor. It does mean that my upper lip and eyebrow regions break into salty droplets with only the slightest provocation. Now, this is not the worst occurrence in the world, except that once my body's radiator gets out of balance, it is difficult to correct the problem. A poor wardrobe choice can lead to a night of sleeve-wiping and awkward looks from the people with whom I am conversing.

While in San Antonio, with us hoping to climb out of the 0–2 series hole over which the Spurs were standing, shovel at the ready, I spent the evening with a college friend of mine and his wife. Because we were staying near it, we set off down the Riverwalk with the hopes of finding a promising restaurant. Along the way, I noticed that I had made a regrettable decision when I had spurned shorts as the evening's apparel. Subconsciously, I must have thought that San Antonio would be cool at night. Apparently my thinking was that since Phoenix is the hottest place in the world, everywhere else must be cool enough for long pants. I forgot that the only truly appropriate clothing choice in Phoenix is complete nudity; by comparison, San Antonio is easily shorts-worthy. (On a side note, it is humid in San Antonio, which reminds me of home, where it is disgusting in the summertime. People in Kansas love to speak of the humidity as the cause of their discomfort. However, I take little solace in the dry heat of Arizona. My oven puts out dry heat as well; I'm confident that I would not be comfortable in there, either.)

About the time my revulsion at the BMIs of the Riverwalk passersby had run its course, we found a restaurant that appeared tolerable. I hammered down an overpriced ribeye that was presented covered in barbecue sauce—a concept that offends me greatly as a former caretaker of steaks on the hoof back in Kansas. Our visit was lovely; when we finished, we hiked back to the hotel and said our good-byes. The walk home in the muggy evening air had done little to refrigerate my core; consequently, my brow was still damp and I was anxious to get back to my hotel room so that I could crank the thermostat down to 60 degrees and finally cool the nuclear power plant that seems to run my body. On the way to the elevators, I noticed the entire brains behind the operation that is the Phoenix Suns closing quickly. Included were Mike D'Antoni, Jerry and Bryan Colangelo, and David Griffin (director of player personnel), with wives and families in tow. They're good people and I get along relatively well with all of them, so I was not displeased to see them. They are, however, my bosses, on various levels, so such of a collection of power—and me— on an elevator provided an awkward situation. Especially for them. They were forced to make conversation with an interloper when they were looking only to get up to their rooms after a long night of planning the future of basketball. They all knew that I wasn't going to play in the next day's game, so that discussion was out. Bryan and I had already talked about the bad beat I took in the poker game on the plane. (Joe Johnson caught one of two nines that would help him, and I was sunk.) David Griffin was in said poker game. Coach D'Antoni is funnier than I am, so any remark he would have made would have gone over my head, and Jerry Colangelo has seen about eight thousand basketball players in his day and certainly didn't need a twelve-second conversation with the likes of me. It was all very *Seinfeld*-esque. The situation was made worse because my face remained coated with a thin film of San Antonio–induced sweat. Which means that the entire front office now thinks either that I have a very hard time dealing with social situations or that I have a rampant drug problem. Note to self: further wardrobe consideration the next time I leave the room.

I can joke about an encounter in the elevator with the entire Suns front office because such a comfortable atmosphere surrounds the team. In fact, I've never been involved with a more positively charged basketball team. Someone obviously made a conscious decision to take a positive approach with this particular grouping of personalities; I think Coach D'Antoni had a lot to do with that plan. I can't say that I know D'Antoni well enough to judge his character too deeply, but I can tell, even with my somewhat limited intuition for these things, that there is a fair amount of fire and brimstone lurking just beneath the calm visage he presents most of the time. At times during games, he will turn to the bench after a particularly boneheaded play and make a face that says, *I would like that player to no longer receive a paycheck from this organization. In fact, I think it would be best if his right arm were chopped off at the elbow so that he will never again perpetrate such an action on a paying audience.* But, in a microsecond, he takes control of his facial muscles and smiles the frustration away, internalizing it so that he can one day pay for some psychiatrist's Porsche.

I think the positive approach was a good decision on his part. My team plays fast and loose and without regard to mistakes. To allow pessimism into the equation would be to invite second-guessing and hesitation—two actions that do not promote standing in the deep corner and making a three-pointer with a hand in one's face. Strangely enough, the effervescent aura that surrounds our team has resulted in some success—enough that my teammates truly believe they can win any game in which they play.

With the attitude that has been bred into my team comes a feeling of invincibility. I've felt all along that everyone involved with the organization assumed that we would play well into the late spring, and no one would be surprised to see us win it all.

Everyone's confidence was shaken with our second loss to the Spurs. I don't think the defeat itself was all that unnerving; it was the way it happened that was so deflating. San Antonio ground out the win, much the way they did in the first game of the series. I think my teammates felt powerless to stop the Spurs because they kept making timely baskets and we could do nothing about it.

I've been caught up in the season-long fervor. Our series deficit and the real possibility of our season's end has caused me to consider three things:

1. How happy I've been with the Suns
2. That my happiness could end quickly
3. Whether or not I've taken appropriate advantage of my celebrity-by-association to up my career sexual output

My approach to my life and my basketball career is based on logic. Too much so, in fact. I'd be a better player if I could think less. The benefit of my reasoned approach is a fairly strong sense of self-awareness. I know my role with the Phoenix Suns. I'm the white guy at the end of the bench who doesn't play very much. For now. But because of the way I played in training camp, I've never felt as though my status would last forever. When I returned to the team after the Russian experiment, Coach D'Antoni was using eight players in each game, and the team was winning. There was no need for me, or for anyone else, to gum up the works.

It would have been easy for those associated with the team to see me as a mascot. There aren't very many of us in the NBA, so it's easy to take us lightly. (White guys, not players who overthink everything.

Although those are few and far between as well.) But I don't think anyone affiliated with the organization laughs about my place on the team. I could be wrong, but I think they see the situation as I do—that there is no real need for me. Or for Bo Outlaw. Or for Jake Voskuhl. Or for Walter McCarty. We're on the bench not because we're charity cases but because the players ahead of us happen to be really good.

I sometimes do a poor job of expressing my opinion of myself to the public. I've embraced my job in a self-deprecating way. Now that I'm writing about it—and now that people are reading that writing—it's evident there's an audience that's interested in the lot of an in-between basketball player.

The resulting attention hasn't been all that surprising. NBA fans are desperate for some hope that players remain human. They are bombarded with news of huge salaries, outlandish purchases, and late-night arrests. They need to hear that players think the way they do. Or, at least, sometimes think the way they do.

And they need to see someone white. The majority of the American population remains white. The majority of the NBA remains black. Every person in history, regardless of remarks to the contrary, has an easier time rooting for someone who looks like him.

Enter me. (That was gross.) I should write: Enter . . . me—sort of normal-looking, pale-faced, somewhat witty. I'm the liaison between the fan and the sport that left him behind when Larry Bird's back began to ache.

Since I was living it, I embraced my role. Fact: I don't play much for the Phoenix Suns. When asked about that, I had two options. I could furrow my brow and act angry that I'm not playing twenty minutes a night. Or I could laugh, enjoy the moment, and make a quip about the superiority of fake breasts in LA over those in Phoenix. I assumed that people understood my self-deprecation. I obviously think I can play or I wouldn't be in the NBA. I don't need to talk about my abilities—that's what insecure people do.

I hope the management of the Phoenix Suns understands. I hope they remember that I can play. I hope they haven't been participating in an elaborate cover-up by acting as if they like having me around. It would be nice to stay here.

June 10

I write on my last night in Phoenix. The only things left in my apartment are the awful rental furniture I have endured for three months, the computer on which I currently type, and some leftover cereal boxes.

Our season ended with a whimper. The San Antonio Spurs eliminated my team in the Western Conference Finals, winning the series 4–1. I reported to America West Arena the day after our final loss and immediately began searching for as many pairs of Phoenix Suns shorts as I could carry.

That the end came so abruptly was not new; my every year of basketball has ended before I could really grasp that it was happening. But this year seemed especially shocking. When the final horn sounded after Game 5 with San Antonio and there were no more sporting contests for my purple-and-white-clad teammates, everyone in Phoenix found themselves in a state of disbelief. I was no different.

When I signed with the team in late January, my contract included a clause that gave the team an option on my services for next season. Said option would have to be exercised by June 15 of this year. On June 16, there will be a line under the "Transactions" section of many a local sports page that says, "Phoenix Suns decline option on F Paul Shirley." In my postseason meeting with the powers that be, phrases such as "contract flexibility" were bandied about and I was, in essence, fired. I have been in such meetings way too many times for someone as young as I; because of that, I know that the real meaning of those words is, *We do not think enough of your basketball skills to pay you the minimum salary required by the NBA, so find a different job.* One day, I was the twelfth player on one of the four best basketball teams in the world. The next, I was unemployed.

When I joined the Suns after a long two months in Russia, I was as fed up with basketball as I have ever been. The positive attitude here was—as clichéd as it may sound—a breath of fresh air. In the end, this was my longest stay in the NBA, and that stay was with by far the best team of my young professional career.

That being said, no one likes rejection. Actually, some people do. I think they're called masochists. (Or is it sadists? I can never remember.) I know I don't enjoy being told that I'm not good enough at something—especially when that something is the one thing upon which I've built my entire existence and self-esteem.

Not to overdo it.

There is some truth to that sentence, though. My life has been oriented around my own basketball success. Basketball is what I do the best. It is likely that I'll never be as good at any one activity.

I suppose I should be well equipped to deal with rejection at the hands of the Phoenix Suns. I've certainly experienced it enough. (By "it," I mean rejection in general. Although this is now twice the Suns have sent me away. They're like the dysfunctional girlfriend that everyone has. Well, that people who have long-term relationships have.) I'm not that well equipped. I don't know what I'll do next. I wanted nothing more than to keep playing for the Phoenix Suns. I'm left to start over. Again.

But I suppose I'll find another home. This is what I do. People tell me no, I pick myself up, and I move on. I'm a nomad, albeit an oft-kicked-to-the-curb one. I don't know what it says about me that the longest I have been in any one place since college is seven months, but I am getting used to the life. (Note to self: sign one of those seven-year, $100 million contracts soon—it will make for fewer gray hairs.) I think maybe I should be nicer to people or learn how to play basketball a little better. Or perhaps I should avoid massive internal injuries and/or angering foreign general managers. Obviously something needs to change.

Oddly enough, I am intrigued to see what comes next. Although I suppose that's my only real option. There's suicide, I guess. But I feel like that would make my mother sad. Earlier today, I finished a poor effort at packing my car with the clothes and few possessions with me in Phoenix. (Unfortunately, I was not blessed with my father's car-packing prowess, so the whole process was an absolute debacle. I did manage to keep the blind spot clear, which should make him happy, if I do in fact survive the eight-million-mile drive back to Kansas.)

As I have been saying my good-byes to the people I have gotten to know while here, I have been asked several times how I deal with this level of ignorance regarding my own future. I don't really have an answer, except to say that I am getting used to it. If I had three kids and a wife, it would be tough; I can't imagine saying, "Okay, darlin', load up Rusty, Darryl, and li'l Bobbie Sue. We's a-fixin' to get on back to Kan-zass." (That would be assuming I had grown up in Dodge City, I sup-pose.) At any rate, it would be a lot more difficult to live this life if I had anyone depending on me. But I avoid both commitment and re-sponsibility like it's my job, so the life I lead works. For now.

It promises to be an interesting summer. I suppose there is a chance the Suns' management could come to their senses sometime before next season and realize how much they would miss my bright-eyed, ever-cheery presence. But I'm not going to hold my breath. That eventuality would be too easy. And it would completely obliterate my migrant persona. I'd actually be in one city for a whole year. I'd have to put decorations on my walls . . . and relearn Spanish . . . and date girls for longer than two months at a time. I can't be expected to live such a normal life.

So tomorrow will come. I'll awake jobless and think about not get-ting out of bed. But then I'll remember that I've figured it out before, so I'll probably figure it out again. I'll drive by the arena, where I will—for nineteen of the twenty seconds it takes to pass it—think wistfully of my time with the Suns. And then I will spend one second making obscene gestures directed at those who just fired me. But then my anger will pass. I'll realize that, despite its ups and downs, my life could be a lot worse. As my father would say, I could be digging ditches.

Most important, I'll ride off into the sunset . . . er . . . sunrise happy. Because at least the Suns, unlike the Lakers so long ago, let me keep my jersey.

Acknowledgments

The book is finished, which means that you're reading this page for one of two reasons:

1. you really, really liked it;
2. you really, really hated it and are looking for contact info to be used in sending hate mail.

Those whose interest is related to reason number two should turn to the about the author page.

This book probably could have been written without the people in the list below. However, it would not have been worth a damn. Some of the people listed helped directly with the book, some helped me in other ways. To

my editor, Chris Schluep; my literary agent, Jay Mandel; my basketball agent, Keith Glass; Jeramie McPeek and Steven Koek, for launching my writing career; Bill Simmons, for drawing attention to it; Royce Webb, for keeping it going;

Chuck Klosterman;

Lynne Shook, Doug Gillispie (who, in a way, started it all), Tara Goedjen, Julie Flory, John DuPre, Erin Tyler, Kate Zenna, Fred Tedeschi, Dr. Tom Greenwald, Anne Beddingfield, Hap Eiche, Maynard James Keenan, Tom Shook, David Hamers, Ryan Broek, Brian Hagen, Derek Grimm, Bob and Meg Beck, Jerry Wilson, Ellen Suwanski, Mark Gretter, Chris Anstey, John Galt, Mark Fox, Joe Gerber, Eric Swanson, Randy Brown, Steve Krafcisin, Elliott Smith, Larry Kennedy, Neil Hayhurst, Jeff Lolley, Tucker Max, Mike Elliot, Erik Phillips, Jeff Nordgaard, Conor Oberst, Mike D'Antoni, Nina Peterson, Matt Santangelo, Rod Smith, Eric

Waters, Trent Reznor, Jeremy Goldstein, Peter Cornell, Christos Marmarinos, Eva Charney, Phil Hay, Alex Jensen, Katie Benton, Ron Adams, Matt Condon, and Tim Floyd.
Scott Wedman;
my family, for reading and criticizing;
some other people, who I probably forgot to include, mostly because this page was done over the course of one afternoon.
Thanks.

ABOUT THE AUTHOR

PAUL SHIRLEY is a human being who sometimes plays basketball and sometimes writes books. Although, to this point, he has done more of the former than the latter, as evidenced by the number of basketball games in which he has played (approximately seven hundred) versus the number of books he has written (exactly one).

myspace.com/paulshirley

ABOUT THE TYPE

This book was set in ITC Century Light, a member of the Century family of typefaces. It was designed in the 1890s by Theodore Low DeVinne of the American Type Founders Company, in collaboration with Linn Boyd Benton. It was one of the earliest types designed for a specific purpose, the *Century* magazine, because it was able to maintain the economies of a narrower typeface while using stronger serifs and thickened verticals.